raised eyebrows

My Years Inside Groucho's House

By Steve Stoliar

Introduction by Dick Cavett

BearManor Media

Published in the USA by:
BearManor Media
PO Box 1129
Duncan, Oklahoma 73534-1129
www.bearmanormedia.com

Library of Congress Cataloging-in-Publication Data

Stoliar, Steve.
Raised eyebrows : my years inside Groucho's house / by Steve Stoliar.
p. cm.
Includes index.
ISBN: 978-1-59393-652-5
1. Marx, Groucho, 1890-1977. 2. Stoliar, Steve. 3. Comedians--United States--Biography. I. Title.
PN2287.M53S76 1996
792.7'028'092--dc20
[B] 95-47750
CIP

ACKNOWLEDGMENTS

This book is not intended as a comprehensive examination of Groucho's life. It is a record of my experiences while working for him during his final years. As such, it is mostly the result of my own recollections, coupled with notes, audio and videotapes, photographs and letters that I've held on to over the years. This is not to say that I did not welcome and receive help and guidance, in various forms, along the way.

I would like to thank Jim Bell, Bob Garrick and especially Diane Szasz Ziccardi for their foresight in saving my old letters. For helping to keep me on track, affectionate nods to Henry Golas and Nat Perrin. For helpful feedback—pro and con—and much-needed support, I'm grateful to Woody Allen, Daryl Busby, Dick Cavett, Bobbi Goldin, Jay Hopkins, Larry Hussar, Jerome Lewis, Angela Mancuso, Mark Petty, Chris Porterfield, William Poundstone, Bill Rosen, Kathleen Rowell, Sela Seal, Melissa Silva, Nina Skahan Sheffield, Jennifer Sloan Kirmse, Pati Stoliar and Paul G. Wesolowski.

For the publication of the original 1996 hardcover edition, my sincere thanks to agent Mike Hamilburg and the Group at General Publishing.

Regarding this new, expanded paperback edition, my great thanks to Monte Beauchamp, Lon Davis, Sandy Grabman, Ben Ohmart, Brian Pearce—and especially *artiste extraordinaire* Drew Friedman for his magnificent cover drawing and supportive efforts.

Lastly, eternal love, gratitude and appreciation to my lovely and talented wife, Angelique, for remaining so supportive during the creation of the original 1996 edition—and for coming up with three-sevenths of the title.

INTRODUCTION

A marginally talented film director named Sam Wood once complained about one of his actors, in this case, Groucho Marx: "You can't make an actor out of clay." The subject of this book replied: "Nor a director out of Wood."

Who would not want to meet such a man?

Steve Stoliar says that had a gypsy told him, back in St. Louis as a kid, that he was destined not only to meet his idol but to work for him *in his house* (italics mine; get your own), he would have told her to try some new tea leaves.

But that's just what happened.

This book tells the story. It is at once an adventure, a good gossip, an improbable through-the-looking-glass tale, a tear-jerker, a belly-laugh maker and a cautionary tale about the mixed blessing of getting what you wish for.

If, at this moment, you happen to be browsing for a good read, let me help you. If you're already a Marx fan, you need no prodding. If not, here's why you should snatch up this volume anyway.

Haven't we all wished to meet someone we idolize? A movie star? A sports hero? A great writer, philosopher, religious leader, even (rarely) a politician? Steve Stoliar had an advanced case of this affliction, and in his case the luminary was born Julius Marx. The desire was so keen that he would readily have made the Faustian bargain for his soul in exchange for merely an autograph and a handshake.

He got much more.

Writing students will note (or have pointed out to them by their teacher) how form follows function. The naive wonder of the opening chapters gives way to a wiser, more mature prose style as the story progresses. The "gee-whiz" kid from St. Louis becomes the mature, reflective and experienced participant in the final years of one of America's human landmarks. (A subtitle for the book might have been, "Or How I Went from Wide-Eyed Innocent to Open-Eyed Realist.") Along the way, gratification, shock, hilarity, sadness and insight occur and a good bit is learned about—pardon the expression—Life Itself.

For me, the book has all the real page-turner qualities of a good novel. Besides the windfall of Groucho-iana and -isms reported here for the first time (with which one can delight and astonish one's friends at the next dull cocktail party), there is genuine drama, psychological and otherwise; particularly from the point when the mercurial Erin Fleming enters the scene.

Thanks to Steve's unique ringside seat, the court battle and other *Sturm und Drang* of Groucho's final years are illuminated here, and there is a trove of new and priceless anecdotes along the way, any one of which is worth the dust-jacket price.

I'll shut up now so that you can walk over to the cashier, part with the requisite kale and delay no longer the delights that lie ahead in this well-wrought tale that is as credible as it is incredible.

As Groucho might have said in an occasional lapse into the dialect of both his youth and the vaudeville stage: "Try it. You vouldn't be sorry."

And how.

Dick Cavett

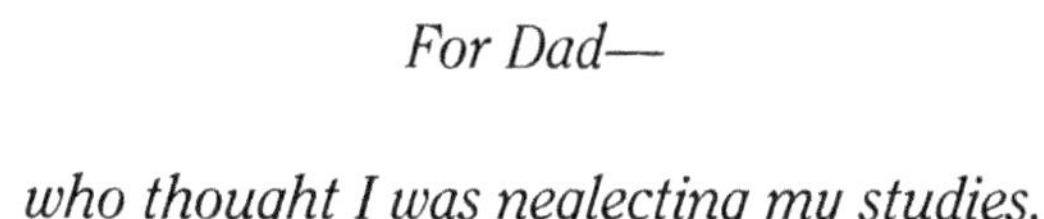

For Dad—

who thought I was neglecting my studies.

ONE

On a Tuesday morning in August of 1974, I stood outside Groucho Marx's Beverly Hills home and rang the doorbell. I'd been working there for about three weeks and was finally allowing myself to feel as though I actually belonged. After a couple of weeks spent testing the waters and settling in, I felt that Groucho and I were developing a genuine rapport. I was beginning to get to know him as a person and not just as "Groucho Marx."

Every day in that house had been an adventure, and I was eager to immerse myself in more Marxiana. I was going to put in a full day's work—if you could call it that—and then there was going to be a small party that evening in honor of Erin Fleming's birthday.

I reflected on my good fortune as I waited for the door to open. I figured I must be the luckiest Groucho fan in the world. Maybe others had seen the films more times or had a larger collection of memorabilia, but how many of them were working for him? In his *home*? By any definition, it was a dream job.

My reverie was interrupted when Agnes, the maid, opened the door and said in a gentle but firm voice, "Please be quiet. Mr. Marx has had a stroke."

My heart sank. He'd had a stroke two years earlier and it had changed him immeasurably. He couldn't possibly handle another. I remember thinking, *Please. Not yet*. It had taken me so long to get there and now my coach was about to turn back into a pumpkin.

I asked Agnes if Erin was with him. To my surprise, she said she hadn't arrived yet but that Julie, one of Groucho's young nurses, was there and had asked that I be sent to his bedroom as soon as I arrived. Warily, I made my way down the hallway, its walls covered with framed photographs of Groucho at various ages, posing with his brothers, his family and his famous friends. I entered his bedroom expecting to find him lying comatose, Julie hovering over him, her face filled with grave concern.

Instead, he was sitting up in bed in his polka-dot pajamas, casually browsing through the *Los Angeles Times*.

"Is the ambulance here yet?" he asked. For all his concern, he might have been inquiring if the mail were here yet; something I'd heard him ask me many times before. I told him it wasn't. Annoyed with the ambulance's tardiness, he shook his head and returned to his reading. His speech was a bit slurred, but all in all it was a great relief to find him in reasonably good shape and grouchy spirits.

Groucho needed to relieve himself, but since his equilibrium was a little off he required more support than Julie could give him. I was glad to be of assistance. I helped Groucho to his feet and into the bathroom, and with one arm on my shoulder to steady himself, he proceeded to urinate. I stood there thinking that as a fan, all I had ever really wanted was the chance to thank Groucho Marx for all the laughs he'd given me, and now here was my hero, holding on to me to keep from falling over. It was a strange moment, one that filled me with a mixture of pride and sorrow.

I helped him back to bed just as a very agitated Erin Fleming breezed in. She surveyed the situation, said a perfunctory hello to Groucho, then did an about-face and screamed "FUUUUUUUCK!" as she stormed off down the hallway. She went straight into her office and slammed the door so hard it rattled the pictures, not to mention our nerves.

Erin didn't come out until after the paramedics had arrived, loaded Groucho into an ambulance and spirited him away to the hospital. She was furious. She was convinced that Groucho had had that stroke on purpose, just to spoil her birthday.

Groucho would bounce back from this minor stroke in record time, so it wasn't my last day on the job after all. Far from it. Although I couldn't have known it then, I would continue working there for another three years. But my initial panic over Groucho's condition, coupled with Erin's bizarre reaction, really threw me. It was a lot for a nineteen-year-old fan to handle in one morning.

What exactly had I gotten myself into?

Two

I suppose I've had a fascination with celebrities for as long as I can remember. Psychologists might say it stems from some deep-seated desire to feel more important by making a connection with a famous person, and there's probably something to that. We're assured that movie stars put their pants on one leg at a time, same as you and me, but if we weren't made to feel that they were different from us somehow, they wouldn't be able to command those hefty fees for their services. We'd say, "What does Sean Connery have that I don't have? I'm not gonna pay $7.50 to look at something I can see staring back at me every morning when I'm shaving." But celebrities *are* different. While the rest of us must content ourselves with being merely life-sized, genuine stars are larger than life.

Seeing a celebrity in person was a rare occurrence for a little boy growing up in the late fifties and early sixties in University City, Missouri, a small suburb of St. Louis. Making contact with a celebrity—be it an autograph, a letter or a simple "hello"—was, for me, a close encounter of another kind altogether.

I think I can trace this feeling back to my childhood Christmases. There was nothing to equal the thrill of waking up and being struck by the sudden realization that Christmas Day had finally arrived. I'd run down the stairs and, just as I'd hoped, there would be presents under the tree with my name on them. But in addition to the presents there was usually a note that read, "Dear Steve, Thank you for the Coke. Rudolph enjoyed the orange. Merry Christmas Santa."

Imagine that: A letter from Santa himself, thanking me for the foodstuffs I'd left out the night before! I knew of no other kid on my block who received such letters, and it made me feel special to get that kind of personal attention, what with all the other deliveries he had to make. I mean, for a five-year-old boy, could there be a bigger star than Santa Claus?

I had two further celebrity encounters during my seven years in St. Louis. The first was seeing Captain Kangaroo. It was exciting to view the star of my favorite show in person, even if my mom and I didn't have the best seats in the auditorium.

My second brush with fame occurred a year or two later when the Three Stooges made a personal appearance in St. Louis during a promotional tour for one of their feature films. This was a big thrill, because I'd recently become a major Stooges fan as a result of seeing their short films on TV. But when I saw them in person, there were certain discrepancies that puzzled me.

For one thing, they looked so much *older* in person than they did on our television set. For another, Curly Joe didn't look much like the Curly I was familiar with. And at one point, Moe made a joke about how Larry combed his hair with an eggbeater. It was a funny remark, but it really didn't work because the Larry I was looking at had only a few strands of gray hair, slicked back along the sides of his head—hardly the bird's nest I was used to seeing. Of course, what I didn't know at the time was that the shorts I was laughing at on TV were twenty or thirty years old and the original Curly had ceased acting in 1947 after suffering a stroke.

Even then I was having to grapple with the difference between fantasy and reality when dealing with the surviving members of old comedy teams.

In 1962 my dad's job caused us to move from St. Louis to Los Angeles, which seemed like an exotic, faraway place. One thing I knew about California was that Disneyland was there. I'd seen it on "The Mickey Mouse Club" and I couldn't wait to go. My mom had visited relatives in L.A. a year earlier and had brought me back some souvenirs from Disneyland—two animation flip books and a Donald Duck pencil eraser. This was the equivalent of an explorer having returned with rare spices from the Far East.

The other thing I knew about California was the result of my having been an avid watcher of "I Love Lucy," and that was that it was filled with movie stars. Why, wherever Lucy turned, there was John Wayne, Rock Hudson, Harpo Marx.

As if to confirm my suspicion about the abundance of celebrities in California, we found ourselves seated directly behind Red Skelton on the St. Louis-to-L.A. plane. And several rows in front of him sat Andy Griffith. At the time, both of them were at the height of their popularity.

Griffith seemed a bit grumpy when I asked him for his

autograph, but Skelton was an absolute delight. As a matter of fact, he turned out to be fairly indispensable. My oldest sister, Carole, was upset because her boyfriend hadn't made it to the airport in time to see her off, so Skelton gave her his monogrammed handkerchief to dry her tears. My other older sister, Pati, was something of an amateur artist, so Skelton, an accomplished artist himself, swapped drawings with her. She still has the pencil sketch he made of the still life from the menu cover hanging on her wall.

Skelton was charming to me as well. In addition to signing a sketch, he would turn around from time to time and fire a cork-on-a-string popgun at me. He kept the gun concealed inside his sport coat; I wonder if he would've made it past the X-ray scanners in today's airports. So all three Stoliar children were kept entertained by Red Skelton on the journey from St. Louis to Los Angeles.

Maybe life *was* like "I Love Lucy."

Once we arrived in California, it was years before I saw another celebrity, and that was veteran character actor Jesse White, eating a sandwich at Nate 'n Al's Delicatessen in Beverly Hills.

Maybe life *wasn't* like "I Love Lucy."

We settled into a spacious, three-bedroom, ranch-style house in the San Fernando Valley. As fate would have it, our next-door neighbor was Hollywood columnist Marilyn Beck. Marilyn wrote a column called "Over the Beck Fence." Since *we* lived over the Beck fence, we never understood why she didn't just call it "The Stoliars." Although I never seemed to be at her house when she was entertaining celebrities, it was still pretty nifty knowing that our next-door neighbor made her living by rubbing shoulders with the rich and famous.

Amid the various celebrity photos on Marilyn's walls was one showing her husband, Roger, as a contestant on a game show called "You Bet Your Life." Seated behind a desk next to Roger was a man with a moustache and glasses. His name was Groucho Marx. He looked a little familiar but I wasn't really a *fan* at the time, so the picture didn't make much of an impression on me.

Toward the end of elementary school, I came under the influence of *Mad* magazine, developing a particular fondness for their parodies of songs, movies and TV shows. For our sixth-grade graduation skit, my schoolmate, Ricky Mann, and I wrote a spoof of the Academy Awards ceremony, complete with references to Bob

Hope being perennially passed over for an Oscar. In retrospect the jokes don't seem quite so funny, but it constituted deft satire when we were eleven, and it succeeded in amusing the graduating class of Collier Street School in 1966.

By junior high I had developed a fascination with old Hollywood, especially horror movies and silent comedies. My mom would drive my friend, Gerry Kroll, and me to a nearby bank that ran silent movies in its community room every Saturday. Occasionally one of the old stars, such as Keystone comic Chester Conklin or early-talkies ingenue Fifi D'Orsay, would stop by and talk to the dozen or so people who bothered to attend the screenings. They also had a display case filled with movie memorabilia, including an officer's hat worn by Lon Chaney Sr. in *Tell It to the Marines.* It was a fun way to spend a Saturday afternoon.

My other pastime was collecting "old stuff." Ever since I stumbled across a fossil shell in St. Louis, I'd been crazy about paleontology. At first I was only interested in things that were millions of years old, but I eventually came to appreciate what man had been able to accomplish over the years, and I expanded my interests to include Roman coins and Indian arrowheads. I always had friends to play with, but much of my childhood and adolescence was spent discovering old movies and collecting old stuff.

When I was fifteen my mom died of cancer, which was the first big emotional crisis in my life. Both of my sisters were married and out of the nest by then, so my dad was on his own in trying to keep my spirits up. He'd take me fossil hunting and bring me back old coins whenever he'd go out of town, but I was pretty much in shock. I still wonder how I managed to get through that first year of high school in one piece.

Some months after my mom died, my dad took me to the MGM auction, which was the most amazing thing I'd ever experienced. I was really able to see what Hollywood (or, more accurately, Culver City) was like behind the scenes. The Universal Studios Tour purports to show the visitor how movies are made, and it succeeds to a certain degree. But wandering around the MGM lot in 1970 was a much better education in filmmaking than I could ever have gotten at an amusement park. Fifty years of moviemaking magic had been tagged and laid out for browsers to rummage through.

In addition to being able to touch costumes worn by Fred

Astaire, Greta Garbo and Clark Gable, I was able to observe, up close, miniature ships from *Mutiny on the Bounty* with dozens of little wooden "mutineers" still on deck. I saw wind machines that used huge wooden airplane propellers to generate hurricanes; plaster "marble" statues from *Ben-Hur*; and the show boat from *Show Boat*. I even got to sit in *The Time Machine*. Immersing myself in all those costumes, props and memorabilia greatly fueled my fascination with old Hollywood and even helped take my mind off my mother's death.

About this time, I wrote some jokes and sent them in to "Rowan & Martin's Laugh-In," one of which I'm convinced they stole. It went as follows: "Mexico is so unstable, even their records have 45 revolutions per minute." Several weeks later, Alan Sues stuck his head through the joke wall and said, "What do you get when you cross Brazil with a phonograph record? Thirty-three and a third revolutions per minute!"

You be the judge.

Although I received no remuneration, I did get a very nice letter from Allan Manings, the show's head writer, which said, "You obviously have an ear for humor and should be encouraged to keep at it." I made a mental note of his suggestion, which I filed away for future reference.

A few months later my dad married a woman named Penny, whom he'd been dating for several months. Suddenly having a stepmother and two stepsisters in the house, less than a year after losing my mom, was another big emotional adjustment. And our cat, Patches, had to cope with the sudden intrusion of a miniature dachshund named Krissy. But at least I had friends I could hang out with, and if they weren't around I could always lose myself in old movies and old stuff.

It was around this time that I discovered the Marx Brothers.

This is not to say I hadn't been aware of them before then. I'd seen bits and pieces of their movies, which my dad used to quote whenever appropriate ("You must've been vaccinated with a phonograph needle!"). There were hazy childhood memories of a funny-looking duck dropping down from the ceiling during a game show. And my uncle Joe, a balding man with a moustache and glasses, had a suspiciously familiar habit of wiggling his eyebrows and flicking his cigar whenever he'd say something funny.

But it wasn't until high school that I really came to appreciate how wonderful the Marx Brothers were. I couldn't imagine where they'd been hiding all my life. And so I began ferreting out Marx Brothers movies on TV and reading as much as I could about them.

It's a little difficult to explain why I responded so strongly to the Marx Brothers. Why, for instance, is someone wild about the Beatles but indifferent to the Rolling Stones? All I can say is that after being exposed to other classic comedians—W.C. Fields, Laurel and Hardy, Mae West and so on—the Marx Brothers, like cream, just seemed to rise to the top. This isn't to say that I didn't enjoy the others. I did, and do. It's just that there was a freshness and a timelessness about the Marx Brothers that, for me, set them apart from the rest.

Perhaps it was their seamless blending of physicality and wordplay that attracted me. A generous portion of their movies consists of unadulterated slapstick, yet much of their material could easily be classified as "humor" rather than "comedy." Indeed, some of the wittiest, most sophisticated wordsmiths of their day provided material for the Marxes, including Broadway playwright George S. Kaufman and *New Yorker* writer S.J. Perelman.

Each member of this curious triumvirate was a colorful and distinctive character, yet they meshed so smoothly with one another. Someone once described the Marx Brothers as "gall divided into three parts," and the whole clearly seemed greater than the sum of those parts. Harpo's puckish personality and pantomime routines remain just as delightful today as they were sixty years ago, not to mention his skill with a certain stringed instrument. Chico's malaprops and piano-playing gymnastics are still great fun to listen to and watch.

And Groucho, their iconoclastic ringleader, had a striking appearance and a wisecracking, pomposity-deflating personality that were, quite simply, unique. Iconoclasm was an appealing trait to an introverted adolescent in the late sixties and early seventies. And I suspect, given my essentially shy nature, that I experienced a certain vicarious thrill watching Groucho blurt out whatever was on his mind to pretty young things, stuffy old things and figures of authority, regardless of the consequences. If only *I* could've gotten away with that.

But analyzing comedy is, ultimately, pointless. The bottom line is, the Marx Brothers were—and are—funny. To paraphrase an old adage: For those who are into the Marx Brothers, no explanation is necessary; for those who aren't, none is possible. And if anyone could be said to have been into the Marx Brothers, I was that person.

I may not have been aware of it at the time, but Groucho's style began to have its effect on me. I remember Miss Harper shocking our eleventh-grade history class by informing us that Benjamin Franklin had fathered thirteen illegitimate children during his lifetime and that he had kept a sixteen-year-old mistress when he was eighty. "Well, he did invent the lightning rod," I muttered, which had an explosive effect on the room.

Although I think I always had the capacity to find the humor in almost any situation, it's unlikely I would've had the audacity to verbalize something like that, right in the middle of class, had I not come to appreciate Groucho's seemingly effortless ability to drop a bon mot at just the right moment and bring the house down.

The following year I was voted Class Clown.

Nineteen seventy-two marked my transition from Taft High School to UCLA. It also marked the first time I actually *saw* Groucho Marx. In the flesh. I'd been inundating myself with anything and everything connected with the Marx Brothers; hitting the revival houses and remaining ever vigilant for books, articles, records and movie stills. I knew that Chico and Harpo were long gone, but Groucho—instantly my favorite—was still around and had recently been touring with a series of one-man concerts entitled *An Evening with Groucho*, the most famous of them at Carnegie Hall.

It was announced that Groucho would be appearing in late September at the Dorothy Chandler Pavilion in Los Angeles. There it was. My chance to be in the same room, however cavernous, as Groucho Marx. My best friend, Daryl Busby, and I pooled our limited resources, purchased two tickets—at a hefty $9.50 per—and waited impatiently for September to arrive.

September came, and with it some frustrating news: According to the papers, Groucho had been hospitalized for a deep depression triggered by the murder of the Israeli athletes at the Munich Olympics. The concert had to be postponed until December. So after having waited impatiently for September, we now had to wait three *more* months before we could enjoy *An Evening with Groucho.*

I soon made an offhand decision that resulted in my missing out on seeing Groucho in person before his appearance at the Dorothy Chandler. Although I'd begun living at a UCLA co-op, which was sort of a cross between an apartment and a dorm, I would return to the family home in Tarzana for weekends and holidays. One weekend in November, Woody Allen was set to perform at the Valley Music Theater in Woodland Hills—a theater not five minutes from my home—during what turned out to be the waning days of his career as a stand-up comic. Despite my growing admiration for Woody Allen, I elected not to go.

However valid my reason may have seemed at the time, it haunts me to this day. A schoolmate, Keith Elliott, attended and reported, "It was great! *Groucho Marx* was there! He got up onstage with Woody Allen and everything! After the show, his car went past us and Groucho rolled down his window and said, 'Don't you kids *ever* go home?' You should've been there!"

Thanks for not rubbing it in.

Also around this time, I'd begun hearing references to the toll that the years were taking on Groucho. He was, after all, eighty-two. And there was that business about being hospitalized for depression. I remember watching the Hollywood Christmas Parade and seeing Groucho sitting on a float, dressed as Santa Claus (two of my heroes for the price of one). He looked old and tired. An unctuous parade commentator ran up to him, stuck a microphone in his face and said, "Happy Thanksgiving, Santa! How do you feel tonight?" to which Groucho muttered, "Very unfunny."

But, as the date of the concert grew nearer, newspaper and magazine articles had led me to believe that, for all intents and purposes, I was in for an entertaining evening with the same ol' Groucho I'd grown to revere; perhaps a bit older, but still sharp and irascible.

Would that that had been the case.

The night Daryl and I had been waiting for finally arrived: Monday, December 11, 1972. We had lousy seats, but what did it matter? We were *there*. The show opened with a clip of Groucho's entrance as Captain Spaulding in the 1930 film *Animal Crackers*. This was exciting enough, since neither Daryl nor I had ever seen it. Then Marvin Hamlisch, known to me at the time as the man who played piano for Groucho at Carnegie Hall and who, according to the program, had written the musical scores for *Take the Money and Run* and *Bananas*, played a medley of Marx-related melodies, just to set the proper mood.

And then...HE came out. Groucho Marx. In full color and three dimensions. My heart pounded and the applause was thunderous.

But something was wrong. Groucho didn't stride out to the podium, light up a cigar and unleash a stream of ad-libbed insults upon the audience. He shuffled out, very slowly, and went right into a creaky rendition of "Hello, I Must Be Going," accompanied by an attractive, youngish woman named Erin Fleming. He sounded as if he were slightly drunk, and his voice was hard to recognize, all soft and whispery. After he finished the song he stood at the podium, cigarless, took out a stack of index cards and slowly began to read from them.

Verbatim.

I felt as if I'd been hit in the stomach with a sledgehammer. A mixture of sadness and anger washed over me. Sadness, because my eyebrow-wiggling, wisecracking idol had been replaced by a fragile old man. Anger, because I resented the press for downplaying his frailty and keeping up the image of a Groucho still razor-sharp after all these years. In time, I learned that he hadn't been hospitalized for depression at all. It had been a major stroke, and it had changed him forever.

Nevertheless, it was an inarguable thrill to watch him read anecdotes off those index cards and struggle mightily through a few songs, which were interspersed with more scenes from Marx Brothers movies. As each film clip would start up, the spotlight would dim and we'd see Groucho silhouetted against the screen, watching his brothers and himself cavorting, decades earlier. It was a strange, almost surreal image.

When he finished, the standing ovation was deafening and endless. My hands still stung the next morning from clapping so hard. It made me feel good to believe that applause generated by *my* hands was reaching *his* ears. Some sort of connection, however tenuous, had been made. As I watched him shuffle offstage, tired and frail, I knew in my heart that it was the last chance I would ever get to see Groucho Marx in person.

It was a powerful experience.

While Daryl and I were in the parking garage wending our way to the car, there was an unscheduled bonus. I spotted Zeppo, the fourth brother from their early films, whom I recognized from recent photos. He had a years-younger blonde in tow and appeared to be hunting for his car. He may not have made much of an impression on-screen, what with Groucho, Harpo and Chico crowding him out, but in the parking garage of the Dorothy Chandler Pavilion it was absolutely galvanizing to see Zeppo Marx.

I mustered all my courage, strode over to him and said "Mr. Marx, I just wanted to tell you how much I've enjoyed your work over the years." "It wasn't *me* you enjoyed," he protested, "It was my brothers." However right he may have been, there was no denying how exciting it was to have been admonished by a genuine Marx Brother.

Seeing two Marx Brothers in person in one night only fueled my fervor. (After all, what is *fan* but a shortened version of *fanatic*?) I continued to consume—and be consumed by—anything relating to them. I had committed many of their funniest lines and routines to memory, as had most of my closest friends; it was almost a prerequisite to friendship.

I even grew a moustache.

During this period, as with the infamous Woody Allen concert, I continued to be plagued by reports of various sightings of Groucho Marx. People who had absolutely no interest in the man would say, "Oh yeah, I saw him taking a walk last week. He looked really old." Why couldn't *I* have been the one to judge how old he looked? Where was the fairness in this?

One day I stopped in a Beverly Hills pizza parlor called Jacopo's and noticed they had a Groucho Special on the menu. Skeptically assuming he'd dropped by maybe once, several years earlier, I asked, "Does Groucho Marx really come in here?" The waitress said, "Yeah. He was in here—lemme see—yesterday, as a matter of fact. Always comes in right after we open and asks if we can change a hundred-dollar bill. And he knows darn well there's nothing in the register. What a character!"

It was excruciating.

I even entertained the idea, fleetingly, of staking out Jacopo's in the hope that our paths would cross. I suppose I had something in common with the obsessive fans of today, except that my ambition was merely to *meet* Groucho, not marry or murder him. I only wanted half a minute to thank him for all the laughs and maybe get his autograph. That was my list of demands in its entirety. Would that be tilting the gods' pinball machine? It sure seemed that way.

Sometime in 1973 I got a call from my stepmother, Penny, informing me that she and a friend were walking their dogs in Beverly Hills when whom should they spot but Groucho! She dashed over to him and begged him for an autograph. While she was rummaging through her purse for some paper and a pen, Groucho glanced down at Krissy, our dachshund, and said, "Whaddaya got there, a bulldog? He looks pretty ferocious." She produced pen and paper and got "To Steve from Groucho" laboriously scribbled upon it.

The Shroud of Turin is treated with less reverence than that with which I treated that scrap of paper—and *my* relic was genuine. There they were, my name and his, on the same piece of paper, in his own hand. It was even better than getting those notes from Santa Claus. I put it in a small frame and kept it on my desk, where I could look at it whenever I wanted. I was extremely grateful to Penny but I still had not met the man personally. It used to seem like a pipe dream, but if my own stepmother could run into him, why then, oh why, couldn't I?

I continued at UCLA, a History major with a more-than-passing interest in motion pictures, my Marx Brothers obsession reaching a feverish pitch. I even began dreaming about Groucho. I remember one in which I saw him sauntering down the street, smoking a cigar. I figured his cigar would make a great souvenir, so I walked up to him and timidly said, "Um, excuse me, Mr. Marx, but would it be possible—" Without letting me finish, Groucho simply handed me the cigar, prompting me to say, "Gee, I guess nobody ever asks you for these things, huh?"

If only dreams really did come true.

I went into the UCLA Research Library one day and began searching through their bound volumes of *Time* magazine. I found the object of my desire: A 1932 issue with the Four Marx Brothers on the cover, standing in a garbage can during the shooting of *Horse Feathers*. It was already a hard-to-find, sought-after collectible, and I was tempted to swipe it, but my conscience got the better of me and I decided it wouldn't have been fair to deprive future Marx fans of the opportunity to look through this rare magazine.

I did, however, vow to reconsider my decision before I graduated.

During winter break in December of 1973, something happened that changed my life forever. My friend, Bob Garrick, informed me that the Old Town Music Hall in Anaheim was going to be showing *Animal Crackers.*

This was the Holy Grail of Marx Brothers movies. There was a good reason Daryl and I had never seen any of *Animal Crackers* except for that clip at the Dorothy Chandler Pavilion. Their second film, made in 1930 for Paramount, *Animal Crackers* had been unavailable for theatrical release since the mid-fifties and had never been shown on television. When Paramount sold their older films to Universal in 1959, a few titles weren't included because the licenses had expired. In the case of *Animal Crackers*, the rights had reverted to the authors and composers of the original Broadway play, George S. Kaufman, Morrie Ryskind, Bert Kalmar and Harry Ruby.

None of this legal folderol mattered to me at the time, however. What *did* matter was the current gas shortage. It was no small sacrifice to wait in line for over an hour at a gas station and then blow almost an entire tank of the stuff on a round-trip junket to Anaheim just to watch a Marx Brothers movie. But that's exactly what my friends and I felt compelled to do. It was a horrible, murky, headache-inducing, bootleg print of what appeared to be a very funny movie. And it contained Groucho's theme song, "Hurray for Captain Spaulding."

After returning home, I got this crazy notion that I wanted to let Groucho know that *Animal Crackers* was playing, just in case he wanted to see it. I knew Groucho had an unlisted number, but I also knew, from idle snooping through the Beverly Hills phone book, that Harry Ruby did not.

So I stared at the phone, took a deep breath and dialed. I was nervous. After all, in addition to being the man who had penned "I Wanna Be Loved By You (Boop-Boop-a-Doop)" and who had cowritten some of the Marx Brothers' funniest films, he was one of Groucho's oldest and closest friends. A nurse answered. She told me that Mr. Ruby was napping and jotted down my number. Had he answered the phone, there would've been no reason to take my number and none of what transpired thereafter would have taken place. Consequently, I'm glad he was napping.

Sometime later Harry Ruby called back. It was a thrill to speak with him, if only for a few minutes. He even said he'd tell Groucho that *Animal Crackers* was playing in Anaheim. That call, in late December of 1973, generated enough excitement to last me a lifetime—or at least until New Year's Day of 1974. On that day, I received a call from a woman who identified herself as "Groucho's secretary."

She said her name was Erin Fleming.

THREE

I recognized the name from recent articles and, of course, from her having accompanied Groucho on his shaky duets at the Dorothy Chandler Pavilion.

Erin was a Canadian-born actress whom some say bore a slight resemblance to Vivien Leigh. Her most memorable role had been—and, in all likelihood, would forever be—the woman who gets laid in the backseat of the car in *Everything You Always Wanted to Know About Sex (But Were Afraid to Ask)*. Who can ever forget Woody Allen, dressed as a sperm, preparing to "enter" her? She also appeared in a low-budget horror film entitled *The Demon Hunter* and as a minor Greek goddess in *Hercules in New York*, which, believe it or not, starred both Arnold Schwarzenegger and Arnold Stang. Erin's real name was Marilyn, and she must've been the only actress on record to have changed her name *from* Marilyn to something else.

She had met Groucho in the summer of 1971 through *The Odd Couple* producer Jerry Davis and had quickly become a combination secretary/personal manager/adviser. But she was usually referred to in print as Groucho's "companion," quotation marks and all. Odd couple, indeed. Erin was someone whose unique standing I'd come to envy—imagine being Groucho Marx's secretary—and here she was, calling *me* on the phone. Between Harry Ruby and Erin Fleming, I felt I'd succeeded in cracking Groucho's inner circle.

True to his word, Harry Ruby had phoned Groucho to tell him about the theater that was showing *Animal Crackers*. Erin had answered Groucho's phone and taken the message. I thought she was calling to get the name of the theater, but it soon became apparent that her motives were far more serious than a night at the Old Town Music Hall.

She wanted to know how they had managed to get their hands on a print of the film, since it was "illegal for them to be showing it." I, of course, hadn't the slightest idea. Also, according to Erin, she and Groucho had been trying to get the film officially rereleased for some time but Universal didn't think there was enough of an audience to warrant clearing the rights and striking new prints. Erin said she wanted to take me with her to show off to the executives at Universal as a sort of Exhibit A, a person who would go all the way to Anaheim during the gas crisis just to see *Animal Crackers.*

I was flattered all to hell.

During the course of our conversation, I mentioned that I had just picked up an old photograph of Groucho taken on the set of *A Day at the Races,* and that I liked it particularly because it was a candid shot showing him playing his guitar between takes, sitting next to Gus Kahn, who had composed the songs for that film. Erin said it sounded like an interesting picture and that she was sure Groucho would be happy to sign it for me. It didn't matter that the photo was a dark one, not particularly conducive to inscribing; I fully intended to take her up on the offer at some point in the very near future.

She had to leave to take Groucho to see *Sleeper,* so I told her I'd call her after my new phone was installed in my room at UCLA. Before we hung up I said, "While I have you on the phone, I was wondering if you could clear up a question that's been bothering me for some time. Some of the books I have say Groucho was born in 1890 and some of them say 1895. Which date is right?"

To my astonishment, I heard her call out, "Groucho! When were you born?" Faintly, in the background, I could hear a familiar, nasally voice call out, "October 2, 1890!" "Did you hear?" Erin asked. I heard. He had been sitting in the same room with her during our entire conversation.

I was getting close (but still no cigar).

Sometime between that call and the next one, a week or so later, the idea of my going personally to Universal expanded into the idea of starting a petition drive at UCLA to show those skeptical studio executives that there were hundreds, perhaps thousands, of young people who wanted to see *Animal Crackers.* Erin talked it over with Groucho's publicity people, who deemed it a worthy idea.

In mid-January I applied at the dean's office to set up a table on Bruin Walk and launch our drive. The people in the dean's office thought what we were trying to do was highly commendable and foresaw no problem in getting approval for a table. Almost as an afterthought, they inquired as to the name of our organization. I said we didn't really have one, and they told me, using true Marxian logic, that unless we had a name, we couldn't have a table.

And so, the Committee for the Rerelease of *Animal Crackers* was born. We called it CRAC for short. (This was before that word had any nefarious pharmaceutical connotations.) CRAC consisted of my roommate, Daryl, several co-op friends and me, although our intention was to send petitions to friends at other campuses and make it a nationwide campaign.

We soon became the envy of every activist group on campus—legalizing marijuana, gay rights, the Hare Krishnas, to name a few—because, while controversy swirled around the other tables, few people had any qualms about endorsing our "cause." After all, what harm could there be in trying to get an old Marx Brothers movie rereleased? The occasional student would stop by to complain that our time would be better spent trying to end world hunger or promote peace, but we felt getting *Animal Crackers* off the shelf was enough of a benefit to mankind.

Some students sympathized with us, saying they loved the Marx Brothers but couldn't quite bring themselves to sign because they were afraid the FBI would get hold of the petitions and there was "no telling *what* might happen." Watergate was, after all, a current event. Speaking of which, after one particularly paranoid student was assured that none of the petitions would be sent to any government agencies, he reluctantly signed. As he walked away, Daryl and I glanced down at his signature. It read: "H.R. Haldeman Jr." Others wanted to know if they had to be citizens of California, UCLA students or registered voters in order to sign. (None of the above.) In three days we gathered two thousand signatures. We even made the cover of the *Daily Bruin*. Twice.

Erin arranged for us to use, as an attention-getting backdrop, a ten-foot-high, circular wooden caricature of Groucho—actually, a prop from Groucho's appearance on Bill Cosby's variety show the year before. It succeeded in attracting attention, but it was hell rolling the thing back and forth from Bruin Walk to the storage room up the hill every time we set up or took down our table.

Erin accompanied the delivery of the wooden sign and so we finally met. She struck me as extremely friendly and down-to-earth, although the full-length white fox coat she was wearing was a little incongruous with the T-shirted, blue-jeaned students who gave her weird looks as they strolled past our table. She told me that the fur had been a birthday gift from Groucho and that he liked her to wear it. "I *wanted* a dining room set," she explained, "but Groucho *insisted* on a fur coat." Getting into the spirit of the campaign, Erin even signed our petition. Under "Comments" she added, prophetically, "I deny everything!"

My conversations with Erin had gotten quite frequent and I was flattered that she would phone me day or night to chat, sometimes for hours, about whatever was on her mind: Groucho, his friends, the Hollywood scene. It didn't matter if it was 1:00 A.M. on a school night; I felt that I had tapped into a magical pipeline that gave me access to a new and wondrous world. And I had no reason to doubt any of the revealing and fascinating things Erin shared with me about Groucho and whatever else was going on in her life.

When I mentioned, diplomatically, how weak Groucho had appeared at the Dorothy Chandler Pavilion, she shrugged it off, explaining that he had been sick that evening but that he was perfectly fine now. I was relieved to hear it.

Eventually, I would come to realize that she and I had different definitions of "perfectly fine."

And when I broached the idea that, based on newspaper and magazine articles, people had the impression that she was Groucho's girlfriend, this appeared to be news to her. She was absolutely dumbfounded, saying, "Oh, you're kidding! Who thinks that?" as though I could provide her with names and Social Security numbers. As time went by, I began to see that taking what Erin had to say at face value had its pitfalls, but for the time being I accepted it all as the gospel.

I remember commenting how wonderful it must be to be able to spend time with Groucho and his longtime writer friends such as Harry Ruby, Nunnally Johnson and Nat Perrin. She agreed halfheartedly but said that frankly, it got pretty dull listening to all those old stories all the time. I couldn't imagine how she could feel that way and I thought that, were *I* in her position, I would see things differently. After all, I'd been fascinated by old stuff all my life.

Erin provided me with an intriguing bit of gossip during one conversation. She said that Harry Ruby, at seventy-seven, was going to be marrying the widow who lived down the street and that Groucho was going to be his best man. I asked her if they'd set a date and she said, "Yes, but Harry keeps forgetting when it is! He knows it's the same day as his birthday, but he can't remember when *that* is either!"

During another call, I asked her how Groucho was doing and she simply said, "Here, I'll let you talk to him." Suddenly on the spot, I did the best I could.

Groucho: "Hello?"

Me: "Hi, Groucho. How are you doing?"

Groucho: "How am I doing *what*?"

Me: "How are you doing whatever you're doing?"

Groucho: "I'm telephoning. What are *you* doing?"

Me: "I'm telephoning, too. Isn't that a coincidence?"

Groucho: "Yes, it certainly is a small world."

Erin told him I was the one who was trying to get *Animal Crackers* rereleased. He asked if I'd succeeded; I told him we were working on it. Then he said, "I'll let you speak to my secretary, Miss Fleming." I told Erin that we'd made the front page of the *Daily Bruin*, and she said maybe she and Groucho could drop by the following evening and pick up some copies on their way to producer Irwin Allen's birthday party. I gave her directions to the co-op and thanked her for letting me talk to him.

In order to avoid a possible stampede, Daryl and I told no one about who might be dropping by, for which we were universally and understandably despised once the truth eventually surfaced. We meandered downstairs and milled around out front as nonchalantly as possible. After a while a silver Mercedes pulled into the driveway with Erin at the wheel and, sitting beside her, a familiar figure in a dark blazer and black beret. I handed Erin a small stack of *Bruin*s and then I shook his hand.

Me: "Groucho, I am *very* happy to be meeting you after all this time."

Groucho: "Well, you *should* be."

Erin explained that I was the young man he'd spoken with who was trying to get *Animal Crackers* rereleased.

Groucho: "Did you do it?"

Me: "No, but we hope to."

Groucho: "You'd better, or I'll *fire* you!"

Me: "I didn't realize I was working for you. How much are you paying me?"

Groucho: "A little less than nothing."

And off they went to Irwin Allen's birthday party.

I'd finally met Groucho Marx.

FOUR

A few days later, publicity agent Bill Feeder arranged for Groucho to make a personal appearance at Bruin Walk on February 7. Together, I was informed, we would speak with reporters and spread the word about our campaign. I was still high from our tantalizingly brief rendezvous in the driveway of the co-op, and now we were going to be having a joint press conference? This was pretty intimidating stuff, but I wasn't about to say no.

The day arrived. Our table was set up and students were busily scribbling away when Groucho appeared, accompanied by Erin (who was dressed more appropriately this time in a "Tell 'Em Groucho Sent You" T-shirt and jeans), Bill Feeder and a large contingent of reporters from print and television. Erin also brought along two college-age kids dressed as young Grouchos with greasepaint moustaches and cigars. They were supposed to spruce up the place with their eyebrow-wiggling and wisecracking, but, in my view, all they did was underscore the contrast between what Groucho used to be and what he had become.

He was still the frail, hazy man I'd seen at the Dorothy Chandler in 1972—probably even hazier—but it soon became apparent, as I watched him handle the questions those reporters were firing at him, that the basic mechanism which made him "Groucho" was still functioning. It's just that it had rusted over somewhat and was badly in need of a tune-up.

My behavior alternated between gushing and cavalier, but I had to keep in mind where my head was: My goal in life had been to meet Groucho Marx, and here we were, sitting side by side, chatting with reporters. Except he was as calm as could be, and I was trying not to explode.

Reporter: "What is the purpose of your appearance here today?"

Groucho: "I expect to get lunch."

Reporter: "Besides that."

Groucho: "I may get dinner."

Reporter: "What do you think of all the attention you're getting from these college kids?'

Groucho: "I'm flattered. I think the college kids of today will be the producers and directors of tomorrow. They're hip and they're smart and they know what they're doing. Last Halloween, three kids came to my house dressed as Groucho, Harpo and Chico."

Reporter: "What did you give them?"

Groucho: "I sent for the police."

Reporter: "What do you think about what this committee is doing?"

Groucho: "I think they're doing a fine job in trying to persuade the studio to put out *Animal Crackers*. It's a good picture and it should be released. Why Universal won't do it, I don't know. People like to laugh, and there's not much to laugh at these days. Even our *bad* movies were funny."

Me: "*Love Happy* was on the other night."

Groucho: "That was one of the bad ones."

Me: "Wasn't Marilyn Monroe in that?"

Groucho: "Yeah. She wore a dress that was cut so low, I couldn't remember my dialogue."

Reporter: "Groucho, do you have any special, funny memories about *Animal Crackers*?"

Groucho: "While we were doing the stage play, the stock market crashed—which *wasn't* very funny—and—"

Reporter: "I'm sorry, Groucho; I couldn't hear you."

Groucho: "You're very lucky."

There were hundreds of students hanging on his every word and Groucho's thin, papery voice only made them crowd in closer. Periodically, Erin would force them back, screaming, "He's very fragile! Please keep back!" But as protective as I felt toward Groucho in his diminished condition, I really couldn't blame them for wanting to get in as close as they could. And he did seem to be enjoying all the commotion he was causing.

After discussing the *Animal Crackers* campaign, Groucho touched on a number of other topics, including a piece of advice he'd gotten from Charlie Chaplin when Chaplin had returned to the States in 1972 to receive a special Oscar.

Groucho: "Chaplin said to me, 'Groucho, keep warm.'"

Me: "What did he mean by that?"

Groucho: "Well, he meant that you should always try to keep

warm, because when you get old, it's easy to catch cold and die. And when he said it, he took my arm like this."

And he reached over and grasped my arm the way Chaplin had, which gave me a jolt. Then a reporter asked about recent movies, wanting to know if he'd seen the controversial *Last Tango in Paris*:

Groucho: "I saw it. It was a pretty good picture. The only objection I had was that Marlon Brando laid that girl and kept his overcoat on."

Me: "At least he kept warm."

Groucho: "He kept the *girl* warm."

Then he noticed a photo button I was wearing showing him in *A Night at the Opera.*

Me: "Anybody you know?"

Groucho: "Yeah, I think that's one of the Ritz Brothers."

After fifteen or twenty minutes of answering questions, Groucho took advantage of the crowd to plug his memoirs, which had just been reissued.

Groucho: "There's a very good book I want to recommend called *Groucho and Me*. It's all about my early years. It's out in paperback now and I think you should all buy a copy."

Me: "Who wrote it?"

Groucho: "Who *wrote* it? Al Ritz!"

As with all good things, Groucho's visit came to an end. The crowd followed as he and Erin slowly made their way down Bruin Walk, back to his Mercedes. Just as he was getting in, he smiled at all the co-eds crowding around, pointed to Erin and said, "You're wasting your time, girls. *This* is the woman I love." And he gave her a little kiss. I thought it was cute, and after observing how responsive and playful he was toward her during the press conference, I remember thinking how lucky he was to have Erin around at that point in his life.

After Groucho left, some news cameramen were packing up their video gear. I overheard one of them saying to his partner, "Save this. We'll need it for the obit." I could've strangled him for saying that, especially while my head was still spinning from all that had just taken place. It was obvious from Groucho's condition that he wouldn't be around too much longer. I just didn't like to be reminded of it.

We received quite a bit of coverage on television as well as in print. In addition to local papers, I received clippings from my hometown of St. Louis and even such faraway places as Mexico and London, all discussing our campaign. In some papers there was an AP Wirephoto showing Groucho and me surrounded by students and reporters. I even got a few fan letters of my own from Marx Brothers enthusiasts in other cities who were also sympathetic to our cause.

A week or so after the press conference, Groucho and Erin were guests on "The Merv Griffin Show," and they arranged for Daryl and me to attend the taping. At one point Groucho told Griffin, "All my friends are either sick or dead. Harry Ruby is very ill in the motion-picture hospital and Nunnally Johnson has emphysema. All you smokers out there should go visit Nunnally and see where smoking will get you." Then, as a tribute to his ailing friend, Groucho and Erin did a duet of Harry Ruby's song "Dr. Hackenbush," which had been written for (and deleted from) *A Day at the Races*. Regardless of the sometimes morbid tone of the evening, however, the audience was excited to be seeing Groucho Marx in the flesh.

I knew just how they felt.

Erin told Merv about what our committee was trying to do and indicated that we were in the audience. Unlike some audience members on the "Ed Sullivan Show," however, we weren't asked to stand up and wave. Still, it was a charge to hear my name bandied about on national television and it struck me how far Daryl and I had come, from squinting at Groucho through binoculars from the back of the Dorothy Chandler Pavilion to sitting a few rows from the Merv Griffin stage—as Groucho's personal guests, no less—in a little over a year.

A few weeks later I got a call from my friend, Bob Garrick, who was attending Brigham Young University in Salt Lake City. He wanted to know if I could do him a big favor: ask Groucho if he would be willing to record a story he had told about encountering a Mormon woman at Disneyland during the "You Bet Your Life" era. I told him I'd see what I could do.

Still feeling rather pleased with myself after the UCLA encounter, I attached a tape recorder to my phone and brazenly dialed Groucho's number. He answered. I told him my name, which he couldn't place, so I reminded him that I was the kid who had launched the *Animal Crackers* campaign and who had sat next to him at UCLA. It sounded as though he'd replied, "I'm sold," but when I listened to the tape later, I realized he had actually said, rather sarcastically, "I'm thrilled." Nevertheless, I told him that a Mormon friend of mine was attending Brigham Young University and that it would mean the world to him if he could relate the Disneyland story. Rather than brushing me off, he agreed to my request.

Groucho: "Do you have a pencil or a typewriter?"

Me: "I've got a tape recorder."

Groucho: "OK. I was at Disneyland and a woman came up to me and said, 'Aren't you Groucho Marx?' I said, 'Yes.' She said, 'I wouldn't watch your show for a hundred dollars a night. The way you treat those people is disgraceful. My husband watches it every week, but I can't stand it.' I said, 'Where are you from?' She said, 'Salt Lake City.' I said, 'Are you a Mormon?' She said, 'Yes.' I said, 'If they still allowed polygamy in Salt Lake City and you were one of ten wives and your husband came home with that certain look in his eye, *you* would be the last one he'd choose!'"

I thanked him profusely for the favor and then sent the tape off to Bob, who later told me that his film class had roared at the story and that they couldn't quite believe that Groucho Marx himself had related it just for their amusement. It made me feel good to be able to share my increasing good fortune with friends.

In April, we received an answer from Universal. According to Vice President Arnold Shane, they were "delighted with the response of the students." I couldn't help thinking that, rather than delight, they were probably feeling something closer to annoyance or embarrassment, since we were publicly calling them stupid and short-sighted for preventing the world from viewing a nearly lost work of art. And how must it have looked to have Groucho, a frail eighty-three, pleading with Universal to grant his wish and release the movie that he and his brothers had made so long ago?

So they agreed to release it. Cautiously. In May, they would run the film in one theater, the U.A. in Westwood, right next to the UCLA campus. If it did halfway decent box-office, they'd release it nationwide. They didn't want to take any chances. In the event that only a handful of die-hard Marx Brothers fans showed up, the studio wouldn't be out that much money.

Universal issued a press release saying that there would be an official "repremiere" on May 23, with Groucho and the Committee for the Rerelease of *Animal Crackers* in attendance. I was elated. Posters touted the film as being "In Glorious Black & White!" It was a parody of the Glorious Technicolor ads of old, but in this day of artist's rights and colorization, such a claim would have been taken much more seriously by film buffs.

In the few months between the Bruin Walk appearance and the premiere, two important events took place in Groucho's life. The first was a sad one: Shortly after Groucho mentioned him on "The Merv Griffin Show" and just before the rerelease was announced, Harry Ruby died. Even though Groucho had been expecting it, it was a major loss, as they had been close friends since before World War I. Later Groucho would say, "When Harry Ruby died, a part of me died, too." And it was personally frustrating for me because it meant I'd never get the chance to meet the man whose work I'd admired for so long and whose phone call had set everything in motion. He never did get around to marrying that widow who lived down the street.

The other event was a much happier occasion. None of the Marx Brothers had ever been nominated for an Academy Award, much less won one. The only Marx Brothers film to be nominated was *A Day at the Races* in 1937, and that was for the dance direction of a musical number called "All God's Chillun Got Rhythm," which featured a flute-playing Harpo leading dozens of black singers and dancers through a barnyard—hardly quintessential Marx Brothers.

This oversight was rectified when, on April 2, Groucho was presented with an honorary Oscar by his good friend, Jack Lemmon—the same man who had presented one to Charlie Chaplin two years earlier. Groucho accepted on behalf of his brothers, and he acknowledged three important women in his life: Minnie, his mother; Margaret Dumont, the stuffy dowager in many of their movies "who never understood any of our jokes"; and Erin Fleming, "who makes my life worth living and who understands *all* my jokes." Watching Groucho's acceptance speech on TV, I thought, "Hey—I *know* them!" I was no longer just another Groucho fan watching from a distance.

About this time, Daryl and I decided to stop kidding ourselves with regard to our majors. We were both fascinated by show business and we thought we might like to become comedy writers. (After all, hadn't the head writer of "Laugh-In" encouraged me to keep at it when I was fifteen?) It was time to put History behind me and change majors for the fall quarter, so we applied to UCLA's Motion Picture/Television department, which was notoriously difficult to get into.

We were told that we needed to submit portfolios containing "anything creative" along with letters of recommendation. A panel would then review the portfolios and decide who would be admitted to the department and who would not. We didn't have much. Some people already had feature-length scripts or student films to submit. We had a few film-class essays and an audio tape of an ill-fated stand-up routine we'd performed at a club in front of half a dozen drunken patrons, wherein three phone callers got their lines crossed and zany hijinks ensued. And we were completely stuck in the "letters of recommendation" department.

Almost on a dare, I called Erin and asked her if Groucho would be willing to write one for Daryl and for me. She asked what sorts of things the letters should cover and where they should be sent. We told her they should mention the *Animal Crackers* campaign and our sincere interest in show business. She said she'd take care of it.

Sometime later, Daryl and I received notification that we'd been accepted to the Motion Picture/Television department for what would be our junior year. Since the reviewing panel was so secretive, there's no telling if it was our portfolios or the letters from Groucho that tipped the scales. Regardless, we were grateful that Erin and Groucho were willing to do us that kindness.

May 23 arrived and I was thrilled to be going to an honest-to-goodness Hollywood premiere, even if it was the premiere of a forty-four-year-old movie. I eyen rented a tux. It was supremely gratifying, after all our work, to look up and see "The Marx Brothers In *Animal Crackers*" on the marquee of the U.A. Westwood while cameras flashed and onlookers gawked.

Accompanied by my friends and family, I entered the theater and plunked myself down in the row in front of Groucho, who happened to be sitting next to Carl Reiner. Shortly before the movie started, I overheard them discussing *Blazing Saddles*, which had been directed by Reiner's friend, Mel Brooks.

Reiner: "What'd you think of *Blazing Saddles*?"

Groucho: "That scene around the campfire was pretty funny."

Reiner: "Well, that's what happens when you eat lots of baked beans and black coffee."

Groucho: "You fart."

Reiner: "Exactly."

And then a nice, fresh print of *Animal Crackers* unspooled, light years sharper than the murky copy we'd squinted at in Anaheim. (Had it really been less than six months since that night?) Not surprisingly, it was an enthusiastic audience. In addition to Groucho, cowriter Morrie Ryskind attended, as did composer Bert Kalmar's widow. It felt good to be able to, in a sense, help give this film back to them, although I was sorry that Harry Ruby hadn't lived to see it.

There was one point during the premiere when my thoughts turned to Ruby and a story I'd heard. During the Broadway run of *Animal Crackers*, the four Marx Brothers, George S. Kaufman, Morrie Ryskind, Bert Kalmar and Harry Ruby began a tradition of kicking in ten dollars apiece in order to buy an eighty-dollar bathrobe for whomever was having a birthday. Everyone else had received his, but when Ruby was next in line, the others suddenly decided they were tired of the tradition and weren't going to get him one. Ruby was annoyed. After all, he'd chipped in for all the others. It was only fair that he, too, should get his bathrobe. He sent out telegrams to the other seven reminding them that his birthday was just around the corner, but when his birthday arrived, there was no robe.

There was a scene in the play in which Captain Spaulding orders a large wooden chest to be brought onstage and opened in order to show what he'd brought back from Africa. During that evening's performance, when the chest was opened, Harry Ruby suddenly leapt out and demanded, "Where the hell is my bathrobe?" leaving the audience bewildered and Groucho speechless—a rare occurrence. The following day, Ruby got his robe.

When I watched them bringing out the wooden chest in the film, all I could think about was Harry Ruby and caskets.

After the premiere, everybody headed to the Bratskellar restaurant next door to celebrate. I figured I'd be able to share in the post-premiere triumph with Groucho and Erin, but their entourage glided past our table and went upstairs to a private room while the rest of us remained below. I guess I had overestimated the extent of our relationship.

At one point during our meal, I threw caution to the wind and bounded upstairs, just to say hello. I never felt so out-of-place in all my life. Everybody turned and looked at me and then went back to whatever they were doing. Erin said hello and Groucho shook my hand, but it was clear I didn't belong on the first-class deck so I said good night, poured myself down the staircase—which seemed to have doubled in length since I'd ascended it—and made my way back to the steerage section where my friends and family awaited. Despite the somewhat chilly reception at the Bratskellar, it was a triumphant night.

As it turned out, Universal had little reason to worry about *Animal Crackers*' performance at the U.A. Westwood. For months, there were lines around the block, and it ended up breaking the house record, which had been set by *The French Connection* several years earlier. Groucho and Erin would attend another repremiere in New York in late June—this time without our committee—and then, true to their word, Universal would open it nationwide.

Animal Crackers took in a considerable amount of money, some of it from my very own pocket since I got into the habit of taking first dates to see it, just to show off. This accounts for my less-than-stellar success with women during my collegiate years.

One night shortly after the premiere, Daryl and I were grabbing a bite at Arthur J's coffee shop, across the street from the U.A., where a long line was forming for the next screening of *Animal Crackers*. Although it was unquestionably satisfying to see this, something was bugging me. The film was out. I'd served my purpose. My goal had been to meet Groucho Marx and I'd certainly accomplished that. But now that I'd spent a little time with my hero, I didn't want it to end. I had hoped to remain in at least sporadic touch with Erin and Groucho, but I wasn't fooling myself: There just wasn't much of a reason for them to maintain the connection. I mean, we weren't really friends. And, unfortunately, there weren't any other Marx Brothers movies that needed rereleasing.

Summer vacation arrived and I had two potential employment opportunities. Job possibility number one was returning to the soda fountain at Farrell's Ice Cream Parlor in Woodland Hills, where I'd worked during vacations ever since high school. As it turned out, there was a new manager who didn't know me, and since my employment record at Farrell's appeared so spotty, he wasn't interested in rehiring me.

But that was OK, because I was secretly rooting for job possibility number two. In the course of the *Animal Crackers* campaign, Erin had put me in contact with an entrepreneur named Abe Shapiro. He was in charge of manufacturing the official Groucho wristwatch, which had eyes that shifted from left to right with each passing second.

During our campaign Shapiro said he'd been impressed with my initiative, and I had been helpful in suggesting certain Marx Brothers photographs which might be appropriate for promoting the wristwatches. He said he just might have a summer job for me with his company, perhaps writing advertising copy. This was pretty exciting given the fact that I was only nineteen and still in college. I mean, if things worked out, maybe I'd have a career in advertising waiting for me upon graduation! It might not be comedy writing per se, but it'd be a hell of a start.

Then came the gradual realization that Mr. Shapiro wasn't exactly Honest Abe. I was supposed to call him on Monday, but he was all tied up Monday, so maybe I should try again on Wednesday. No wait—he'll be out of town on Wednesday. Better make it next week, just to be on the safe side. That sort of thing. He kept insisting there'd be something for me "real soon; maybe in a week or so," but it was becoming increasingly apparent that a job wasn't in the cards, and probably never had been.

My father was pestering me to find employment, so figuring I had nothing to lose, I gave Erin a call. I explained to her that Shapiro had been stringing me along and wondered if there wasn't something—anything—I could do for her and Groucho, workwise. Just for the summer. I fully expected to hear, "I'm very sorry, dear. Of course we'd help if we could, but there's simply nothing that needs doing." Instead, she said something that would forever make me grateful to Abe Shapiro for the shitty way in which he'd led me on.

Erin explained that she had been handling Groucho's fan mail and correspondence, but that lately, with all the renewed interest in Groucho, her responsibilities as his personal manager had grown to the point where she just didn't have time for that anymore. They needed someone to handle all of the mail. In addition, they were looking for someone who was familiar with the Marx Brothers and their careers to act as an archivist and organize all of Groucho's memorabilia for eventual donation to the Smithsonian Institution. She went on to say that, based on my vast knowledge of Groucho and his various brothers, I was that person.

This was a dream job. Even better than making banana splits or selling wristwatches.

She said that they were preparing to go to New York for the second repremiere of *Animal Crackers*, but that when they got back we'd work out the details.

In my wildest dreams I hadn't expected anything like this to land in my lap. I had envied Erin for years because of her unique status as Groucho's secretary and now *I* was about to take over that exalted position. I prayed that Erin wouldn't change her mind between that day and their return from New York.

Animal Crackers had its East Coast repremiere at the Sutton Theatre on June 23, and, by all accounts it was a riot. Literally. According to the papers, Groucho was nearly crushed to death by a throng of adoring fans as he and Erin tried to make their way to the theater. There were even policemen on horseback trying in vain to keep the mob in order.

When Groucho stood up to say a few words before the film began, he remarked, "I'm delighted to be here, although I was almost murdered." Erin later said that a No Parking sign outside the theater had become a piece of twisted metal by the time the night was over.

But they returned intact from New York in early July, and Erin hadn't changed her mind about the job. She asked if three dollars an hour would be acceptable. Acceptable? I would have been making close to minimum wage at Farrell's, which was two dollars an hour in the summer of 1974. And frankly, I'd have paid *them* three dollars an hour just for the experience. Four, even. Erin had a few things to get squared away, so we agreed upon the last Monday in July as my official starting date.

One last detail: I needed to know where to go. I assumed I'd be working in some towering Wilshire Boulevard office building and that I'd be afforded the rare opportunity of catching a glimpse of

Groucho from time to time, when he'd come in to handle important business matters.

"Oh no," Erin corrected me, "You'll be working right in Groucho's house. There's a room there you can use for an office." And I could make my own hours, coming and going as I pleased.

Holy shit.

FIVE

Shortly before my first day of work, Erin informed me that Groucho was in the hospital with a chronic urinary problem—nothing to worry about—and that he wouldn't be at the house when I arrived. But she said she'd meet me there and explain what my duties would be. Although many people assumed she lived at Groucho's house, Erin had her own house off Doheny Drive in West Hollywood, about five minutes away.

Since I didn't own a car yet, I borrowed the family Cutlass and headed to work. I took the familiar freeway route from Tarzana to the Sunset Boulevard off-ramp, only this time I wouldn't be stopping at UCLA. I would keep going down Sunset, right into the heart of Beverly Hills. I found Hillcrest Road, made a left through the stone gates announcing Trousdale Estates, and began a steep, twisting ascent up Hillcrest, watching the numbers increasing along the way. Getting there was, literally and figuratively, a long and winding road. I drove past Barbara Stanwyck's house, past Morey Amsterdam's house, but not quite to Danny Thomas' house, and pulled into the driveway of 1083 Hillcrest.

Even though it was only a one-story, ranch-style home—hardly one of those "Beverly Hillbillies"-type mansions that people assume all celebrities inhabit—it was, to my eyes, an imposing structure. I walked up the white marble steps to the immense front door and rang the bell, my heart pounding. Agnes, the maid, answered and inquired as to my business. I explained that I was starting work there as Groucho's secretary and that Erin was supposed to show me what to do. Agnes said that Erin wasn't there yet but that I was welcome to come in.

So I went in.

I'd made it. I was actually *inside* Groucho Marx's house. The only analogy I can come up with that can begin to describe the feeling I had as I entered that house for the first time is when Dorothy opens her door into Munchkinland and everything turns to Technicolor.

Glorious Technicolor.

Although it would become almost a second home to me in the years ahead, that day the house seemed to stretch on forever. It was certainly much larger than our house in Tarzana and downright vast compared to my tiny cubicle at the co-op.

Just inside the front door was a hall tree with various hats, berets and wigs hanging from it. Past that, along the right wall, was a small table holding a vase and a silver dish. Hanging above the table was a massive oil painting of the Four Marx Brothers by John Decker, hard-drinking buddy of John Barrymore and W.C. Fields, which had been done in the style of one of the Dutch masters (the artists, not the cigars).

To the left, an original William Hamilton *New Yorker* pen-and-ink cartoon hung on the wall. It showed a hip, young college professor sitting at a table, conversing with his students. The caption read: "The tautology of their symbolism thus begins to achieve mythic proportions in *A Day at the Races*, *Duck Soup* and *A Night at the Opera*." Groucho was regularly amused by pretentious, pseudointellectual attempts to analyze and find deep meaning in his work. He always said he was just trying to be funny.

On the other side of the wall was a modest but ample kitchen that had a small dinette table and chairs situated beneath a window looking out onto the circular driveway and street. Just beyond the kitchen were the servant's bedroom and bathroom. Even those looked luxurious compared to my lodgings at UCLA.

Adjacent to the kitchen was the dining room, which had red wallpaper, a long table and high-backed, red velvet chairs. There was a buzzer on the floor beneath Groucho's chair so that he could summon the cook. The dining room was to become an important location for reasons beyond the fine cuisine.

Past the dining room was a den that doubled as a screening room. There was even a small projection booth, filled with cans of film, including an entire print of *A Night in Casablanca*, half a print of *Animal Crackers*, some of Groucho's television appearances from the fifties and sixties and home movies.

Groucho's home movies, incidentally, proved to be something of a disappointment. I had imagined them as lost masterpieces, filled with brilliant comic touches. Unfortunately, they ended up looking pretty much like everyone else's home movies. Most of them consisted of Groucho in various holiday locales, trying and failing to get his squirming children to wave to the camera.

One reel, however, was a little more interesting than the others. It dated from the early thirties and showed Groucho and his first wife, Ruth, handing sack lunches to their children, Arthur and Miriam, kissing each of them on the forehead, waving to the kiddies as they skipped off to school and embracing each other at the film's close. It was obviously a parody of sentimental family scenes and it still held up as such.

Another film can had a particularly tantalizing label, written in pencil in Groucho's youthful hand. It read, "Marx Brothers/ Minnie/Harry Ruby on horseback/Central Park." What a find! I was eager to view this particular reel for obvious reasons. Alas, when it was about to be loaded into the projector some months later, we noticed that the sprocket holes on the film had been badly damaged. Rather than risk ruining the rest of the reel permanently, we put it back into its canister.

I'd still like to see that one.

The wall of the den held, in addition to foreign posters of Marx Brothers movies, a gold record from the Queen album *A Night at the Opera,* which the rock group had presented to Groucho. If nothing else, it was an eclectic assortment of memorabilia.

On the other side of the dining-room wall was a very spacious living room that featured a hi-fi center, a massive fireplace and a baby grand piano that NBC had lent Groucho for rehearsal purposes during "You Bet Your Life" and which he had somehow never gotten around to returning. On the piano was the sheet music to an obscure World War I song entitled "Stay Down Here Where You Belong," which had been inscribed to Groucho by its composer, Irving Berlin, who had told Groucho that he'd give him a dollar for every time he *didn't* sing it. That piano had been and would be the focal point for many a gathering at Groucho's. Outside the living room was the swimming pool and the patio, which afforded a breathtaking view of the hills.

Continuing down the hall past the living room was "my" office. It was a small room that originally had been used as a painting studio by Groucho's third and last wife, Eden, for whom he had built the house in the mid-fifties and who had divorced him in 1969. Some of Eden's canvases were still being stored in Groucho's garage. He had held on to Eden's paintings, but he hadn't managed to hold on to Eden. As I recall, they were mostly still lifes and landscapes that seemed fairly good for an amateur but not quite up to professional standards.

On the wall just outside my office was a framed poster that had been used to promote the picture book *Why a Duck?* several years earlier. It featured a large sepia-toned photo of a thirty-nine-year-old Groucho flirting with Margaret Dumont in their first film, *The Cocoanuts*, with some memorable lines of dialogue printed below. ("I can see you now, you and the moon. You wear a necktie so I'll know you.") Nearby hung a disarmingly whimsical oil painting of Hansel and Gretel and a snowman standing outside a charming little gingerbread house, which Groucho had painted in the early fifties.

From my office the hallway made a sharp left past a long table upon which sat various trophies and curios from Groucho's past and present. Among them were his recently acquired Oscar, his 1950 Emmy and a Peabody Award for "You Bet Your Life," a 1951 *Time* magazine with Groucho on the cover, a medal he'd received from the French government in 1972 and the key to the city of Beverly Hills, "which is worth nothing," as Groucho would later confide to me.

Across from the trophy table was a wall of photos showing Groucho with (please hold your applause till the end) Chico, Harpo, Zeppo, Gummo, John Barrymore, Al Jolson, Noel Coward, Carole Lombard, Edward G. Robinson, Carl Sandburg, Rex Harrison and Cary Grant and many others. There were also original pen-and-ink drawings of Chico and Harpo by James Thurber, along with another Thurber drawing of a horse, on the back of which (the drawing, not the horse) was his rendition of Groucho. In addition, there was a Thomas Hart Benton pencil drawing of a pensive Groucho smoking a pipe, plus letters from Harry Truman, Booth Tarkington and Irving Berlin.

At the end of that section of the hallway was a large, circular bedroom that had been Eden's but which Erin had converted into her office. Adjacent to the bedroom/office was a bathroom containing a massive, circular, sunken tub—the last word in fifties luxury.

There was one more hallway, its walls bedecked with additional photos of family and friends, at the end of which was Groucho's bedroom. Just before Groucho's room, on the left, was the guest bedroom and bathroom, which had been his younger daughter,

Melinda's, until she'd moved out on her own in the late sixties.

Groucho's bedroom was spacious without being extravagant. In addition to the bed, there was a large desk with a wooden "You Bet Your Life" nameplate on top, a few family pictures, and a tall bookcase that took up most of one wall, jam-packed with volumes inscribed by Robert Benchley, S.J. Perelman, George S. Kaufman, Moss Hart—even Margaret Dumont, who had presented Groucho with one of Russell Baker's books when she had appeared with him on "The Hollywood Palace" in 1965. This bookcase would become one of my favorite hangouts as time went on.

But on that first day, I didn't do much exploring. The house was simply too intimidating. I felt that at any moment someone was going to collar me and say, "I'm sorry, sonny. You don't belong here. Go back to St. Louis." But that didn't happen. Instead, Agnes led me down the hallway to Erin's office, where I was introduced to two young men in their early twenties, one of whom was Groucho's grandson, Andy. I seem to recall they were working on a script.

I liked Andy immediately and found him to be very friendly and amusing, not to mention a pretty good jazz pianist. Andy was the son of Groucho's only son, Arthur. Although I didn't detect a strong family resemblance at first, I soon discovered that Andy could do the best "Gookie" around. If he didn't look like Groucho, he could manage to look almost exactly like his great-uncle Harpo (without the blond wig, of course).

For those who have done other things with their lives besides absorbing Marx Brothers trivia, a "Gookie" is the face that Harpo used to make wherein he would puff out his cheeks, cross his eyes and grimace. The word is a corruption of "Gehrke," a tobacconist from the Marx Brothers' old New York neighborhood who used to make just such a face, inadvertently, while rolling tobacco leaves into cigars. Now you know.

Andy didn't live at Groucho's. Part of his reason for being there was that he was in the midst of putting in order hundreds of 16mm prints of "You Bet Your Life" episodes so that KTLA, a local television station, could begin running them in the fall—another sign of the renewed interest in Groucho.

Andy wasn't sure what my job would entail, but he said I was welcome to hang out with him and his friend until Erin got there. I enjoyed talking with him and it helped take the edge off my nerves on that first day through the looking glass.

After a while, Erin arrived and showed me where I would be working. My office was certainly adequate for my needs. It had a desk, a chair, a couple of file cabinets, a tall wooden cabinet with a few drawers and a bulletin board holding up, among other things, a sheet of paper on which was written, "Marx Brothers Writers Still Alive and in Town." The paper listed, should the need arise, the names, addresses and phone numbers of Groucho's extant collaborators. And my office had windows.

I was all set.

Erin explained what would be required of me with regard to the fan mail. In addition to the letters that arrived daily, there were drawers filled with unopened mail, the postmarks of which dated back to mid-1972! If her idea of handling the fan mail was tossing it into a drawer, there was clearly a need for someone such as myself. It would take weeks for me to process the mail in those drawers before I could even think about the current stuff, which continued to accumulate at a steady pace.

Apart from the fan mail there was the matter of Groucho's memorabilia, which needed to be organized so that it could be donated to the Smithsonian Institution after Groucho's death—an eventuality I preferred not to think about. Much of Groucho's "stuff" was crammed tightly into a closet which, if you opened it, threatened to spill out onto the floor, and sometimes did. To the disinterested it was a colossal mess, but to a Marx Brothers fan it was paradise.

Groucho had dozens of vintage photographs dating from the turn of the century through the current year including candid shots of the Marx Brothers out of makeup, in various plays and films and with their families. Only a small portion had ever been published, and it was mind-blowing to sort through so much theatrical history and begin to organize everything thematically and chronologically.

There were scripts going back to the Marx Brothers' Broadway careers in the twenties and Hollywood in the thirties, some with Groucho's handwritten revisions on them. I unearthed not only familiar final drafts of scripts for Marx Brothers films, but also early drafts of those scripts as well as *only* drafts of scripts for films that never got made.

I remember thumbing through an early draft of *Go West,* which had been written by Bert Kalmar and Harry Ruby in 1940. It was looser and more absurd than the final draft by Irving Brecher, a close friend of Groucho's, and contained a number of memorable jokes. One of them had Groucho flirting with a woman and saying, "It's women like you who make men like me make women like you!" This might have become an oft-quoted Grouchoism, except for the fact that it was never uttered.

On the other hand, there was a first draft of 1941's *The Big Store* that had a deleted scene in which Groucho is trying to prevent some guy from beating a dog. "Hey, don't hit her! She's man's best friend!" Groucho pleads. The man stops hitting the dog. Then Groucho turns around and the dog bites him on the rear, prompting him to snap, "Go ahead! Beat the hell out of the bitch!" It struck me as far too nasty, even for Groucho. And besides, if the Hays Office had hemorrhaged over Clark Gable's "Frankly, my dear, I don't give a damn!" in 1939, I couldn't imagine them even considering "Beat the hell out of the bitch!" two years later.

Groucho also had some mimeographed pages from *Go West,* which were used when several scenes were taken on the road in 1940 and performed in front of audiences in order to polish them up before filming began. They had used this method of testing scenes live, which was producer Irving Thalberg's idea, before shooting *A Night at the Opera* and *A Day at the Races,* and it had resulted in better-paced, higher-quality films. Why *Go West,* which had also employed the same method, didn't end up a better film is anybody's guess. Possibly it's because they didn't have Thalberg around to supervise the production, as he had passed away several years earlier.

I was reading through one set of notes from a performance at the Paramount Theatre in Los Angeles when I ran across this matter-of-fact remark: "After Harpo's solo in the last show Sunday evening, Harpo made the following speech." I stopped and read the sentence over again just to make sure I hadn't misread it. And then, incredibly, there was the transcript of a long, rambling speech by Harpo Marx.

For the record, here is what the "silent" Marx Brother had to say that night: "Ladies and gentlemen, I appreciate to the fullest this outburst and applause which conclusively proves my knowledge of dramatic arts. I would indeed be ungrateful were I not to acknowledge even in this inarticulate manner your generous yet wholly spontaneous (*sound of a gun shot*). That'll never stop me! And in conclusion, may I not have the rather unusual privilege of tendering to you, my audience, the warm congratulations which are rightfully yours for the keenness and perspicacity which you have shown in recognizing true genius, accomplished artistry, and monumento-monumania. Thank you."

In the midst of Harpo's speech, Groucho blurts out: "Now you know why he never talked!" It was astonishing to uncover written proof that, contrary to legend, Harpo did speak onstage, if only occasionally. The speech, of course, never made it into the filmed version of *Go West*. Once I was settled in at Groucho's I made my own copy of that historic address for future reference.

Then there were the clippings. Groucho and his various wives had kept fairly meticulous track of his career through newspaper articles. There were a number of old scrapbooks with reviews of the brothers' Broadway shows, films and radio and television work, not to mention items about their personal lives, spanning more than fifty years.

The albums seemed to taper off in the early sixties, which coincided with the tapering off of Groucho's career. For items after that period, there was a large footlocker brimming with whole sections of newspaper which, after careful scrutiny, would yield some piece of news about Groucho. Slowly I began to sift through that trunk of newspapers, snipping out the pertinent blurbs and then arranging them, first by decade, then year, then month, then day. Eventually I filled three huge scrapbooks with nothing but newspaper clippings from the mid-sixties through the early seventies, adding to them as new items appeared. It was an exhausting but gratifying undertaking.

In addition to the photos, scripts and clippings, there were boxes of letters, programs and posters, plus reel-to-reel audio tapes and records that also needed sorting out. In almost every room of the house there was some piece of Groucho's past that needed organizing.

In terms of Groucho's personal wardrobe, there was a pith helmet and swallowtail coat that Erin claimed were from the stage production of *Animal Crackers*, but which felt newer, somehow. There was one item, however, whose authenticity I never doubted.

I was in Groucho's bathroom some weeks later, looking through drawers for the skin lotion that a nurse had requested, when I noticed a pair of round, gray, wire-rim glasses. Without lenses. They were unmistakable, and the worn chrome plating coupled with the slightly greenish oxidation around the metal rim attested to their vintage. It seemed to me that they deserved a more noble place of honor than inside his bathroom drawer.

After giving me an overview of the enormous task ahead, Erin left the house to see how Groucho was doing. Sometime later Andy and his friend took off. I wasn't sure where to start; I only knew that I couldn't wait to dig in. While I was trying to make a dent, Groucho's weekday cook, Martha Brooks, came into my office and asked what I wanted for lunch. I couldn't think straight at that point so I deferred to her judgment. She prepared a tuna sandwich and a Coke, which I ate in the kitchen. We talked while I ate.

Martha had been working for Groucho for nearly fifteen years. I envied her having known him for so long. It occurred to me that Martha had begun working there while Groucho was still starring in "You Bet Your Life" each week. She must have seen and heard so much over the years. In the course of our conversation, I asked her how long it'd been since Groucho had been able to drive a car for himself. She laughed and recalled the last time she and Groucho had gone down to the Department of Motor Vehicles to renew his license, sometime in the late sixties.

Martha had been drilling him on the various rules and regulations in the driver's manual, and she even succeeded in slipping him an answer or two while he was taking the written test. But when it came time for Groucho to take the wheel, there was no way out—he had to do that part all by himself.

"He came back from that driving test looking just as sad as could be, and he said, 'Martha, I don't understand it. I gave that man a picture, a book and one of my *best* cigars—not the cheap ones—and he *still* failed me!' He just couldn't understand how they could do that to him. After that, they wouldn't let him drive anymore."

For a time Martha had been, in effect, the lady of the house, as well as a good friend to Groucho during a period when his last wife had left him and not much was happening professionally. She told me that quite often she'd be cleaning up in the kitchen at night and Groucho would amble down the hall in his pajamas and sit and talk with her for hours, asking her advice about whatever was troubling him. Clearly she had been much more than just the cook.

I liked Martha right from the start. She was warm and funny and she clearly had Groucho's best interests at heart. In later months I would be treated to sumptuous feasts in Groucho's dining room, imported gourmet foods and five-course meals. But on that first day I sat in the kitchen talking with Martha, eating a tuna-fish sandwich and drinking a Coke, and it was probably the best tuna-fish sandwich and Coke I'd ever tasted.

The rest of my first day was uneventful. I stayed until around five trying to make some sense out of the mail and memorabilia mess, then I said good night to Martha and Agnes and left. As I pulled the door closed behind me, it locked. The loud *click* caused a twinge of apprehension about leaving. After all, I'd just spent the day inside Groucho Marx's house, the culmination of years of loyal fanaticism from afar. It had taken me so long to cross that threshold, in more ways than one. What guarantee did I have that I'd be allowed back in the following day?

Eventually I would have my own key to the house, but for the time being I had to depend on the kindness of whomever happened to answer the door. But I had a sneaking suspicion that things would work out after all. So I started up the Cutlass and headed home, eager to share my first impressions with family and friends.

SIX

It wasn't long before Groucho returned from his hospital stay, and when he and Erin sauntered past my office for the first time she reintroduced me. Although I may have looked familiar to him from the *Animal Crackers* campaign several months earlier, he could hardly have been expected to have retained the name. In a sense Groucho's hazy memory gave me the chance to enjoy meeting him for the "first" time on several occasions: Over the phone, at Bruin Walk and now in his own home.

Erin: "Groucho, this is Steve. He's going to take care of the fan mail."

Groucho: "You're Steve, huh?"

Me: "Yes."

Groucho: "Well, you don't *look* like him."

After tossing off that bit of absurdity, he shuffled off down the hall, back to his room.

That first week I worked from Monday through Saturday and then I figured I'd give myself a break and take Sunday off. I woke up Sunday morning, got dressed and sat in my room in Tarzana wondering, *What am I doing here when I could be at Groucho Marx's house! Who needs a day off from that?* So I flew out the door, got in the car, drove back to Groucho's and leapt back into my work. I ended up working there seven days a week for quite a while during that first summer.

When I began sorting through those drawers of unopened fan mail that had accumulated over the previous few years, I had what I consider to be the closest I have ever come to a psychic experience. I opened the first drawer and noticed a fan letter from someone with a name like Steve Sandler. For some reason the name reminded me of Steve Singer, one of the friends I had to leave behind when we moved from St. Louis to Los Angeles in 1962. I hadn't thought about Steve Singer in years, nor had I been in contact with him since the move, and it was only the similarity in names that caused me to think of him in the first place.

After looking through the first drawer, I opened a second drawer —a drawer into which I had never peered—and there, buried beneath a large clump of fan mail, was a letter asking if it would be possible to meet Groucho after his Carnegie Hall concert. It was from Steve Singer in University City, Missouri.

It gave me the creeps.

I cannot say with certainty that this was a bona fide psychic experience (after all, I'm from Missouri, the Show-Me State), but no one has ever been able to explain it to my satisfaction. Skeptics tell me it was either a coincidence or I'd probably seen the envelope sometime earlier while absently glancing through the drawers of mail. But I swear I hadn't even *opened* that drawer, much less begun sifting through its contents.

After I regained my composure I sent Steve a letter explaining what had happened and reintroducing myself as his buddy from the old neighborhood, but I didn't hear anything back. Almost twenty years later, through another series of stranger-than-fiction circumstances, I came in contact with Steve for the first time since St. Louis. He said that he had indeed sent that letter to Groucho, but he didn't remember ever receiving one from me. So a certain measure of mystery still surrounds the incident.

In time I worked out a routine for handling Groucho's fan mail. But be forewarned: In the event you wrote to Groucho during the mid-seventies requesting an autograph, you will either be delighted or disheartened by what I am about to divulge, so read on at your own peril.

If someone sent something of his or her own to be autographed, such as a book or a picture, I would set it aside with other, similar items and periodically take them in to Groucho to be personally inscribed by him. He almost never varied from a "To/from" format ("To Mary from Groucho"), which may have disappointed some of the fans who wrote in requesting specific, elaborate inscriptions. I remember one Canadian fan who sent in a poster and who wanted Groucho to write on it, "To my pal, Mike—Hands across the border and friends forever. Your friend, Groucho." Groucho wrote, "To Mike from Groucho." I hope it was friendly enough for him.

For "regular" fan letters requesting an autograph but not enclosing anything to be signed, there was an alternate plan. I would leave a thick stack of eight-by-ten-inch glossies on Groucho's desk every few months and he would sign "Groucho" on each one with a black Sharpie, leaving some blank space above his signature. The most common photo was a publicity shot of Groucho, Harpo and Chico from *A Day at the Races*, with a caption promoting *An Evening with Groucho*, the two-record set of his one-man show. I also had portraits from the fifties and some recent shots printed up in order to respond more precisely to the requests. If they said, "I loved you on 'You Bet Your Life,'" they'd probably get one of the fifties portraits, and if they said, "You look so dapper in your turtleneck and beret," they might get a recent one. I aimed to please.

After Groucho would go through the stack of photos, signing only his name on each, I would take them back to my office. As requests came in, I'd take a black Sharpie and personalize each photo above his signature, emulating Groucho's handwriting as best I could. It would have been nice to have been able to honor each request with an inscription entirely in Groucho's hand, as with the special items people sent in, but there was simply too large a volume of fan mail, so most of the photos sent out were hybrids. But they could all truthfully be said to have been "signed" by the man himself.

In fairness to Groucho, this was above and beyond what many younger, less legendary celebrities are willing to do. Some of them have pictures printed up with photographic facsimiles of their signatures already on them. Others have their signatures made into rubber stamps that their secretaries use on whatever comes their way. Some simply have their secretaries forge their names. And still others hire fan-mail services, which intercept and respond to the letters, preventing them from ever reaching the celebrity in the first place. So it counts for something that a man of Groucho's stature, in his mid-eighties and in diminished health, bothered to personally autograph as much as he did.

As I was leaving his room one day after he'd signed a particularly large stack of pictures, I thanked him on behalf of the fans, saying that a lot of celebrities wouldn't have taken the trouble. He simply said, "It's my job."

If you're curious as to why he signed only "Groucho" and left off the "Marx," there's a reason for that. For decades, whenever

Groucho was asked for an autograph, he would scribble "Groucho Marx." One day in the mid-fifties, baseball great Leo Durocher noticed Groucho signing his full name and said, "Why don't you just write your first name? Everybody knows who Groucho is!" And that was that. From then on, it was rare for Groucho to bother signing his full name on autograph requests or letters.

He did, however, write his full name on checks. During my initial weeks there, he would personally fill out my paychecks, including my name, the date and the amount, putting me into a quandary as to whether or not to cash them. Being keenly aware of the value of autographed celebrity material, I wondered if a check made out entirely by Groucho Marx wasn't eventually going to be worth much more than whatever the amount was. On the other hand, I needed the money, and a hundred and twenty dollars was a hundred and twenty dollars.

My financial situation being what it was, I decided to Xerox one as a souvenir and then cash the original checks, causing more than one bank teller's eyebrows to rise when they'd notice the signature. Even though Groucho's real name was Julius Henry Marx, his checks were signed "Groucho Marx." And they went through. Eventually, due to slip-ups in keeping his checkbook balanced, Groucho's accountants printed out the checks and he would only sign them. This kept the balance accurate—and made the checks less of a temptation to hoard.

In the event a letter seemed particularly worthy, I would bring it in to him. Certainly letters from old friends would receive his personal attention, but it was difficult to gauge which of the other letters he'd care about and which he would not. There was one letter from a man who had been the Marx family's chauffeur in New York in the twenties, and who had said it was always a laugh a minute when they were in the car. I figured he'd appreciate hearing from someone who went back that far, but when I showed him the letter, he looked up at me and said, "So? What do you want me to do about it?"

Conversely, there was a letter from a man who said he'd seen *Duck Soup* twenty times and who wanted to name his horse after Groucho. He would frequently recount this to lunch guests. It wasn't the part about naming his horse that impressed Groucho; it was the fact that this guy had seen *Duck Soup* twenty times! Well, I had seen *Duck Soup* about sixteen times by then and didn't feel it was particularly noteworthy, but he could never get over that guy who'd seen it twenty times.

One man wrote in and asked if Groucho had developed his distinctive, forward walk in order to conceal an erection. I didn't show him that one. Over the years people have told me that I should have given it to him, but I still think my judgment at the time was sound. Groucho was a liberal in many ways—particularly for a man from the nineteenth century—but when it came to overtly sexual references, especially from someone he'd never met, he sometimes remained truer to the Victorian times in which he'd been born. I'm convinced he would have taken offense at such a brazen query from a total stranger.

Andy Marx told me about an incident that illustrates Groucho's aversion to tastelessness. Groucho was at a party where some of the guests were amusing themselves by standing outside a bathroom door and listening to people peeing, then giggling at the noise and making snide remarks. Irked by what he perceived to be their sophomoric behavior, Groucho excused himself and went into the bathroom. As soon as the door was locked, people gathered 'round to listen to Groucho relieving himself, but were flabbergasted when the ensuing tinkling sound seemed to go on for five or six minutes nonstop.

What they didn't know was that Groucho had quietly retrieved a garden hose from the adjacent patio and had been standing over the toilet letting the water trickle steadily into the bowl. Groucho's ploy succeeded in shaming the guests and discouraging them from further eavesdropping.

If a fan had a question about Groucho or the Marx Brothers, I would take a piece of stationery—which had his caricature on it—and answer it as best I could, signing my name as Groucho's secretary and enclosing one of the signed pictures. Occasionally I had to give them a bit of bad news, such as the time a man wrote in saying he loved "You Bet Your Life," he played the accordion and, if he could just get on the show, he'd donate all his winnings to the Veterans of Foreign Wars. I wrote him and told him that the shows he'd been watching were mostly from the late fifties and that "You Bet Your Life" was no longer in production. I hope he didn't take it too hard.

Only once did Groucho receive what I suppose could be called hate mail. It was a letter from a Southern "gentleman" who had just seen an episode of "You Bet Your Life" wherein Groucho had, apparently, been lenient in judging a black contestant's response to a question. The letter-writer accused Groucho of "gypping for the nigger"—a particularly offensive phrase I'd heard neither before nor since—and he vowed never to watch the show again as a result. Somehow I don't think Groucho would've minded losing such a viewer, and I chose not to bother him with that letter either.

There was another letter that stands out because it illustrates Groucho's approach to fans way back when. A man wrote to him saying that when the Marx Brothers were appearing in the stage version of *Animal Crackers* in 1928, he had written to the theater requesting an autographed picture. Groucho had written back saying, "Please send us fifty cents in coin, to cover the cost of the picture." The man sent them a half dollar and shortly thereafter he received a signed picture of the Four Marx Brothers, along with his half dollar back and another note from Groucho, this one saying, "Here's your fifty cents back. We just wanted to make sure you were serious about wanting our picture."

Another aspect of the fan mail intrigued me. A couple of years earlier, I had written Groucho a fan letter. But I hadn't just scribbled down a note off the top of my head and dropped it in the mailbox. I had laboriously gone through draft after draft, making sure my letter was unlike anyone else's. Although I had managed to unearth Groucho's street address, I wasn't sure of the ZIP code for Beverly Hills. (This was years before those five digits were known to every television-watching teenager in America.) But I went ahead and sent the letter minus the ZIP code. I never received a response and I'd always assumed it was because I had failed to include the proper ZIP code.

Once I was handling Groucho's fan mail, however, I began to see how difficult it was *not* to get a letter to him. Not only did many people leave off the ZIP code, they left off the address as well. Sometimes it simply said, "Groucho Marx, U.S.A." Occasionally, it just had his picture pasted on the front of the envelope.

But my favorite was from a fan in South Africa who had addressed the envelope: "The Three Brothers, Hollywood, Culver City, London." Somehow it had found its way into Groucho's mailbox! How did the post office know it wasn't intended for the Ritz Brothers or the Kennedys or Manny, Moe and Jack? To this day, I remain baffled—and impressed.

I had made sure my fan letter was typed on a clean sheet of paper and didn't have a single error, spelling or typographical. Many of Groucho's fans weren't quite so finicky—I was aghast at how people would write to him. They used diagonally torn sheets of notebook paper. They scrawled handwritten letters in pencil that *I* could barely read, much less a man in his eighties. And they misspelled his name so frequently—"Grocho," "Graucho," "Marks"—that it was downright depressing. But it didn't matter. The fans were sincere in their admiration for Groucho, so despite their slovenly ways they were still rewarded with a signed photo. And the postage was on the house.

Occasionally a rumor would spread that the best way to reach Groucho was to write to him somewhere *else*. Some years earlier, when a fan had heard that Groucho was a frequent patron of Nate 'n Al's Delicatessen, she had sent him a letter in care of the noted eatery. Groucho was presented with the letter upon his next trip to Nate 'n Al's, and in replying to her letter he'd said, "I'm thinking of having all my mail forwarded there."

And when someone in Seattle wrote in to their local newspaper's celebrity-questions column asking for Groucho's address, the printed reply was, "Your best bet is to write to Groucho c/o The Beverly Hills Hotel in Beverly Hills, California." It didn't matter that Groucho rarely went there. Scores of Seattle fans figured, if it's in the paper, it must be true.

Consequently I had to drive over to the Beverly Hills Hotel, inform the parking valet that I was only going to be a minute, then dash inside, elegantly attired in blue jeans and old tennis shoes, retrieve Groucho's mail from the front desk and drive back to Groucho's house. This ritual continued for a number of weeks, until the Seattle item had run its course.

Although the bulk of Groucho's letter-writing days were behind him, he would occasionally want to send a note to an old friend or respond to a letter. I didn't know shorthand, but I scribbled as fast as I could, just managing to get down what he was saying as he was saying it.

Once, after jotting down a couple of letters Groucho wanted to send, I said, "I'll type these up for you," to which he replied, "Yes, and then throw them away." I flashed on the dictation scene in *Animal Crackers* in which Zeppo had to "take a letter" from Groucho to his lawyers: Hungerdunger, Hungerdunger, Hungerdunger, Hungerdunger and McCormick. After Zeppo had patiently taken down Groucho's nonsensical dictation, Groucho instructed him to "make two carbon copies of that letter and throw the original away."

At Groucho's house, life really *did* imitate art.

Even though I'd spent some time with him during the *Animal Crackers* campaign and had Erin's seal of approval, I was still nervous about being in Groucho's house during those initial days, especially while Groucho was in it. It was intimidating when I had to ask him a question or bring in something for him to sign. Walking down the hallway toward Groucho's room, I found myself feeling a little like the Cowardly Lion when he had to walk down that long corridor and approach the Wizard's throne room.

I could never quite shake the feeling that somehow, in the course of my duties, I'd do something terribly wrong and that would be it as far as Groucho was concerned. I'd be out the door before I knew what hit me. After all, his name was Groucho, not Cordialo or Warmo. This never happened, mind you, but I always felt that it could occur without a moment's notice.

Part of my paranoia, it turned out, was justified. One aspect of growing older is inconsistency. Something could be just fine for five days in a row, and then, on the sixth, it would suddenly be unacceptable. I learned this the hard way a few weeks into the job.

I enjoyed having music playing in the background while I was working on the fan mail. It helped keep me company when no one else was around. Erin had let me borrow a small radio to listen to in my office, saying that Groucho never used it and wouldn't mind. Indeed, Groucho had strolled past my office on several occasions when the radio was on and he hadn't said a word about it.

Then one day, I was coming out of the guest bathroom near my office. I opened the door and there stood Groucho, holding the radio, waiting for me. Startled, I smiled and said, "Oh! Hello there!" but he was in no mood to chat. "What makes you think you can borrow this?" he snapped. "It isn't your radio, you know!" I told him that Erin had OK'd it and he said, "It isn't *Erin's* radio either! It's mine!" Then he marched off toward his room, taking the radio with him. I nearly burst into tears. This was the person I'd most wanted to please and somehow I'd angered him.

I had to run an errand later that day and when I returned, I heard Groucho calling, "Steve!" from down the hallway. Oh no. What now? I made my way into his room rather tentatively. He simply said, "You can listen to the radio if you want," and he handed it back to me. I thanked him and took it into my office, where I would continue to enjoy music whenever I was in there for any length of time.

Apparently Erin had interceded on my behalf and cleared everything up. As far as Groucho was concerned, the incident was forgotten. But I still felt badly that he'd snapped at me when I really hadn't done anything wrong.

Another example of his inconsistency involved some visiting fans. There was a standing rule at the house that no one was to bother Groucho if fans came to the door; they were to be politely turned away. Frankly, I could never quite understand how a fan could be so audacious as to just show up that way, unannounced, but it happened. It wasn't that Groucho didn't appreciate his fans; he did. But they wanted to visit and talk with him and ask him a lot of questions, and he tended to avoid that sort of thing.

One day, however, the doorbell rang and I was nearby, so I answered it. It was a family who had driven from the midwest in their camper and who wanted very much to meet Groucho. Of all people, I could certainly understand their quest, but I informed them as graciously as possible that this simply wasn't done. As a consolation, I told them that if they waited a minute I'd get them a signed picture. They were disappointed but glad to hear about the photo. As I walked down the hallway toward my office I passed Groucho, who wanted to know who was at the door. I told him it was some fans and that I was about to get them an autographed picture and then send them away.

"Why? This isn't your house!" he said sharply. And he went to the door, greeted the startled fans and proceeded to make their entire trip worthwhile, wiggling his eyebrows, doing "the walk" and chatting with them. I guess from time to time he needed that interaction with his adoring public.

Once again, I'd only been following orders (although that's

what they said at the Nuremberg trials). But this time I didn't feel all that badly that Groucho had reprimanded me; the delight he had given that family was worth my discomfort. Even though I ended up spending three years working for Groucho, I never took my inside position for granted or grew complacent about it, and I never lost sight of what it felt like to be on the outside looking in.

As a matter of fact, on several occasions when I was sitting by the kitchen window, I'd wave as the tourist vans cruised by, hoping to give them a little thrill. They could go back to Montana and boast, "We drove past Groucho Marx's house and he waved to us! At least I think it was him."

Despite the occasional reprimand, it was fairly smooth sailing between Groucho and me. After I became a familiar presence in the house, he'd often stop by my office on his way to or from his room and we'd chat briefly about whatever was on his mind: a book, a movie, something in the news.

I never took *that* for granted, either.

Seven

During my second week on the job, I was in Groucho's bedroom sifting through some old recordings when I ran across a 78 of Groucho, George S. Kaufman and Irving Brecher, who had written *At the Circus* and *Go West*. Despite Groucho's longtime friendship with Kaufman, I was unaware that anything like that existed. Intrigued, I showed it to Groucho, who said, "We can listen to it if you like." So I fired up his record player and we listened to the old transcription disc, just the two of us. The material wasn't all that funny, but it was nice to be able to share the experience with Groucho, one on one.

It was at that point that I felt we were beginning to develop a rapport. We weren't exactly friends, but our relationship was certainly friendlier than merely employer and employee. Maybe something like having a funny, unpredictable old uncle. At any rate, it was after we listened to that record that I decided to ask him to sign a picture that I'd been keeping in my office ever since my first day on the job.

It wasn't that dark picture of him playing the guitar on the set of *A Day at the Races,* which I had mentioned to Erin over the phone. It was a beautiful, matte-finish portrait of Groucho from 1939, complete with greasepaint moustache and cigar. I wanted to wait until just the right moment, and I felt that moment had arrived. After having had him sign picture after picture for anonymous fans, it was my turn.

A word about autographs in general: Some people don't understand what the big deal is in asking a person to scribble his or her name on a picture or a cocktail napkin, except perhaps for the increase in monetary value the signature adds. But for fans, it is a very big deal and it has nothing to do with what they could sell the item for. I suppose this gets back to my contention that celebrities really aren't "just people," at least not to their fans.

For me, an autograph serves several purposes. First off, it is a tangible memento of a point in time at which two paths crossed, however fleetingly. A handshake or a hello is fine, but it's not very durable. Second, I can continue to get a charge, as time passes, by taking out the autographed item and reflecting on that moment in the past when it was freshly signed. Finally, it's an ego-boost to show it off to envious friends and acquaintances.

In truth, I'd become a bit spoiled. "To Steve from Groucho" was fine for that piece of paper my stepmother had given him a year earlier, but I was holding out for something special. I handed him the picture and said, "I'd like you to write something so that someone looking at it won't think I just ran into you on the street. You know, something personal." He looked at me and said, "What do you want me to say? 'I love you'?" He took Sharpie in hand and proceeded to write, "To Steve—A great secretary—Groucho." There could be no higher praise.

Actually, that's not entirely accurate. On one occasion he called me a genius. In front of witnesses. Granted, I'd earned that accolade because I was the only member of the household who could figure out how to change the needle on his stereo, but the fact remains that Groucho Marx once called me a genius. Can *you* make the same claim?

Bit by bit, Groucho began to see that our tastes were not dissimilar. In my reading about Groucho and his circle, prior to getting the job, I often encountered references to the Algonquin Round Table, but I really hadn't read any of their work. I was browsing through one of his Benchleys one day when Groucho said, "You can borrow that if you like. You can borrow any of my books. Just make sure you put them back." So I began to do just that, in the process receiving a wonderful education in the history of humor. Groucho's room became my favorite library.

There was a reason Groucho was so fond of Robert Benchley and those other Round Tablers. They were witty, entertaining people who wrote witty, entertaining stuff. Groucho had a copy of a book entitled *While Rome Burns*, written in 1934 by the noted critic, Algonquinite and close friend of Harpo, Alexander Woollcott. The book was issued in a limited edition of 500, of which Groucho's was number 106. In addition to the number and signature, Woollcott had added, "For Groucho, who is, evidently, my one hundred and sixth closest friend. A. Woollcott."

I was grateful to Groucho for introducing me to the wonderful world of the Algonquin, a subject about which I remain passionate.

In addition to the Round Tablers, I was exposed to early *New Yorker* writers such as S.J. Perelman, James Thurber and E.B. White. Coincidentally, White had written my favorite book when I was in the sixth grade, *Charlotte's Web*. I was able to appreciate him all over again when Groucho introduced me to his *New Yorker* material. I think Groucho was happy that someone as young as I was taking such an avid interest in those particular people. Maybe we weren't all pot-smoking hippies after all.

Another occasion that made me feel Groucho and I were on the same wavelength was when he called me into his bedroom, peeled off a twenty-dollar bill and told me to run out and pick up a couple of records for him; he'd leave the choice up to me. It was a challenging assignment. I drove down Sunset to Tower Records and after considerable browsing came up with a recording of a forties radio show on which Harpo had guested (playing the harp and honking) and an album of composers singing their own songs (Irving Berlin singing "Oh, How I Hate to Get Up in the Morning," Cole Porter singing "Anything Goes" and so on).

I brought the records back to the house and presented them to Groucho, along with ten dollars in change, which startled him. After listening to the Harpo record and half of the composers album, he turned to me and said, "This is a lot of talent for ten dollars!" So I guess I did good. And it was very gratifying to be working on the fan mail down the hall and hear him singing along with that record, sometimes dancing to it with one of his young nurses. Any pleasure I could bring to Groucho brought me pleasure as well.

Despite our similar tastes, however, I was at a fundamental disadvantage when it came to the nurses: I was male. Even though Groucho seemed to appreciate my interest in his circle of friends, he took a lot more time with his young nurses, slowly making his way down the hall, pointing out pictures and explaining, "That's me and Ty Cobb. . . Sid Perelman. . . Betty Comden. " Often I could tell that the nurses weren't particularly interested in all that old stuff, but they listened patiently and smiled. And I understood: When you're in your eighties, it's probably better to be humored by a pretty young nurse than to hang out with some guy.

But every now and again, word would trickle down that my presence was appreciated. Once, I took a day off to show a visiting friend around L.A. I returned to Groucho's the following morning to resume work and Martha said, "Mr. Marx came up to me yesterday and asked, 'Where's Steve?' I told him you were with a friend and he said, 'Y'know, Martha, he's a nice boy and he really knows what he's doing.'" Later that day, he handed me two "Tell 'Em Groucho Sent You" T-shirts and said, "You're a handy guy to have around." Since such compliments were few and far between, I was quite touched.

I'm often asked about Groucho's health, particularly whether or not he was senile. I'm always careful about how I describe him, because I don't want people to jump to the wrong conclusion. Usually the word *senility* conjures up images of an old man muttering to himself, unaware of what's going on around him, lost in some sort of second childhood. This was not really the case with Groucho, at least not until the very end.

As I explained earlier, he had had a major stroke in September of 1972 and it had changed him forever. There had been a minor stroke the year before, but it was the one in 1972 that took the greater toll. If you had a timeline of Groucho's life, you could draw a thick, black line on that date, delineating the "before" Groucho from the "after" Groucho.

Before the stroke he had already begun to slow down, but he was still, unquestionably, the Groucho Marx people remembered. Afterward, his quick mind was slowed, his speech was a bit slurred and his stroll was reduced to a shuffle. In addition, a certain light behind his eyes had dimmed. It was as if someone had taken a sledgehammer and struck one well-placed blow to a beautiful, smoothly running piece of machinery. It still worked, but it was way out of alignment. In other words, the stroke had turned Groucho into an old man.

That said, however, I hasten to bolster the other side. Despite his gradually deteriorating condition, he never really lost the personality traits that made him Groucho. As I discovered at Bruin Walk, just when people were ready to write him off as a senile old man with no trace of the Groucho that once was, he'd make a remark and phrase it exactly as the young Groucho would've phrased it—only a bit more slowly and softly.

For instance, he always looked forward to the day's batch of mail, particularly the Hollywood trade papers, *Daily Variety* and

The Hollywood Reporter. Even though he wasn't as active a participant as he'd once been, he loved to keep up with what was happening in show biz. One day early on in my tenure there, Groucho came to the lunch table, looked me in the eye and said, "Wonderful mail today. Nothing but requests for money."

Me: "You got a *Variety,* didn't you?

Groucho: "Yes. A variety of requests for money."

And that's how it was. Just when you thought that making a wisecrack was beyond his reach, he'd hit you with something like that. It was very reassuring.

In addition to keeping up with Hollywood, he remained a shrewd observer of the political scene. Groucho had been a staunch Nixon detester for some time. After losing the 1960 presidential election, Nixon moved temporarily into a house in Trousdale Estates, not far from Groucho. Groucho was asked his opinion of his new neighbor. He said, "Better here than the White House."

In 1971, Groucho made it onto Nixon's enemies list by saying that the only hope for this country was his assassination. The FBI even listed Groucho as a potential threat to the Chief Executive's life. Needless to say, Groucho was more than pleased when Nixon was forced to step down. Disgraced by Watergate, he resigned shortly after I began working for Groucho. At the time, I asked him, "Was there ever a president you'd always wanted to meet?"

Groucho: "Yeah, Nixon."

Me: "You never met him?"

Groucho: "No."

Me: "Well, it's too late now."

Groucho: "It's too late for *him*, anyway!"

Me: "So now we have a new president—Ford. What do you think of him?"

Groucho: "Well, he's an honest man. He's not too bright, but he's honest. Someone said that he was playing football once and was hit in the head. But at least he's honest!"

Groucho had a lot of admiration for Betty Ford, however, because she wasn't afraid to speak her mind.

It was during my third week there, the week after he inscribed my picture, that Groucho had the minor stroke I described in the first chapter. The papers said he was in the hospital for tests, but I had long since given up believing what I read in the papers. Just as

I was starting to feel like a part of the household, *bang!* It scared the hell out of me.

And what about Erin's bizarre behavior that morning? After flying into a rage and hiding out in her office until after Groucho had been taken to the hospital, she told me he'd had the stroke on purpose, just to spoil her birthday, as though it had been more a temper tantrum than a cerebral hemorrhage.

What sort of person could make such a wild accusation?

After asking what Groucho was like, people usually want to know about Erin. This is a complex subject and one about which I have many mixed feelings. I often think of the Andre Gide quote that Hector Arce used at the beginning of his section on the Erin years in his excellent biography of Groucho entitled, coincidentally, *Groucho*. Gide said, "The color of truth is gray." Never was this as true as when it pertained to Erin Fleming. When asked about her, I usually begin by saying that whatever they've heard about her is probably true, however flattering or damning or contradictory it may appear.

If they heard that she came along at a time when Groucho was alone, his last wife having left him, his children having found other priorities, and that Erin picked him up, dusted him off and devoted herself tirelessly to helping him go out a living legend, that was true.

If they heard she was eccentric and colorful and unforgettable, that was true, too.

And if they heard that she was extremely hard to get along with, given to wild mood swings, abusive to Groucho—at least verbally and possibly physically—and that she made his final years a much rougher road than they needed to have been, sadly that was true as well.

No single element of Erin's personality is sufficient in summing her up; one needs to combine all of them in order to get a clear picture of what she was like. She could bend over backward to help you one day and then refuse to speak to you the next. There was absolutely no second-guessing her reaction to any given situation, or even to the same situation twice.

If nothing else, she was unpredictable. During a party one hot summer night, Erin was walking around the house in her full-length fur coat. As if that weren't odd enough, she asked me to help her build a fire in the fireplace. Once the fire was roaring, and with everyone already a little on the warm side, Erin said, "Whew! It sure is hot in here!" But rather than opening a window or taking off her coat, she asked me to put another log on the fire. Chaplin may have wanted Groucho to keep warm, but this?

And then there was the time Erin announced that she was going to go skinny-dipping in Groucho's pool and that I was not to peek at her under any circumstances. I had neither the intention nor the desire to peek, so I went into my office and busied myself with the day's mail. A short time later I was walking down the hallway, when I noticed that Erin had opened every single curtain in the living room before going outside, giving me—and anyone else who happened to be walking through the house—an unobstructed view of her floating on a raft, stark naked, in the middle of the pool. These incidents, I hasten to add, were not unusual; they were par for the course.

I can never deny that Erin was generous with me on many occasions. The most obvious kindness, of course, was introducing me to Groucho and getting me the job in the first place. I would have experienced none of these events were it not for her decision to hire me. My dream could never have come true without her help. I doubt that I would even have had the opportunity to see Groucho from the back of the Dorothy Chandler Pavilion in 1972, because it was Erin who had prodded him into accepting the invitations to perform again, which he'd been declining for years.

Also, with the new school quarter about to begin in the fall of 1974, I needed my own wheels. Erin asked how much I was willing to spend and I said, "Fifteen hundred dollars." She told me I could have her 1972 Pinto for just that amount, for which I was extremely grateful. Granted, Groucho had given her the Pinto and had recently given her a Mercedes 450 SEL, but the fact remains that she sold it to me for significantly less than she could've gotten. (This was long before Pintos were discovered to be mobile Molotov cocktails.)

And there were numerous instances when I relied on Erin to intercede on my behalf with regard to Groucho, since she obviously had more influence over him than I could ever have. For all these things and much more, I will always remain in her debt.

I do not believe, however, that my indebtedness dictates that I must have a blind, unswerving sense of loyalty to her. By all accounts Al Jolson was a mesmerizing entertainer in his day, the equal of Sinatra, Presley or the Beatles in theirs. But that did not give him carte blanche to indulge in cruel, abusive behavior toward his wife, Ruby Keeler. Likewise, Erin was extremely attentive to Groucho and I'm personally grateful to her for many things, but that does not in any way excuse the manner in which she sometimes treated him or other members of the household. As Erin herself proudly admitted later, "They live in holy fear of me."

Eventually I developed a facility for divining what sort of mood she was in by how hard she slammed the front door and threw her keys into that silver dish on the entry table. Often the household—if not the house itself—seemed to breathe a sigh of relief after she'd left. Sometimes, that even included Groucho.

On two separate occasions, two separate nurses gave me their professional opinions, unasked, about her mental condition. One said she had never seen anyone as bad off as Erin walking the streets without medical supervision. The other went so far as to say that Erin was "a textbook case of paranoid schizophrenia." Hardly the best choice to look after a frail, increasingly hazy old man.

Although I'd seen her speak firmly to Groucho before that small stroke, it had never seemed particularly noteworthy. It was only after that incident that I became aware of her raising her voice to him more frequently.

After asking about Groucho and about Erin, people usually ask about Groucho-and-Erin. Theirs was, unfortunately, an all-too-common scenario in Hollywood: An aging star, once strong and forceful, allows an ambitious younger woman into his life who alienates family and friends and causes hostility and ill feeling as the curtain descends. It happened with W.C. Fields and Carlotta Monti. It happened with John Barrymore and Elaine Barrie. And it happened with Bela Lugosi and Hope Lininger, who first fell in love with the dashing on-screen Dracula in 1931 but who wasn't quite prepared for the frail old man she encountered twenty-five years later. In each of these instances, however, the couples were romantically involved, and in the cases of Barrymore/Barrie and Lugosi/Lininger, they ended up husband and wife (for better or for worse, in sickness and in health).

What, then, was the nature of Groucho and Erin's relationship?

Again, this is a complex subject. Obviously, not having been behind closed doors with them I can't be certain of anything. I can say, however, that I have never talked with anyone who was close to either of them who felt that there was anything physical going on between them. Groucho himself admitted that he was long past being able to have a sexual relationship with anyone.

Clearly Groucho got a charge out of holding hands with Erin and kissing her from time to time, as he did various young nurses, cooks and whomever else was in his line of fire. But at his age, it was more a flattering ego-boost—like George Burns being seen on the arm of a lovely starlet at an awards ceremony—than a dirty old man who was making it with someone young enough to be his granddaughter. (Or at least his *daughter*, anyway. Although Erin claimed to be in her mid-thirties, I later discovered that she was, in fact, in her early forties by the time I came to work there.)

Was Groucho in love with Erin? Possibly. He said that if he were ever to marry again it would be to Erin, but he knew she wanted to have children and he didn't want to hold her back from realizing her ambition.

And Erin did want to have children. She spoke of it often. She even had a name all picked out for the daughter she would never have: Solange. On the bed in the master bedroom of her own house, Erin kept a stuffed toy sow, with a number of tiny piglets snapped to the mother's teats, suckling away. Also, Erin was allegedly cast as the seductive countess in Woody Allen's *Love and Death*, but, according to her version, she walked out on the film after Woody refused to rewrite the role to allow for her character to have his baby at the conclusion. She just couldn't understand why it was such a big deal for Woody to make what seemed to her to be a simple change in the storyline.

Sometimes Groucho appeared to be a father figure to Erin, but much of the time it seemed *he* was the child and *she* the parent. In the latter case, one is reminded of children who live in an abusive atmosphere at home. They must juggle a volatile mixture of love and fear and the idea of actually leaving seems inconceivable. They crave the love of their parents even as they fear them. This might to some degree explain why Groucho put up with Erin's fits of rage. It's easy for an outsider to tell a battered wife to leave her alcoholic husband, but it's rarely as simple as just *deciding* to get out from under his influence.

And Erin had an influence over Groucho that cannot be overestimated. Although she insisted that *he* made all the decisions, there was a curious similarity between Erin's sudden shifting opinion of someone one day and Groucho's the next. It was obvious to me and to anyone else who watched them together that, for all intents and purposes, she was in charge of his life, personally, socially and financially.

As time went by, Groucho became more and more dependent on Erin's judgment and companionship. And, sadly, as he grew weaker her outbursts became more frequent. Simply put, it seemed to me that Erin was unable to come to terms with Groucho's mortality and somehow felt that if she pushed hard enough, she could actually keep the years from crowding in on him.

But I am, perhaps, getting a little ahead of myself. As I say, the atmosphere was fairly tranquil at the beginning of my tenure in the Marx household and my primary loyalty was, and would always be, to Groucho.

EIGHT

The day after that minor stroke, I came to work not expecting to see anything of Groucho since he was in a private room at Mt. Sinai Hospital (this was before it merged with Cedars of Lebanon). But a nurse called from the hospital and said that Groucho wanted a few necessities from home—his *Variety* for one—so the household elected me to take them to him.

When I entered his room he smiled and said, "Hi," and I got the feeling that I constituted a familiar face, what with all the strangers from the hospital staff milling around. He was glad to receive the things I'd brought, but he'd forgotten to ask for the daily calendar from his desk at home. So I drove back to his house, grabbed the calendar and brought it to the hospital.

Just before leaving his room, I thought of some appropriate words from *Animal Crackers* and said, "Well, I'm glad I came, but just the same, I must be going." This put a big grin on his face. He turned to the nurse and said, "A comedian." I beamed all the way back to his house. I felt that, in a small way, I'd succeeded in cheering up Groucho Marx.

On another occasion I was carrying a tall, teetering stack of empty boxes out of Groucho's bedroom and I guess I hammed it up a bit as I tried to maneuver out the door without toppling the boxes. He seemed to get a kick out of this and he laughed out loud at my comical balancing act.

My status as a fellow comedian was a tenuous one, however. On one occasion I accompanied Groucho to a doctor's appointment. The man who ran the elevator in the medical building smiled at Groucho and said, "You look much better," to which Groucho replied, "Thanks. I wish I could say the same for you." After we got off the elevator, the conversation continued:

Groucho: "That fellow is the fiancé of the woman who operates the other elevator."

Me: "If they get married and still operate elevators, they'll really have their ups and downs."

Groucho: "Was that a joke?"

Me: "Not much of one."

Groucho: "I'll say it wasn't."

A little later, Groucho asked what I wanted to do as a profession.

Me: "I'd like to try comedy writing."

Groucho: "It's a tough business. And your last name is too strange to go up in lights."

Me: "Did you know we both have the same middle name—Henry?"

Groucho: "Well just because we have the same middle name, that doesn't automatically make you funny."

Me: "I don't know. When I tell people what my middle name is they crack up."

Groucho: "Then they're just easy laughers."

I learned early on that even if I had what I felt was a clever remark, it was somehow more satisfying to let Groucho have the last word. I wasn't really interested in trying to top him in his diminished capacity, so I tended to soft-pedal my attempts at wise-cracking in deference to the aging master.

It wasn't long before Groucho reached the point where he could continue his recuperation at home. The household elected me to handle the "errand" of picking him up from the hospital. Although I was honored, I was also a little nervous, but I wasn't about to pass it up. I drove over to Mt. Sinai, pulled my Pinto up to the front of the hospital, opened the passenger door and made sure Groucho was comfortably settled into his seat before driving off.

Despite my privileged assignment, I felt as though I were travelling with a five-foot, seven-inch bottle of nitroglycerin on the seat beside me. He was almost eighty-four years old and had just had a stroke. One slip of the brake pedal and I would forever be known as The Guy Who Assassinated Groucho Marx, like that college student who had sucker-punched Houdini in his dorm room and ended up killing him, however inadvertently.

But we made it back to his house without incident. Thereafter, I was often called upon to take Groucho to one appointment or another, and eventually I got used to having him sitting next to me in the Pinto. One day, however, he suddenly decided to hire a chauffeur-driven limousine, explaining, "Now you won't have to drive me around anymore, Steve. I'm much too rich to go around in that crummy old car of yours anyway." Lest we forget, he had purchased that "crummy old car" for Erin only a couple of years earlier.

Groucho seemed to bounce back from this minor stroke with impressive speed. Although it took him a while to recover the total use of his legs, he had an amazing constitution and will to live. From that point on Groucho took a drug called Coumadin, which was supposed to thin out the blood, thus cutting down on the possibility of another stroke or a heart attack. This was just as well since, with Erin's mercurial temperament, his blood pressure could shoot up without a moment's notice. The down side was that he had to be extra-careful not to cut or bruise himself because the drug made coagulation more difficult.

There were times when Groucho would amble past that "Why a Duck?" poster showing him in *The Cocoanuts*, and it would be difficult for me to accept that the young man in the sepia picture and the old man shuffling down the hall were the same person. At other times, however, he'd strike a pose or have a certain expression on his face, and he would be unmistakably the one, the only Groucho.

I came to appreciate Groucho on three distinct levels. The first and most obvious was that he was "Groucho Marx," the man in the "Why a Duck?" poster. The man who danced a tango with Thelma Todd in *Monkey Business.* The man who sat behind his desk and embarrassed George Fenneman every week on "You Bet Your Life." It was he, himself, *that* man.

The second level was appreciating that he was someone who personally knew so many of the people I admired: George Gershwin, Robert Benchley, W.C. Fields, George S. Kaufman, James Thurber, to pick but a handful of snowflakes from a blizzard of legendary personalities. There were times when I'd sit there at the lunch table listening to Groucho telling an anecdote about Irving Thalberg or Ring Lardner and I'd think to myself, *I've read about these people; he* knew *them.*

The third level was realizing that Groucho was a man from another century. My dad was born in 1916, during World War I, and that had always seemed like a very long time ago. Indeed, when I got him one of those historic birth-year newspapers, I was startled to find that the headline concerned Pancho Villa! But Groucho predated my father by more than a quarter of a century. I'd never really gotten to know anyone who went back to 1890.

One day at lunch, Groucho began describing what it was like when he had to announce to an audience that President Harding had just died. That was in 1923. He had said, "Ladies and gentlemen, the president is dead. A great man is gone. He will be missed." According to Groucho, all he and his brothers could hear after that was the sound of raindrops pelting the aluminum roof of the theater and women weeping. Nobody in the audience was in the mood to laugh. It was a vivid tableau, from so many years back, and he had brought it to life for me. This prompted me to ask him just how far back he could remember. He thought for a moment and then said, "I guess the Spanish-American War."

That was in 1898.

By 1906, he was already enough of a show-business veteran to sing at a benefit at New York's Metropolitan Opera House in order to raise money to help the victims of the San Francisco earthquake. Others on the bill included pianist Ignace Paderewski and opera legend Enrico Caruso. Groucho could still recall what he'd sung that day: "Somebody's Sweetheart I Want to Be." They ended up raising $33,000 in quake-relief money. It was mind-boggling to look at Groucho across the lunch table and think about how much history he had witnessed, from before the Wright Brothers to after the moon landings.

I've made several references to "the lunch table." That is because it was something of a central location for the exchange of ideas, and many of my memories and experiences seem to center on that particular piece of furniture. Despite the fact that I was an employee, I was always welcome to sit at the dining-room table, regardless of the caliber of guest.

During my early months there I was treated to a particularly rich parade of celebrities, partially because Lyn Erhard, who writes under the pen name Charlotte Chandler, had been working on a biography of Groucho and arranged for various luminaries to have lunch there in order to record their conversations with Groucho. Thus I had the pleasure of lunching with George Burns, George Jessel and Jack Lemmon, on separate occasions, within my first few months of work.

Burns was a dynamo. He breezed through the front door and,

never having met me, greeted me with, "Hi! Ya wanna live a long time? Become an actor! You'll live to be an old man like Groucho and me! OK, let's have lunch!" It was a hell of an entrance.

What a treat it was, listening to Burns and Groucho talking over old times. And by old times, I don't mean the early days of live TV; I mean the early days of *vaudeville.* It was fascinating, listening to them discussing small towns, long-dead theater managers and obscure acts such as Swayne's Rats and Cats, which consisted of several cats dressed as horses being ridden by several rats dressed as jockeys. I'd sure like to have seen that.

Groucho asked Burns if he remembered "the hook," which was used by theater managers to pull lousy acts off the stage and into the wings. Burns said that not only did he remember the hook, he also remembered the *hoop,* which was considerably more brutal. According to Burns, a man with a hoop would sit in the front row during the performance, and if he thought the act was lousy he'd use the hoop to pull the performers right over the footlights.

It was on that day that I realized I had misunderstood something important about what old age does to the mind. I had thought, with some degree of logic, that the most recent memories would be the most vivid and the early memories the haziest. But with the elderly, it's just the opposite. Groucho could argue with Burns about the location of a particular vaudeville theater in the midwest, down to the name of the cross street and the type of store adjacent to it, but he would have trouble recalling who his lunch guest had been three days earlier.

Talk turned to Harpo, and Burns told a story about when he and Gracie double-dated with Harpo and his wife, Susan, during World War II. They went to a theater that happened to be next to a candy shop. According to Burns, Harpo had a passion for black jelly beans, so he went into the candy shop and asked the owner if he had any. The owner said that as a matter of fact, he had just received four ten-dollar sacks of black jelly beans that day.

Harpo, figuring the candy store would be closed after the theater had let out, decided to buy all four sacks of black jelly beans. So Burns and Allen and Harpo and Susan had to sit in the theater with huge, ten-dollar sacks of black jelly beans on their laps. The clincher, according to Burns, was that nobody was allowed to touch

Harpo's black jelly beans, "So he bought *ten cents'* worth of *mixed* jelly beans for the rest of us!"

He also told a story about impressing W.C. Fields by giving him an idea for a sight gag involving a glass of scotch and a cup of coffee during the shooting of *International House* in 1933. I had recently seen that film in a class at UCLA, and it was a strange feeling to realize that I was sitting across the table from the very same man I'd watched moving about on-screen in black and white.

After the meal Burns took out a cigar and pushed it into a plastic holder, explaining, "I never smoke expensive cigars. All I care about is if it fits the holder. Milton Berle pays two dollars apiece for his cigars. If I paid two dollars for a cigar, I'd go to bed with it before I'd smoke it!"

Speaking of cigars, while my job may have been a dream-come-true, my *dream* never became a dream-come-true because Groucho had given up smoking cigars several years earlier for health reasons. He kept a few boxes of them in a small compartment in his desk—mostly gifts from well-intentioned but misinformed friends—but since he wasn't actually *smoking* them anymore, I didn't really see the point in asking for one of Groucho's cigars.

For me, it wasn't much of a loss. I couldn't stand the smell of cigar smoke, so I was actually grateful that he'd given them up, trademark or not. Many of his friends and colleagues, however, continued to enjoy a good cheroot, so the house was often filled with their "aroma," even if it wasn't emanating from Groucho's direction.

When Burns and Groucho were arguing about the location of that vaudeville house, it would've been easy to have been reminded of the heated conversations in *The Sunshine Boys*, except for one detail—there was no such film at that time. It was in production, but not with George Burns. Burns' longtime friend, Jack Benny, was in rehearsal in that role, opposite Walter Matthau.

Indeed, Benny was supposed to have had lunch with Groucho not long after the lunch with Burns, but he didn't show up. Groucho was upset at being stood up until he ran into Milton Berle shortly thereafter, who told him that Benny had stomach cancer and did not have long to live. Groucho felt doubly terrible—that he'd judged Jack Benny unjustly for having stood him up, and that Benny, whom Groucho called "a nice man," was dying. Groucho's observation on "The Merv Griffin Show" that all his friends were either sick or dead was becoming increasingly true.

In a strange twist of show-business fate, it was Jack Benny's death the following month that allowed Burns to take over and, in the process, embark on a whole new career. Burns' performance in *The Sunshine Boys* not only earned him an Oscar, it also marked the beginning of his status as a cherished living legend.

George Jessel was a curious fellow. Like Burns, he had interesting stories about vaudeville, but unlike Burns, he almost never smiled. There was a certain bitterness about him. Noticing a photo of Groucho and Al Jolson on the wall, Jessel said, "Look at Jolson with that big, phony smile of his! Whenever there was a camera around, he'd stick that stupid smile on his face!" I had a theory, as we sat down to lunch, as to why Jessel might be bitter about Jolson.

Jessel had starred in the popular stage version of *The Jazz Singer*, and the Warner brothers had asked him if he wanted to recreate the role for that first-ever sound film in 1927, in exchange for a percentage of the film's profits. Not having any faith in talkies, Jessel insisted instead on a large sum of money up front. The Warners balked and hired Al Jolson. The rest, as they say, is history. I guess if I'd made that decision, I might have a certain bitterness about me, too.

Jessel always called Groucho Julius because he'd known him since before the Marx Brothers took their stage names. Groucho didn't mind being referred to as Julius, but Jessel also had a habit of referring to Erin as Eden, the name of Groucho's most recent ex-wife. Erin wasn't too thrilled about that. The one time he did remember to call her Erin, when he was hosting a testimonial dinner for Groucho, he managed to refer to her not as Erin Fleming, but as Erin *Flynn*, giving her a certain swashbuckling quality I'd never noticed before.

Jack Lemmon is one of the warmest, most likable people I've ever met. Indeed, at Groucho's eighty-fourth birthday party in October of that year, I overheard Harpo's son, Billy, talking to Lemmon. Billy said, "You know, there are so many nasty, phony people in this town, but I have to tell you, you are a genuinely nice guy." Lemmon instantly replied, "Well, thanks, but there's no reason not to be." At the time I thought it was just an obvious, casual reply, but the more I've thought about that over the years the more

I've realized what a wise philosophy it is: There *is* no reason not to be a nice guy.

Lemmon was about to begin shooting the television remake of *The Entertainer*, which Laurence Olivier had done on stage and screen and for which Groucho's old accompanist, Marvin Hamlisch, was composing a score. Lemmon said he had met Olivier and had asked him how he'd done such a convincing job of playing Archie Rice, a song and dance man who wasn't really lousy, just third-rate. Olivier had told him, "By singing and dancing the very best I could!"

In addition to this trio, I also had the pleasure of lunching with some of Groucho's longtime writer friends. Often, when we encounter someone notable, it's not until years later that we come to realize who they were and what they'd accomplished. We say, "If only I'd known that at the time, I could've asked him about such-and-such." But because I'd so immersed myself in Marx lore before getting the job, I was able to fully appreciate the people from Groucho's past as I encountered them. My brain would simply flip to the proper Rolodex card when they'd show up for lunch:

Ryskind, Morrie: Cowrote the theatrical and motion-picture versions of *The Cocoanuts* (1925 and 1929) and *Animal Crackers* (1928 and 1930) for the Four Marx Brothers. Cowrote *A Night at the Opera* (1935) and adapted *Room Service* (1938) for the Three Marx Brothers. Won a Pulitzer Prize for coauthoring *Of Thee I Sing* (1931) along with George S. Kaufman and George and Ira Gershwin. Although he and Groucho had been close friends since the twenties, Ryskind had become an extremely right-wing columnist for the *Los Angeles Herald-Examiner* while Groucho had remained a staunch liberal. As long as they stuck to reminiscences and steered clear of politics, they were fine.

Perrin, Nat: Wrote dialogue for *Monkey Business* (1931) and *Duck Soup* (1933) for the Four Marx Brothers, with his longtime partner, Arthur Sheekman. Cowrote radio show, "Flywheel, Shyster, and Flywheel" (1933) for Groucho and Chico. Wrote initial draft of *The Big Store* (1941) for the Three Marx Brothers. Groucho's nickname for Perrin was "the Deacon" because Nat wore spectacles that made him look a little like a clergyman. Nat struck me as an extremely friendly and engaging man and, although no one knew it at the time—least of all, Nat—he was to play a crucial and controversial role in Groucho's life toward the very end.

Brecher, Irving: Singlehandedly wrote *At the Circus* (1939) and *Go West* (1940) for the Three Marx Brothers. Cowrote *Meet Me in St. Louis* (1944), a film that holds a soft spot in my heart for obvious reasons. Created "Life of Riley" for radio and television. During lunch, Brecher scoffed when I mentioned I was taking a class in screenwriting at UCLA. "How can they *teach* screenwriting?" he asked skeptically. I suppose to someone who learned the ropes the hard way as a junior writer at MGM in the late thirties, the idea might seem a little foreign. For Brecher, experience was the only real teacher. Actually, I *don't* believe one can be taught how to be funny or how to have an ear for humor. But there *are* certain basics about screenwriting that one can learn in a classroom, such as format, plot and character development.

Kanter, Hal: Wrote for Groucho for radio and television. Cowrote *My Favorite Spy* (1951) and *Road to Bali* (1952) for Bob Hope. Created "Julia," with Diahann Carroll, which was one of my favorite TV shows in the late sixties. Hal and I got to be quite friendly and I spent a considerable amount of time with him and his delightful wife, Doris, over a number of years, both at Groucho's and at the Kanters' home in the San Fernando Valley.

I felt an innate affinity for the writers and I often found them more interesting than some of the other, higher-profile lunch guests. They were witty raconteurs with humorous and perceptive things to say about what was happening in the world. Apparently I wasn't alone in feeling this way. Despite Groucho's popularity as a star in the thirties, he always said he preferred having lunch at the MGM writers' table, foregoing the alleged honor of eating with the other stars, whom he found to be self-absorbed and rather dull.

Another thing I noticed during those celebrity-studded meals was that, almost instinctively, I preferred Groucho's circle to Erin's—at least as lunch guests. I thought back to that conversation we had had during the *Animal Crackers* campaign, where she had told me that sometimes she found Groucho's friends tiresome. My hunch had been right: While she found them dull, I couldn't get enough of them.

Conversely, whereas Erin seemed to thrive on the company of friends such as Elliott Gould, Sally Kellerman, George Segal and Bud Cort, I found them a little too quirky and offbeat for my generally down-to-earth tastes. This is not to say that they weren't nice people or that I didn't appreciate their considerable talents. I was a big fan of *M*A*S*H*, *Who's Afraid of Virginia Woolf?* and *Harold & Maude*, particularly the latter. It's just that for company and conversation, I found myself more naturally drawn toward Groucho's pals than toward Erin's.

In addition, I noticed that there was a graciousness and a geniality among the older people that seemed to be lacking in some of the younger set. It struck me that the people who had had money and success over a long period of time were more comfortable with it, while those who had achieved some measure of fame relatively recently were the ones who had the attitudes.

Even Groucho, who had a healthy ego when it came to being appreciated for his talent, was scrupulously honest about giving credit where credit was due when exchanging funny lines with guests. He would never, to my knowledge, appropriate someone else's remark and try to pass it off as his own. He would say, "Benchley had a funny line about health. He said, 'I feel fine, except for an occasional heart attack.'" Or, "Woody Allen said, 'I don't mind dying; I just don't want to be there when it happens.' That's a great line. He's a big talent."

It certainly wasn't necessary for guests to be present in order to have an enjoyable time at the lunch table. Even when it was "just" Groucho, something memorable was bound to occur. One day, after he'd finished eating half a grapefruit, Groucho put down his spoon, picked up the bowl and proceeded to pour the remaining juice directly down his throat. While he was doing this, I said, "What would Amy Vanderbilt say about your etiquette?" He turned to me, calmly replied, "Fuck her," and continued to enjoy the grapefruit juice right from the bowl. It may not have been his wittiest line, but it sure took me by pleasant surprise.

Another time, I happened to notice some people on the hill beyond the dining-room window, watching us through binoculars. I pointed this out to Groucho, who looked over his shoulder, waved to the voyeurs, then said, "They probably think I'm Danny Thomas," referring to his up-the-street neighbor.

I never knew ahead of time what sort of tasty morsel might be dropped into the lunchtime conversation. It could be an impromptu witticism, a political observation or an obscure bit of trivia from his lengthy career. Once, when I mentioned my admiration for Fred Astaire's dancing artistry, Groucho said, "When I was fourteen I was in an act with a tap dancer. One night, he danced with such exuberance that his shoe flew off into the audience and hit someone in the head. We got forty dollars instead of sixty that week."

He's lucky they didn't give him the hoop.

And when the Pinto that I'd purchased from Erin came up in conversation one day, Groucho said, "I used to have a car that if you leaned on it with your elbow, the door flew open. I had a girl in the car once and she leaned on it and slid into a drugstore."

One time, we were served a lamb chop that had apparently been cooked a bit too long.

Groucho: "This lamb chop is like rubber."

Me: "It tastes good, though."

Groucho: "Yes. It's the best-tasting rubber I've ever eaten."

And there was the day we were served some fish that hadn't been thoroughly fileted.

Groucho: "What's the matter?"

Me: "I think I found a bone in my fish."

Groucho: "What are you gonna do? Bury it?"

I never counted lunchtime as part of my work hours. I felt guilty enough accepting a paycheck in the first place; I wasn't about to charge Groucho for listening to stories about Swayne's Rats and Cats or for having coffee with George Burns.

Speaking of coffee, one other aspect of lunching with Groucho stands out and that was his fondness for Brim, the decaffeinated coffee substitute. I cannot count the number of times I witnessed his unsolicited testimonials on behalf of this particular beverage. Coffee would be brought to a guest and, while Groucho sipped his Brim, the conversation would go something like this:

Groucho: "What have you got there?"

Guest: "Coffee."

Groucho: "Coffee's bad for you. You should drink Brim. It *isn't* bad for you and it tastes wonderful."

I can only imagine the money Brim might've made off Groucho had they recorded these "endorsements." But, of course, Groucho's comments were intended for home use only. I have the feeling that if the Brim people had furnished Groucho with a script for a commercial wherein he said words similar to the preceding, he'd have tossed the pages against the wall and thrown the advertising people out. But left to his own devices, he was more effective than Mrs. Olsen.

Nine

In the early fall of 1974, a charity event was held at a privately owned equestrian center and Groucho was the guest of honor. They even called it "A Day at the Races," because there was going to be a short horse race within the grounds.

For the kiddies, the 1937 Marx Brothers classic of the same name was screened inside a barn, which was either appropriate or insulting depending on your point of view. But the main event was a talent show inside a giant circus tent. A number of picnic tables were set up under the big top, with wealthy arts patrons and their families seated at them, eating lunch and waiting to be entertained.

Groucho made some humorous remarks ("No matter how rich you are, sometimes you have to take a leak") and sang a few numbers, which were received with great enthusiasm by the crowd. Bud Cort also sang a song, which was politely received. And then Marvin Hamlisch, who had become a popular, Oscar-winning composer in the two years since he'd acted as Groucho's accompanist, came out to play the piano. In order to generate some more money for the charity beyond the substantial amounts the audience had already paid for their tickets, Hamlisch announced with great flourish that he was going to auction off his performance.

He even acted as his own auctioneer. The bidding quickly reached $100—and stayed there. Hamlisch said that wasn't good enough and that he wasn't going to play for them until the amount hit at *least* $250. Despite his admonition, the bidding did not budge.

After some moments of awkwardness as Hamlisch tried in vain to coax the bidding in an upward direction, Groucho raised his hand, indicating that *he* would pay the $250, but Hamlisch said, "No, Groucho. I don't want *your* money," and rejected the bid. Apparently, Hamlisch had lost sight of the fact that the money was going to charity and not into his own pocket.

Frustrated that the bidding wasn't going any higher, Hamlisch finally relented, saying, "OK, I'll play, but I'm going to do it for *nothing* rather than for such a small amount." Thus he rejected even the $100 which, I'm sure, the charity would've welcomed.

Frankly, I couldn't believe the audacity of turning away money for charity simply because it didn't measure up to his notion of what it was worth for them to be able to watch him perform. Nevertheless, the audience enjoyed his medley of Marvin Hamlisch tunes.

The last bit of entertainment was comedian Albert Brooks performing his hilarious "Danny and Dave" ventriloquist routine, wherein the dummy proceeds to fall apart, one limb at a time, while a panicky Brooks presses gamely onward. I'd seen him do it on TV and it was even funnier in person.

When the local paper's society column about the event was forwarded to Groucho, it was placed on my desk so that I could put it into one of those large scrapbooks. I laughed out loud when I read the review of the festivities: "The entertainment included comedian Groucho Marx, actor Bud Cort, composer Marvin Hamlisch, and a ventriloquism act." Apparently the reviewer had neither seen nor heard of Albert Brooks and thought he was just some poor ventriloquist who had a run of particularly bad luck that day.

A short time later, Groucho mentioned that he'd really like to have a new camera. Since he was due to turn eighty-four in only a few weeks, Erin said, somewhat suggestively, "Well, if you're good, maybe someone will get it for you for your birthday. Some nice-looking woman with *great legs!*" Groucho perked up and said, "Betty Grable?"

October second was Groucho's eighty-fourth birthday. My roommate, Daryl, and I attended the party and we felt honored to be a part of the evening. There weren't too many guests, so for me it was a comfortable gathering. I've never been able to tolerate wall-to-wall people.

Among others, Marvin Hamlisch was there, once again drafted into playing the piano for free. Groucho, in good spirits and good form, ran through about a dozen of his favorite songs. Also in attendance were Hal Kanter, Bud Cort, Elliott Gould, Tom Smothers, David Steinberg, Flip Wilson, Morrie Ryskind and Groucho's son, Arthur. Although I'd heard a lot of unflattering things about Arthur, mostly from Erin, I didn't spend any time with him so I was hardly able to make much of a value judgment that night.

Valerie Harper was also there, nervous because her new TV show, "Rhoda," had only recently premiered. We talked a little and I wished her much success with the series, which was a spinoff of

"The Mary Tyler Moore Show." I guess it worked. "Rhoda" ran for four years.

The guests at Groucho's house were usually friendly toward me regardless of their "rank." I suppose they figured, "Maybe that's Groucho's grandson. Whoever he is, if he's on the inside he must be OK." So I was able to wander around the party, drink in hand, and chat with whomever I wanted without arousing suspicion as to my credentials.

As a matter of fact, there's really only one time that I can recall being officially snubbed at Groucho's house. It was when Elliott Gould arranged for his ex-wife, Barbra Streisand, to come with him one Sunday afternoon along with their young son, Jason. Streisand never made eye contact with me the whole time she was there, nor did she acknowledge my presence in the room even when I was speaking. It was as though I didn't exist. Others spoke to me and Streisand made comments to the people around me, but to her I was apparently invisible.

I remembered that Streisand had come into Farrell's Ice Cream Parlor a few years earlier on a night when I wasn't working. The day after, all anybody had to say about her was that she was extremely demanding and left no tip.

Streisand and Hamlisch. The way they were.

For a birthday present, I'd given Groucho a new biography of another transplanted Missourian, T.S. Eliot. As Groucho passed by me at the party, he said, "By the way, thanks for the book." I asked him how it was and he said, "It's OK. It's mostly about his early years. But thanks just the same." After Groucho ambled off, Daryl just looked at me and said, "You have arrived."

I recall one woman making repeated references to Groucho's brother, whom she kept calling Gumbo. Finally Groucho stopped working on his roast beef, put down his fork, leaned over to her and said, "Look, will you stop calling him Gumbo? Gumbo's a type of *soup*. My brother's name is Gummo!"

In addition to the stellar array of celebrities, some other things stand out from that night. One was walking down the hallway toward my office and catching sight of David Steinberg, who was absorbed in the "Why a Duck?" poster and the *Cocoanuts* dialogue printed on it. After taking in the poster he looked over at me, smiled and said, "I never get tired of it." I knew how he felt. Even though Steinberg was a popular comedian and I was merely a kid from UCLA, at that particular moment in that particular hallway, we were just a couple of Groucho fans.

An especially unforgettable moment occurred after we'd sung "Happy Birthday" to Groucho and he'd blown out the candles on his cake. To my amazement, while Groucho's cake was still being divvied up, Martha brought out a second, smaller cake in my honor, since my twentieth birthday had been two days earlier. Then all those stars of stage, screen and television were drafted into singing "Happy Birthday" to *me.* I wondered if I wasn't about to wake up and find that this had all been a product of my fertile imagination. A birthday party held side-by-side with Groucho's would've seemed inconceivable only a year earlier.

After everyone had finished their cake, Harpo's son, Bill, sat down at the piano and Groucho led us all in a rousing chorus of "Take Me Out to the Ballgame" in honor of the Dodgers having won the pennant. After a few more tunes, a slightly tipsy Jack Lemmon took over the keys and began pounding out an exuberant version of "There's No Business Like Show Business" while simultaneously executing a wild, high-kicking dance, which really cracked Groucho up.

In short, it was your typical quiet evening at home.

At 11:10, Groucho looked at his watch and said, "Hey, my show's been on for ten minutes!" At which point he deserted his well-wishers and made a beeline into the den, where he enjoyed the remainder of "You Bet Your Life." A few guests left, and at 11:30 Groucho excused himself to "brush his fangs" and go to bed, which caused almost everyone else to depart as well. But Daryl and I weren't about to miss a thing, so we plunked ourselves down on the living-room floor and listened to Jack Lemmon improvise jazz on the piano. Eventually, we were the only ones left.

It was like being in a nightclub just before closing time—except it was Groucho Marx's living room and we'd just finished a dual celebration of our birthdays. It was a wonderful, magical moment, and I was sorry when Lemmon finally glanced at his watch, said, "Oh, jeez, I gotta get home!" and bade us farewell. Daryl and I went back to our co-op room and, despite the lateness of the hour on a school night, sat up for a long time rehashing the evening's events.

I had, indeed, arrived.

TEN

By that time I had cut back my work days to weekends plus a couple of afternoons during the week because the fall quarter had begun. One of my classes during that first quarter as a Motion Picture/Television major was in Television Production. As an assignment, the class was broken up into three groups and each group was given the assignment of producing a videotaped documentary on a subject of their own choosing.

One group decided to focus on the defunct Pacific Ocean Park amusement park, another centered on a homeless shelter, and then there was my group, which also included Daryl. While ideas were being bandied about, I mused, "Wouldn't it be something if we could do one on Groucho?" The others were all in favor of giving it a shot, so I promised them I'd check it out.

Not wanting to confront Groucho with it directly, I asked Erin if such a thing were possible. She said it was fine with her but I'd still have to ask Groucho. Drat. So I went into his bedroom where he was sitting in a chair reading, and I asked him if it would be OK if I were to do a short documentary on him for school. He asked what it would entail and I said, "A short interview. Maybe a song or two, if you feel like it." He said, "OK," and went back to his reading.

It was that simple.

Erin and I set up a mutually agreeable date and our group prepared for what we fully believed would be the coup of the school year. We arrived at Groucho's house at the appointed hour, videotape camera and microphone in hand, and rang the bell. My classmates were understandably nervous, but I assured them that we had both Groucho's and Erin's approval and that everything would be fine. After a moment, a very formally dressed Erin Fleming answered the door and looked us over quizzically.

With a gradually sinking feeling, I spluttered out, "Hi, Erin. We're here to do that documentary. You know, for school?" She said, "Oh no, dear. We can't do this tonight. Can't you see Groucho is having a dinner party?" And then she closed the door and went back to her dinner while the rest of us made a meal out of the egg on my face. Clearly, it wasn't going to happen that night.

With the project deadline rapidly approaching, I began to worry that we were going to have to come up with another subject, and fast. Mercifully, Take 2 was considerably more successful. We agreed on another day a week or two later. This time, Groucho *wasn't* having a dinner party. My classmates and I entered the living room and our teaching assistant, Irwin Hale, told us that the available light from the windows would be sufficient, which was comforting to hear since we'd brought no lighting equipment with us.

The plan was for me to spend a little time interviewing Groucho, then perhaps he would sing a few songs accompanied by Morgan Ames, a composer/musician friend of Erin's. Finally, time permitting, there would be a brief tour of his trophy table.

We set up the camera and I went to fetch Groucho. On our way back to the living room, he turned to me and muttered, "OK, Mr. Producer, let's go." There would be no retakes or dubbing in voice-overs at a later date. We had one chance and that was *it.* It would be fair to say that I was a little on the nervous side.

Groucho's voice was a bit more gravelly than it had been during the UCLA interview, but the trade-off was that it was a much less hectic atmosphere and I felt much more comfortable conversing with him. By this time I was familiar with many of Groucho's anecdotes, so rather than conducting a formal interview I felt my job was to play straight man and set him up so that he could tell a few stories. Since it was just before the gubernatorial election in which Ronald Reagan was stepping down, I thought I'd start with something topical:

Me: "Well, Groucho, there's an election just around the corner, and—"

Groucho: "Around which corner?"

Me: "Just 'around the corner.' And—"

Groucho: "You can't just say 'the corner.' It has to be a *specific* corner."

Me: "Anyway, we have an actor leaving—"

Groucho: "Good!"

Me: "—leaving the governorship of California, and I was wondering if you've ever considered running for office."

Groucho: "Yes. I once had an offer to run for governor of

California. I asked them how much money it paid. They said, '$37,000 a year.' I told 'em I was making more than that on the quiz show every three weeks!"

Me: "Do you watch 'You Bet Your Life'?"

Groucho: "Every night."

Me: "It's on at eleven o'clock, which is opposite the news. I wonder why people would prefer your show to watching the news each night."

Groucho: "Who wants the news? There's nothing but *bad* news. If they watch my show, they can *laugh.*"

Me: "Do you think we're headed for a depression?"

Groucho: "Yes. Nothing you can do about it."

Me: "No? What do you think the country needs?"

Groucho: "Nobody knows what it needs."

Me: "Well, who do you like in comedy today, aside from—"

Groucho: "Me."

Me: "*Aside* from yourself. Is there anyone else in the field of comedy you enjoy watching?"

Groucho: "Dick Cavett...Woody Allen."

Me: "What other television shows do you enjoy watching?"

Groucho: "Mine."

Me: "How about motion pictures?"

Groucho: "Motion pictures? Yeah, they're good. They oughta make a *lot* of 'em!"

Me: "What sort of films do you enjoy watching?"

Groucho: "Mine."

Me: "You recently celebrated your eighty-fourth birthday. You've seen a lot, you've accomplished a great deal. Do you have any sort of philosophy for the young today?"

Groucho: "Yeah. I wish I was *younger.*"

Me: "Along with the Marx Brothers, W.C. Fields is also quite popular today. Did you know him?"

Groucho: "Very well."

Me: "What sort of a man was he?"

Groucho: "Drunk. I went over to visit him once. He took me upstairs—he had an attic—and we went up there and there was fifty thousand dollars' worth of whiskey. So I said, 'What do you have all this whiskey for? We don't have Prohibition anymore.' He said, 'No, but it might come back!'"

Me: "Who do you like in singing today?"

Groucho: "Me."

Me: "Would you like to do a few songs?"

Groucho: "No."

Me: "Well, then, that pretty much kills the rest of this documentary."

But Groucho was only fooling. He got up and ambled over to the piano where Morgan Ames was sitting at the keys, waiting to provide musical accompaniment. Just before he launched into song, Erin called out to him: "You look pretty sour, Dad! They want this to be about somebody who's *alive!*"

Nobody could ever accuse her of being too subtle.

He started with Harry Ruby's nonsensical "Show Me a Rose," the chorus of which contains the lines:

Show me a rose and I'll show you a storm at sea.
Show me a rose or leave me alone.

This was followed by "There's a Place Called Omaha, Nebraska," an equally silly song Groucho had written with Ruby. It starts out:

A man sat by the fireplace, the fire it was out.
It was out because the logs were soaking wet.
He thought of days when he
Sat on his mother's knee,
Which, by the way, was also soaking wet.

For this particular number, he was joined by Erin. The chemistry between them was palpable. Perhaps significantly, *she* sang the melody and *he* sang harmony. His fondness for her was obvious, as was the effect she had upon him. When she was near, he'd perk up and even laugh a little. As previously discussed, all was not tranquil between Erin and Groucho. But during this duet, at least, they seemed to be having a pretty good time.

It was also apparent—and this was the case during his birthday party—that while it was enormously entertaining to listen to Groucho sing and tell stories in the comfort of his living room, we did so with much more forgiving eyes and ears than would an audience of strangers listening to a personal appearance or television performance.

I don't believe Erin ever bothered to make that distinction.

Between each tune, Groucho would saunter over to the couch and kiss either Erin or Robin Heaney, the attractive, blond weekend cook, or Connie August, one of his pretty young nurses. He showed no prejudice, distributing his affection equally among his three female admirers, sometimes going back for seconds.

After "Omaha," Groucho launched into the fabled "Lydia the Tattooed Lady," which he'd introduced in *At the Circus.* A bonus for my classmates and me was that during this song we were drafted into singing the chorus of "la, la, la's" that was required between each of the intricate verses.

After the final "Olé!" of "Lydia," Groucho took off his beret, donned a Mickey Mouse hat and sang Harry Ruby's "Father's Day." This concluded the musical portion of our program.

After the songs we were treated to a brief tour of his photo walls and trophy table, where he pointed out his Oscar and his Emmy and then held up the medal the French government had given him at the Cannes Film Festival in 1972. "I got one and Chaplin got one," he said proudly.

Afterward, with the camera still rolling, I said, "Do you have any closing words before we wrap this thing up?" Impishly, Groucho snapped, "Yes, get out!" which was a perfect note on which to end. Actually, the true punchline occurred sometime later, after we'd turned off the camera and packed away the equipment. Just before leaving, I went into his bedroom and said, "Groucho, I can't possibly thank you enough for letting me do this." He said, "Sure you can. Don't take a salary."

Around this time, Daryl and I heard through the UCLA grapevine that "The Carol Burnett Show" was looking for young writers with fresh ideas. Figuring we had nothing to lose, we wrote out a series of sketches wherein Carol would play the "extra girl" at a department store, working in a different department each week, always under the watchful eye of her martinet boss, who would be played by Harvey Korman. The quality of our youthful writing may have left a lot to be desired, but we felt it showed a flair for comedy, so we sent it in.

A short while later we received our material back, along with a polite letter from one of the producers informing us that the basic problem with our sketches was that they were too contrived and that "true comedy comes out of real-life situations." With that piece of wisdom in mind, we tuned in to the next "Carol Burnett Show" just in time to catch the end of a sketch that consisted of a twenty-foot-high roll of toilet paper crashing through a bathroom wall and crushing Harvey Korman to death. Real-life situations indeed. William Goldman's dictum about Hollywood was an accurate one: Nobody knows anything.

During the fall quarter, I'd begun dating a young film student whom I shall call Linda, for that was her name. She and I had plans to go out to dinner one night, but just before leaving work, Erin informed me that Zeppo would be coming up from Palm Springs and would I like to have dinner with them at Groucho's. Frustrated, I said, "I'd love to, but I have a date." Erin simply said, "Bring her."

This appealed to my sadistic side, because up to that point Linda had been pretty unflappable. Nothing ever seemed to faze her. I was determined that she be flapped, so I told Erin to count us in, then went back to the co-op and changed clothes.

When I picked up Linda, she wanted to know where we were going for dinner. It was a reasonable request. I told her it was "a little, out-of-the-way place." I think she caught on when I turned from Sunset onto Hillcrest since there were no restaurants in sight, only large, expensive homes. She suddenly got very quiet, then said she did not want to do this. But no dice—we were going to have dinner with the Marx Brothers (*two* of them, anyway), and that was final.

Seeing Zeppo under these circumstances was far different from that quick compliment in the parking garage of the Dorothy Chandler Pavilion two years earlier. For one thing, we were in his brother's house, and for another, I was in the company of a bright, young, attractive blonde.

Neither of these factors can be overestimated.

During dinner Zeppo appeared to be quite taken with Linda, despite the fact that, due to her being a little intimidated by her dining companions, she wasn't contributing much to the conversation. Zeppo's interest, of course, was flattering to me. Here was a man who'd been around the track once or twice, and if he thought she was noteworthy, apparently I'd done well.

Zeppo: "Steve, you and Linda should come down to Palm Springs sometime and visit."

Me: "I don't know. I went there once when I was nine. It was too hot."

Zeppo: "When did you go? During the summer?"

Me: "Yeah."

Zeppo: "You know, it's cold in Alaska during the winter, too!"

I got a kick out of Zeppo. As hard as it is for others to believe, he lit up the room just as brightly as had George Burns. It was often said that Zeppo was the funniest of the brothers, off-screen. Once, when Groucho was hospitalized for appendicitis in Chicago during their stage days, Zeppo pinch-hit for him and reportedly matched Groucho laugh for laugh. The audience didn't miss Groucho because no one knew it was really Zeppo behind the greasepaint moustache and cigar. As a result, Groucho was out of the hospital and back onstage much earlier than anticipated.

People often knock Zeppo for his comparatively wooden appearances in those first five Marx Brothers films, from *The Cocoanuts* through *Duck Soup*, but my feeling is he never really got the opportunity to shine. Since he was the youngest brother and had inherited the "straight man" role when Gummo left the act during World War I, there simply wasn't enough character comedy to go around. Understandably frustrated, Zeppo left acting in 1933 and opened up a talent agency that became the third largest in Hollywood in the thirties and forties, representing, among others, Clark Gable, Carole Lombard and Barbara Stanwyck. He never looked back.

In Joe Adamson's vastly entertaining examination of the Marx Brothers, *Groucho, Harpo, Chico and Sometimes Zeppo*, he has a "Nausea Rating" chart of the various straight, romantic leads who populated their films. Adamson took a good, hard look at the actors who sang the ballads and romanced the ladies and promptly dubbed Zeppo the least nauseating of the lot. Not exactly *high* praise, but praise nonetheless.

He may not have made a strong impression in those early films, but Zeppo was still one of the Marx Brothers, and once he left the act he was missed, if only by comparison with his often sappy replacements. For the record, Adamson considered Tony Martin from *The Big Store* to be their most nauseating romantic lead. I might've cast my vote for Kenny Baker from *At the Circus.*

In person I found Zeppo to be charming, animated and very amusing. And he seemed to be about twenty years younger than he actually was. Earlier in the evening, he had presented Groucho with a number of cans of tuna that, according to Groucho, Zeppo had personally caught on his yacht (or *off* his yacht, I should say). As he was leaving, Zeppo took me aside and whispered conspiratorially, "If you want to know the truth, I buy that tuna at the store whenever I come up to visit Groucho. But don't tell him. He likes to think I catch 'em!" I felt privileged to be in on an interfraternal secret. True to my word, I never told Groucho.

A few months later, Linda and I stopped seeing each other romantically. About that time, I'd found a couple of vintage photos of Zeppo that I wanted him to sign. Figuring that having recently lost his wife to a virulent strain of Frank Sinatra and having, essentially, picked up where Chico left off in the women department, I sent the photos to Zeppo along with a note informing him that Linda and I had broken up, and wanting to know if a man of his experience had any advice for the lovelorn.

I should've seen it coming. Two days later, I received a long-distance call from the Tamarisk Country Club in Palm Springs:

Zeppo: "Steve? It's Zeppo Marx, how are you? I got those pictures you sent and I'll be happy to sign them for you. *God,* I was good-looking back then. Listen, I'm sorry to hear about you and Linda, but I was wondering: Do you think she'd go out with me?"

Me: "Go out with you? I don't know. She *did* enjoy meeting you, so I suppose—"

Zeppo: "I'm not stepping on your toes, am I, Steve?"

Me: "Er, no. I mean, after all, she and I aren't seeing each other anymore."

Zeppo: "Because I wouldn't want to do anything that would hurt you, you understand."

Me: "No. Don't worry about it. Tell you what: I'll give you her phone number, and then I'll let her know that she'll be hearing from you."

Zeppo: "Terrific. You're sure it's OK, now?"

Me: "I think so."

So I gave him Linda's number, then called her to let her know what was happening. She was as amused as I was. I wasn't jealous;

I thought the whole thing was kinda cute. I mean, she was nineteen, I was twenty, and he was seventy-four. She braced herself for the call but the phone didn't ring.

A couple of days later, I received the photos back, inscribed by Zeppo. On the front of the envelope he had penned a cryptic message: "Wrong number for Linda." So I called him up, gave him the number again, and this time he succeeded in getting in touch with her.

I mentioned this to Erin, assuming she would get the same kick out of it that Linda and I had gotten, but she just looked at me in disbelief and said rather sharply, "I can't believe you'd want that wrinkled old man crawling all over your friend!" Suddenly I had second thoughts about Linda going out with Zeppo. But go out they did.

Once.

I talked to Zeppo a short time later and he said, "I took her to dinner in San Diego and then to a jai alai game in Tijuana. But we didn't 'do' anything. I didn't even kiss her, Steve. I swear it. You know, she's very nice, but all she did was talk about herself all evening."

Sometime after that, I ran into Linda on campus. She said, "I had a good time with Zeppo, but all he did was talk about himself."

I think they were probably both right.

From that point on, whenever I'd see Zeppo at a party, he'd razz me about my fluctuating waistline and then introduce me to whomever he was standing next to by saying, "Have you met Steve? He and I went out with the same girl, but he got further with her than I did." It was as though it were my formal title, as far as Zeppo was concerned.

Zeppo also took a fancy to Groucho's weekend cook, Robin Heaney. Tall, slender, with long, blond hair, Robin was another accident waiting to happen. One evening Zeppo and Gummo came to dinner and I was lucky enough to be there.

At the table, Zeppo watched Robin serving the salad. Then, as soon as she went back into the kitchen:

Zeppo: "Robin said she'd marry me, but she's too tall."

Erin: "What part of her do you want?"

Zeppo: "The part I can reach!"

Gummo: "What do you want with her *feet?*"

There are lots of Groucho anecdotes floating around and even a few Zeppos, but I cherish that as my one-and-only Gummo witticism. Actually, that's not true. After dinner, I got Gummo's autograph on an index card. As he finished signing it, he said, "You know, if this were at the bottom of a check, it might actually be *worth* something." It was said that of the various brothers, Groucho had always felt closest to Gummo.

Listening to these three aging Marx Brothers kidding around at the dinner table, I could only begin to imagine what it must've been like when all five were around and at the height of their powers.

In November of 1974, Erin enlisted my help on a project that was separate from the fan mail and memorabilia. The year before, a book entitled *The Marx Brothers Scrapbook* had been published. It was essentially a running interview between author Richard Anobile and Groucho, interspersed with pictures and comments from others, including Zeppo, Gummo and Groucho's longtime writer friends.

Because Anobile had included a number of graphic, off-color comments attributed to Groucho in the book, Groucho, at Erin's insistence, had filed a lawsuit. Erin was of the opinion that Anobile—whose name, she pointed out, means ignoble—had simply whipped up these dirty words out of thin air in order to make a name for himself while simultaneously destroying Groucho's reputation.

My suspicion was that Groucho had probably *said* them, but that they hadn't been intended for publication, and that it had been imprudent of Anobile to have included them in his final draft. But Groucho was certainly capable of using naughty language. Witness the following exchange between Groucho, Bud Cort and myself as I prepared to visit my sister.

Groucho: "Where are you going?"

Me: "Portland, Oregon."

Groucho: "I played there. They call it the City of Roses. Used to go with a girl whose father owned the largest department store in Portland."

Bud: "Do you remember her name?"

Groucho: "No, but I remember fucking her. She knew more about fucking than any whore. Never went out with her again."

Bud: "Didn't you enjoy it?"

Groucho: "Yes, but she knew too much. Knew every position."

Bud: "How'd she learn so much?"

Groucho: "I don't know. She must've fucked every guy in her father's department store."

Bud: "Must've blown your mind."

Groucho: "Why not? She blew everything else I had!"

So Groucho could be unabashedly bawdy when he was around familiar faces—and off the record. But according to Erin, Groucho had approved the *Scrapbook* galleys when he was hospitalized and in no condition to make shrewd legal and editorial decisions.

Despite my skepticism about Erin's allegations, I agreed to help out. If nothing else, it meant temporarily higher paychecks due to the extra hours. My assignment was to sit at the dining-room table in Erin's house on Vista Grande and compare the original transcripts of the Groucho/Anobile interviews with the final, published version, noting any and all discrepancies.

I was assisted in this task by nurse Connie August's younger sister, Penny, and an aspiring, Western-dressed actor named David Hixon who seemed to have modeled himself after the Jon Voight character in *Midnight Cowboy*. It was generally assumed by the Marx household that Hixon was squiring Erin about in the hope that his career might pick up. A short time later, David wore out his welcome by losing his temper and slapping Erin across the face. Groucho thought it terribly unchivalrous, commenting sarcastically, "It takes a big man to hit a woman."

The transcripts were a massive undertaking because Anobile had conducted hours and hours of interviews over several months and then edited them down to a usable size for the book. Consequently there were a number of inconsistencies between the recorded interview and the printed book, but most of them were condensations of Groucho's actual responses; not made up, just compressed for space and clarity. After a number of evenings spent doing this, I came to the same conclusion I'd had before I'd started: Groucho *had* said those things, but he probably didn't think Anobile would have the bad taste to include them in the book. As a result, Groucho tended to refer to Anobile as "a pipsqueak."

It was a stressful assignment for Penny, David and me, because Erin would pace back and forth looking over our shoulders, and every time we found the slightest discrepancy her attitude would be "Aha! *Now* we've got 'em!" We'd then have to trace over the passages in yellow highlighter that, rather than emphasizing the words, tended to smear the poorly Xeroxed pages so that no one could tell what they said. It was an exercise in absurdity.

One marathon session lasted from 10:00 A.M. until 1:00 A.M. the following morning, stopping only for meals. The saving grace of that particular day was that Groucho was there and in rare form. He'd get bored listening to Erin and me trade off on reading the depositions, so every time Erin would turn her back or leave the room, Groucho would make a snide remark about whatever we'd just been discussing.

His impishness led to a sort of exquisite torture, since I wanted nothing more than to laugh but feared Erin's wrath had I given in to silliness. She was taking the whole lawsuit situation very seriously and saw nothing funny about any of it.

Having had a large bowl of chili for lunch that day, Groucho inadvertently emitted a volley of audible explosions. Erin thought it was terribly disruptive of him, but Groucho shrugged it off, launching right into a chorus of "I Left My Fart in San Francisco." This cracked me up, irritating Erin even more, since she was trying to get as much accomplished as possible, what with the court date only a week away.

Later that evening, inspired by a story in the transcripts, Groucho started talking about his vaudeville days when the Marx Brothers rode Harley-Davidson motorcycles. "We used to ride with two girls on each bike, one sitting in front on the handlebars and another on the seat in back of us. One day, Harpo and I were having a race to see who was fastest. We couldn't see where we were going and we ran full speed into a mule. We knocked that ass *on* his ass!" Penny, David and I laughed, but Erin fumed like a schoolmarm who'd caught some students making naughty comments in the back of class.

Erin's irritation at Groucho's seemingly cavalier regard for legal matters was nothing new. Two months earlier, when Groucho's daughter, Melinda, had a daughter of her own named Jade, Groucho wanted to revise his will to include a monetary bequest to his new granddaughter. I was asked to cosign as a witness, but just as I was about to put pen to paper, Groucho's cat, Blackie, wandered into the room. Groucho blurted out, "Wait a minute! Don't sign anything yet! I want to include Blackie in my will! I hereby leave him two cans of salmon!" Erin thought Groucho should be taking his last will and testament a bit more seriously. As usual, Groucho thought otherwise.

There were a few errors that made it into *The Marx Brothers Scrapbook* which were nothing more sinister than sloppy editing or just plain ignorance. Groucho's reference to the Pantages theater circuit came out "Fantasia" in the book, giving it a strange Disneyesque quality. Algonquin member Donald Ogden Stewart came out "Don Martin Stewart." And a photograph clearly showing entertainer Maurice Chevalier with the Marx Brothers had a caption which stated that the man was *Cocoanuts* director Robert Florey. (An ironic error since, in *Monkey Business*, the Four Marx Brothers attempt unsuccessfully to pass themselves off as Maurice Chevalier. Perhaps they would've gotten further had they tried impersonating Robert Florey.)

A more amusing error occurred when Groucho was talking about the funeral of George S. Kaufman, at which their friend, Moss Hart, had delivered the eulogy. In truth, Groucho had said, "And five months later, Moss Hart was dead." But the transcript read, "And five months later, Mort Sahl was dead." Happily, this error was corrected before the book went to print, saving Mr. Sahl the hassle of borrowing Mark Twain's disclaimer that the reports of his death had been greatly exaggerated.

In the end, however, there was no injunction against the book and Groucho lost the suit. The court ruled that Groucho had signed the contracts, allowing the publishers to put the book out in whatever form they chose. Just the same, Groucho continued to refer to Anobile as a pipsqueak.

Also during the month of November, there occurred an incident of considerable intrigue. One evening my phone rang. It was Erin. "I understand you're in on a plot to get rid of me," she stated firmly.

Gulp.

Much of what Erin imagined to be going on around her was exactly that—imagined. Sometimes she misinterpreted things. Sometimes she was completely offbase. In this case, however, there was actually some truth to her accusation.

When I noted that, in my short documentary, Groucho seemed to be distributing his kisses evenly between Erin, cook Robin and nurse Connie, this was not without significance. Despite the fact that all of Groucho's nurses were young and attractive, Connie August had been gaining an increasingly substantial foothold in Groucho's life, which none of the other nurses had been able to do. In addition, she felt that Erin's irrational behavior was detrimental to Groucho and that it had to stop.

Connie believed, as I did, that Erin was essentially "blaming" Groucho for getting older and weaker and that she was incapable of accepting the fact that underneath it all he was an eighty-four-year-old man in declining health. But what could be done?

For starters, Connie had a lot of support. There was instant unanimity among everyone who *wasn't* Erin: cooks, maids, nurses, even secretary-archivists. For although I owed my job to Erin, her increasingly frequent fits of rage aimed at Groucho and almost anyone else within earshot were gradually eroding my sense of loyalty and obligation. In the early weeks of my tenure there, when the nurses would complain about Erin's behavior, I felt they were exaggerating the situation. I found myself rationalizing Erin's conduct and trying to look at the positive side of her effect on Groucho, which was admittedly substantial.

But, as with Fletcher Christian in *Mutiny on the Bounty*, once I'd been won over to the idea of her removal, I was unshakably a mutineer. It was becoming too painful to sit back and watch the way she treated—or mistreated—Groucho. If there were some way to subtract Erin and substitute someone else, someone *capable,* then I was all for it.

It wasn't just the household; Groucho's longtime friends felt the same way. Robin had become friendly with writer-producer Nunnally Johnson and his family. Nunnally had been one of Groucho's closest friends for decades, and he and his family cared deeply about Groucho's well-being. His wife, Dorris, said something akin to, "If there *is* a move under way to unseat Erin, we'll do whatever we can." According to Robin, a number of Groucho's other friends had expressed similar sentiments once they were certain they were out of Erin's earshot.

In the meantime, Connie set to work gently trying to wean Groucho away from Erin—no mean feat. She helped him to understand that his blood pressure would get dangerously high after Erin had been screaming at him and that he didn't deserve to be treated that way. Connie cared about Groucho as a person and not simply as a legendary entertainer who could advance her career. What's more, she had an educated understanding of how to maintain the health of a frail octogenarian. Erin's medical training consisted of dressing up as a nurse for the "Dr. Hackenbush" number in Groucho's one-man show.

And, frankly, Connie was very attractive, so Groucho wouldn't even be losing out on having a pretty lady on his arm whenever he'd go out in public. In short, Connie appeared to be an eminently viable alternative to, and considerable improvement over, Erin Fleming.

Even Groucho began to see the appeal. I was surprised and encouraged by this because I had assumed that Groucho had grown too dependent on Erin's guidance and would never be able to envision a life without her by his side (or *in* his side, as with certain thorns). But things were looking up. Groucho started insisting that *he* was in charge of things, that this was *his* house and that he didn't need Erin making his decisions for him.

This was absolutely revolutionary.

At the same time, Erin was getting increasingly and understandably paranoid that Connie was overstepping her bounds as one of Groucho's nurses. Although she never needed anything more solid than a whim in order to fire someone, for some reason Erin allowed Connie to continue looking after Groucho. I suppose it falls under the heading of Erin's unpredictability and her frequent habit of doing the exact opposite of what the rest of us assumed she would do in a given situation.

I was still sitting in Erin's dining room each night, next to Penny, Connie's *sister,* going over those transcripts of the Anobile book while Erin breathed down our necks. As you could imagine, it was a tense, stressful time. But it began to look as though the coup might actually come to pass. If we could all just hang in there a *little* while longer, things would improve dramatically all the way around.

It all came to a head at a dinner at Groucho's shortly before Thanksgiving. A number of his friends were there, including entertainer Edie Adams and producer Bert Granet and his wife, Charlotte. The plan, such as it was, was for the Bel-Air Patrol to arrive early and, in effect, bar Erin from entering Groucho's house while Groucho was being looked after by his friends and Connie.

Unfortunately, the whole thing backfired.

Erin managed to circumvent the Bel-Air Patrol and entered, screaming. All hell broke loose. The astonished guests were tossed outside, Connie was fired on the spot and that was the end of the Great Rebellion of 1974.

In the end, although she was well intentioned, Connie probably tried to accomplish too much, too soon, thus enabling Erin to get the upper hand. And despite Groucho's increasing attachment to Connie, he was not able to choose her over Erin when push literally came to shove.

Although I had had no active role in the attempted mutiny, I had certainly been rooting for its success. I'm still not sure exactly how I managed to talk my way out of my complicity when Erin surprised me with that accusation over the phone. My head could easily have rolled right alongside Connie's, but it didn't. I guess I had gradually been learning how to handle Erin, if we accept the hypothesis that such a thing is possible.

Eventually I was to emerge the longest-surviving employee of Groucho's household except for the gardener, Arturo, who was, literally and figuratively, on the outside. (As a matter of fact, Arturo would continue to look after the shrubbery at 1083 Hillcrest for almost a full year after Groucho's death.)

After the Connie fiasco, things settled back down to normal, if that word can be applied to life inside Groucho's house. Toward the end of the year I officially met Groucho's son, Arthur, when he came to lunch one day. It was a strange experience. When we sat down, the tension in the dining room was palpable. I knew that things had been strained between them, to say the least, and I was glad that they were having some sort of rendezvous. After all, Arthur was Groucho's oldest child and only son.

Food was served, but very little was said. Mostly there was the sound of three forks poking at salads. When Arthur did speak, he was all mumbly and fidgety, and he struck me as a rather bitter and neurotic person. Suffice it to say it was an uncomfortable gathering.

Although I'd become accustomed to sitting at the table when guests were there, I sensed that I was intruding on something very personal. Erin wasn't around and I felt Arthur would rather be left alone to visit with his father. I excused myself and took my plate into the kitchen, where I sat down at the little dinette table.

As I was sitting down, I happened to look out the kitchen window. I couldn't believe what I saw. It was Arthur Marx, driving away! It didn't seem as though he'd had sufficient time to reach the front door, much less get into his car, in the twenty seconds it had taken me to go into the kitchen and sit down. What had—or hadn't—been said by either of them that might have resulted in Arthur's swift departure? I was baffled.

According to Arthur's 1988 book, *My Life with Groucho*, Groucho had accused Arthur of having written an unflattering article about Erin and had demanded an apology. Arthur claimed he'd never written such an article, so no apology would be forthcoming. Groucho told Arthur he was no good. Understandably upset by his father's response, he'd walked out. That may have been the same day he came to lunch.

Regardless, Arthur didn't see Groucho again until November of 1976, two years later.

What, then, is the full story behind Arthur's relationship with Groucho? Once again, the color of truth is gray. Clearly, Erin's domination of Groucho's life caused enormous friction between her and Arthur and, in turn, Arthur and Groucho. I had heard that Groucho's children had neglected him in recent years, but much of what I'd heard came from Erin. In retrospect those rumors must be carefully scrutinized.

Erin had spent no small amount of time and energy badmouthing Groucho's three children—to Groucho and anyone else within earshot. She resented the fact that Groucho continued to give money to his two daughters, Melinda and Miriam, who "never visited him." Melinda lived with her husband and two children in the northern California town of Mendocino, and Miriam had spent years struggling with the perils of alcoholism and mental institutions. But Erin had no compassion for either daughter. To her, Melinda didn't care about her father, Miriam was simply a drunk and they only called Groucho when they needed money.

With regard to Arthur, Erin kept drumming into Groucho the idea that his own son, if given the chance, was going to put him in "a home," which was something Groucho never wanted to have happen under any circumstances. There's no evidence that Arthur intended doing anything of the kind, and it appears to have been just a ploy on Erin's part to poison Groucho against Arthur.

But Erin Fleming cannot be blamed for all the familial unrest. Arthur and Groucho had a history of troubles that reached back many years before Erin ever came on the scene. Arthur, born in 1921, was the son of Groucho and his first wife, Ruth. Arthur was close to his mother and by the time the marriage ended in divorce in 1942, Groucho's caustic treatment of Ruth had taken its toll on Arthur. Ruth was an alcoholic, and as Arthur grew older he came to understand how much of a strain that can put on a marriage. But as a child, it hurt him to hear the cruel, demeaning things Groucho often said to Ruth.

After a considerable amount of success in the tennis world, Arthur began making a name for himself as a writer. Since Groucho had always aspired to be a writer, one might assume that this would have forged a special bond between father and son. Instead it engendered a rivalry. Groucho would often be highly critical of Arthur's work which, understandably, caused resentment in a son who was looking for his father's approval.

In 1954, Arthur wrote a book called *Life with Groucho*, and, although Groucho had initially been enthusiastic about the project, when he saw the manuscript, he was so upset about how he felt he'd been portrayed that he threatened to take legal action if the book wasn't completely rewritten to his satisfaction. Each party summoned a lawyer. Since Arthur would only agree to make a *few* changes, Groucho threatened to get an injunction against the book. It is not known whether or not Groucho took to calling Arthur a pipsqueak.

Arthur hit upon the idea of sending an unedited version of the book galleys to his publisher and another, "sanitized" version to Groucho, who was pleased to see that Arthur had finally come around to his way of thinking. The deception worked. The unexpurgated book was a success and Groucho never seemed to mind, once it hit print and got good reviews. But his belated cooperation never washed away the fact that he had come perilously close to suing his own son.

Then there was the matter of Arthur's marital record. As children, Arthur and Miriam had been friends with Irene and Donald Kahn, the children of Groucho's friends, composers Grace and Gus

Kahn. In 1943 Arthur and Irene married—a union Groucho initially opposed because he felt Arthur was too young to settle down. Eventually, however, Groucho warmed up to the couple.

Around the same time that Arthur married Irene, Donald Kahn married a woman named Lois Goldberg. In 1961 Arthur divorced Irene and married Lois—his own sister-in-law. Once again Groucho disapproved, and this caused yet another rift between father and son.

As a matter of fact, while he maintained a certain coolness toward Lois, Groucho continued to invite Irene to social gatherings at his home until 1977, when his declining health put an end to partying. Irene was, after all, the mother of Andy Marx, someone who never fell out of Groucho's good graces and was always welcome in the house. For Andy's father and stepmother, things were much iffier.

As if all *this* weren't enough, there was an incident in 1973 that was straight out of a Jackie Collins novel. Erin had told Groucho she couldn't have dinner with him because she had an acting class, but Arthur and Lois spotted Erin dining with a handsome young man at Matteo's Italian restaurant in Westwood that night. Upset that Erin had lied to Groucho and left him all alone, Lois poured a glass of ice water on Erin's head, then left the restaurant. Needless to say, when word of this got back to Groucho, it didn't make things any smoother between Groucho, Arthur and Lois. As a matter of fact, Groucho threatened to cut Arthur out of his will. Not even two cans of salmon.

There were numerous other factors that served to make Arthur and Erin bitter adversaries, mostly centering on money and the influence she had over his father. So between Erin's sweeping accusations and the very real problems Groucho had with his children, it's difficult to separate fact from fiction.

And while Erin might have exaggerated certain problems or made them up entirely, one can't overlook what it must have been like to grow up in the shadow of a man of Groucho's stature—and withering wit. I've never doubted that Groucho loved all three of his children very much. But it takes more than just loving them.

When I started working there, I remember thinking that it would have been the coolest thing in the world to have Groucho as a dad. Now that I'm older and allegedly wiser, I've come to realize that being a successful funnyman doesn't necessarily translate to being a successful father. Children still need emotional support, encouragement and acceptance. Suffice it to say that, for a variety of reasons, Arthur and Groucho were not particularly close during my tenure there except for during Groucho's final months, when there was a certain reconciliation.

As the holidays drew near, Groucho told me, "I'm gonna give you a hundred dollars for Christmas. Get yourself a new pair of shoes." Since I was not given to wearing hundred-dollar pairs of shoes, I followed Groucho's directive and pocketed the difference.

Groucho decided to send out Christmas cards to his friends that year and he took the time to personally sign his name to each of them. One day he received a tin of candied almonds from comedian Fred Allen's widow, Portland. Groucho instructed me to send her one of his Christmas cards. I said, "Don't you want to say anything special?" He thought for a moment and then said, "Tell her, 'Thanks for the nuts; hope you're the same.'" That remains one of my favorite off-the-cuff Grouchoisms from my years there.

But even Christmas had its dark side. It marked Erin's final conflict with another significant employee. After nearly fifteen years of working for Groucho, Martha Brooks finally had her fill of Erin Fleming. She told me, "At first, Erin was very sweet and nice. Everything was, 'Yes, Mr. Marx. No, Mr. Marx.'" Then, as Erin's power grew, her sweetness gradually gave way to tyranny. Martha felt, as did so many others, that Groucho was very fortunate to have someone in his life at such a late date—and very *un*fortunate that it was Erin Fleming. "Why can't he live out his last few years comfortably, instead of having to put up with all *that?*" Martha asked rhetorically.

On more than one occasion, Martha had told me that she was thinking of quitting. I wanted to dissuade her, both because she and Groucho had been together for so long and because she was just about the last of the old regime that Erin had been systematically driving to quit or simply firing. Agnes, the maid, was gone. Groucho's longtime business manager, Alexander Tucker, had been fired. As had his longtime lawyer, Marvin Meyer. As had his longtime stockbroker, Salwyn Shufro, who had helped Groucho rebuild his holdings after he'd lost his $250,000 fortune in the stock market crash of 1929.

The final straw came when Erin insisted that Martha work on Christmas Day. Martha said she had never worked on Christmas and that Groucho had never asked that of her. Erin told her things were going to be different. Rather than acquiesce to Erin's demands, Martha threw in the dish towel, despite the fact that only three months earlier Groucho had revised his will, specifying that she was to receive $10,000 at the time of his death provided she was still in his employ. Apparently getting away from Erin Fleming far outweighed whatever financial rewards she might have reaped had she stuck it out.

The coup had failed, Arthur was persona non grata, Groucho's longtime employees were gone, and as 1974 drew to a close Erin was more solidly in charge of Groucho's life than ever before.

There would be only one other serious threat to Erin's autonomy, but that would not happen for another two and a half years, during Groucho's final days. In the meantime, though the honeymoon period may have ended, there were still many more adventures to come at Groucho's before the clouds closed in for good.

ELEVEN

People seem to have a fascination with round numbers: The Big Three-O, The Big Four-O, Special Fiftieth Anniversary Collector's Edition and so on. It's the same with celebrities. People may keep track of a celebrity's age, but they'll only make a fuss about it if that person has hit some sort of mutually agreed-upon milestone: Fifty, sixty-five, seventy-five and so on. Seventy-three or ninety-one just doesn't cut it. It has to be one of those nice, round, milestone birthdays in order for people to attach significance to the occasion.

And so it was with Groucho. Nothing much was made of his eighty-fourth birthday—and nothing much would be made of his eighty-sixth—but the fact that Groucho was in his eighty-*fifth* year seemed to be extraordinarily meaningful to people, so much attention was lavished on Groucho in 1975. Although technically speaking he would not hit eighty-five until early October, a parade of journalists came by the house to do profiles on "Groucho at Eighty-five" throughout the entire year.

After interrogating Groucho, the reporter or Groucho's press agent would usually send a copy of the final, published interview to the house. It was my job, then, to cut the piece out of the paper and put it into one of the large scrapbooks. I often noted discrepancies between what had been printed and what had actually been *said.* It seemed some of the reporters tended to downplay their own deficiencies and edit the pieces to make themselves—and not necessarily Groucho—look good. Additionally, in the event Groucho had said something that was deemed inappropriate for the purposes of their publication, it was simply omitted.

Unfortunately for them, I was there with my trusty blue Lindy ballpoint.

Although I did not keep a journal per se I did develop the habit of going back to my office after lunch and jotting down interesting or amusing things that Groucho had said at the table, or if there was an interview conducted at the house, I'd write down some of what had been said in the course of questioning. I treasure those scraps of paper, which I have kept in a single, paper-clipped clump all these years. They may not have been the *funniest* things Groucho ever said, but they were still worth noting. Had I not felt almost an obligation to scribble these things down so that I could go home and tell my friends what he'd said that day, these Late Period Grouchoisms would have been lost to the ages.

Reporter: "Why are you so big all over again?"

Groucho: "I'm only five-seven."

Reporter: "Do you enjoy being called a living legend?"

Groucho: "Yes."

Reporter: "Why?"

Groucho: "Because I'm dead."

Reporter: "You're going to be eighty-five soon. How does it feel?"

Groucho: "Sixty-nine felt better."

I was often dismayed at the relative ignorance of some of the reporters who came to Groucho's house. It seemed to me that it was a rare privilege for them to be able to share some of Groucho's increasingly precious time and I felt the least they could do was come prepared. I'd sit there thinking to myself, *You schmuck. Don't ask him* that. *Any movie book can tell you that. Ask him something interesting.*

Of course, for many of them it was just another assignment, and they couldn't be expected to have certain information at their fingertips. Groucho didn't suffer fools gladly, however. If nothing else, their inexperience gave him the opportunity to get off a good line or two at their expense.

Reporter: "What was it like making movies back then?"

Groucho: "It was hard work. They didn't have restrooms near the sound stages. I guess they didn't think actors were human. But all that's changed now."

Reporter: "Oh? How so?"

Groucho: "People don't piss anymore!"

Reporter: "What are you doing with your time?"

Groucho: "Wasting it talking to you."

On one occasion, Groucho treated a reporter to a couple of songs before the actual interview began. Unfortunately, the reporter hadn't realized that music had been a part of the Marx Brothers' performances since their earliest vaudeville days.

Reporter: "Where'd you learn to sing?"

Groucho: "That's a stupid question. I've been singing all my life. Where'd you learn to *write*—or maybe you haven't?"

Once, Groucho managed to turn the tables on his inquisitor.

Groucho: "Enough about me. What do *you* do for amusement?"

Reporter: "I go to the movies, play backgammon and dance."

Groucho: "At the same time?"

In addition to the columnists who came and went, hammering out their Groucho profiles for disposable newspapers, a more ambitious opus was in the works. I spoke earlier of Lyn Erhard, who under the pen name Charlotte Chandler had been assembling material for a book on Groucho. They had met in 1973 when she was assigned to interview him for *Playboy* magazine. Since the *Playboy* interview had gone so smoothly, it was decided that she would write Groucho's official biography, which was tentatively entitled *Groucho Marx and Other Short Stories.*

Lyn's modus operandi was to accompany Groucho and Erin to various events, such as the Oscars and the New York repremiere of *Animal Crackers*, taking notes and keeping her tape recorder running at all times. Lyn was an unusual woman who was of an indiscernible age—she could have been anywhere between thirty and fifty-five—and there was a certain soft-spoken, old-fashioned manner in the way she dressed and carried herself. In some respects she reminded me of an even more reserved Dr. Joyce Brothers. Sometimes Lyn was so unobtrusive she almost blended right into the wallpaper. Despite her demure appearance, however, she managed to secure interviews with an impressive array of powerful personages, including Salvador Dali, Francisco Franco and Charlie Chaplin.

Although her home base was the Hotel Navarre in New York City, from time to time Lyn would come out to California and stay in the guest bedroom that had once belonged to Groucho's younger daughter, Melinda. One day, as she was preparing to return to Manhattan, Lyn came into my office and, knowing of my preoccupation with celebrities, said, "I'm going to be interviewing Gloria Swanson, Lillian Gish and Woody Allen while I'm in New York. Would you like any of their autographs?" To no one's surprise I took her up on all three offers, digging up a trio of nice portraits that, as promised, were handed back to me inscribed upon her return to Beverly Hills.

Lyn interviewed Groucho in depth about his life and career, recorded conversations between Groucho and his celebrity friends, and conferred with me as to which photographs might be the most interesting to include from a fan's perspective. She even used me as source material, interviewing me about the *Animal Crackers* campaign and my subsequent duties as Groucho's secretary and archivist. Eventually Lyn would fall out of favor with Erin and Groucho, but for the time being she continued gathering information for her book.

In late January, Groucho shuffled into my office and dropped off a copy of *Cavett,* written by Dick Cavett along with his former Yale roommate, Christopher Porterfield. Groucho had written a blurb for the dust jacket extolling the book's virtues and had received two copies from the publisher when it was issued at the end of 1974. As Groucho handed me the book, he simply said, "Read this. You'll enjoy it."

It was more an order than a suggestion.

Although I'd certainly seen and enjoyed Cavett's late-night talk show from time to time, I really wasn't much of a fan. He was clearly more interesting than Merv Griffin, but for the most part I tended to think of him as little more than the thinking man's Johnny Carson, and I had the distinct impression that he was one of those New York snobs who loathed anything and everything about California. What's more, I thought he had a lot of nerve publishing his memoirs when he was only thirty-eight.

But I knew that Groucho was a big admirer of Cavett and that he would eventually ask my opinion of the book, as he had with other books he'd lent me, so I figured I'd better get to it. I brought *Cavett* back to my room at UCLA and began reading it.

I don't think I've enjoyed reading a book as much, before or since. I never wanted it to end. Daryl kept wondering why I was exploding into teary-eyed hysterics every few pages and so I would have to stop and read him some of the funnier passages, which were in abundance.

I found myself relating to *Cavett* (and Cavett) right from page one. Far from being a native-New Yorker elitist, Cavett, like me, had hailed from the midwest—Lincoln, Nebraska, to be exact. As in my case, he'd lost his mother to cancer when he was young and had found it initially awkward adjusting to having a stepmother around the house. We also shared an early and profound fascination with old movies and classic comedians. And like me, alas, he'd been painfully shy around girls while he was growing up.

All in all, Cavett struck me as an extremely witty yet thoroughly down-to-earth man. I thought to myself, *I know if I ever meet this guy, we'll hit it off, but I'm never in New York and he's never in Los Angeles. Oh well.*

I considered sending him a letter in praise of the book, but I was far too intimidated by the thought that this Yale-educated intellectual, who was close friends with Woody Allen and the rest of the New York intelligentsia and who was such a stickler for proper English usage, wouldn't give me the time of day. I had visions of carefully crafting a letter, sending it off and either not hearing anything or receiving my letter back covered in red-inked corrections. So I decided not to write to him, rationalizing that if I never sent the letter, he couldn't not answer it.

Nonetheless, I devoured the book in record time and set to work turning on each and every one of my friends to this funny, fascinating and revealing memoir. My friends, in turn, agreed that it was a wonderful book, and began telling *their* friends about it. *Cavett* may well have gone into another printing as a direct result of our campaigning.

So when Groucho finally got around to asking what I'd thought of the book, I couldn't think of enough superlatives. Groucho's hunch had been an accurate one: I had enjoyed it, to say the very least. And I vowed that someday, I would sit right down and write that man a letter.

But not just yet.

One letter I *wasn't* afraid to write was to a young lady in Strongsville, Ohio, named Diane Szasz. Diane had sent a fan letter to Groucho requesting his autograph and I had, in turn, sent her an inscribed photo. She had written back, thanking Groucho for the picture and wanting to know if he had really signed it or if it had just been the work of some secretary.

As previously described, I tended to fill out the fans' names on the photographs, but Groucho did, indeed, sign each of them as well as signing *and* personalizing the books and pictures that some fans took the trouble to send in. Consequently I was a little irked that she would ask for a picture, then turn right around and, in thanking Groucho, question its legitimacy.

So I wrote her back and informed her that Groucho had, in fact, signed her picture—technically the truth—and that, despite his advanced years, he still considered granting his fans' requests to be a part of his job, and why had she asked for one if she was just going to get all suspicious? Diane, in turn, responded to my response, apologizing for her skepticism and asking what it was like to be working at Groucho's house.

After another few letters back and forth, we shifted the correspondence to my UCLA address, since it was getting to be a pen-pal type situation and it was unfair to use up Groucho's stamps, stationery and time with what was becoming personal business. Diane had a sincere admiration and appreciation for Groucho—generally a rare trait in women who, if they do go for the Marx Brothers, tend to favor Harpo. That interest, coupled with a sharp sense of humor, led to a correspondence that ended up spanning several years, and which would, eventually, lead to more serious things (like exchanging snapshots of ourselves). But for now, we contented ourselves with writing each other.

In the spring of 1975, while Lyn Erhard was still toiling away on Groucho's biography, another writer appeared on the scene. His name was Hector Arce. He had spent considerable time as a celebrity columnist and had recently completed coauthoring director Vincente Minnelli's memoirs, entitled *I Remember It Well* after the song of the same name from the Minnelli-directed *Gigi.* Hector told me the title turned out to be an ironic one since, in reality, Minnelli remembered very *little,* well or otherwise, and it took no small amount of research and prodding on Hector's part to elicit reminiscences and anecdotes from the absent-minded director.

Initially Hector was brought in to work with Groucho on a proposed coffee-table book about interior decorator Peter Shore. Shore was a colorful man who had decorated the interiors of a number of celebrity homes, including those of Henry Fonda, Rock Hudson, Steve McQueen, Paul Newman and James Stewart.

At the time of Hector's arrival, Shore was in the midst of refurbishing Groucho's house—a substantial undertaking that had been Erin's idea. Left to his own tastes, it's unlikely Groucho would've elected to spend so many thousands of dollars redoing the home he'd been accustomed to living in for twenty years.

In addition to numerous major and minor decorator touches, Shore found the doors of an old circus wagon in Laguna Beach and had them made into a headboard for Groucho's bed, adding the name Lydia to its center for obvious reasons. Groucho would tell visitors, "I want to show you my headpiece. It's the only piece I'm getting these days." Hector was going to write the text of the Peter Shore book, and Groucho—with a little editorial assistance from Hector—would pen the introduction.

I met Hector on the day he came to Groucho's for the first of what would be many lunches. We became fast friends. Hector was about forty and would eventually be something of an older brother to me. We spent a considerable amount of time lunching and generally socializing together when we weren't at Groucho's. It was interesting and educational for me to learn about the ups and downs of life as a freelance writer, and he was a veritable fountain of Hollywood gossip. In addition to enjoying each other's company, it was fun to be able to rehash a memorable Groucho experience—and therapeutic to be able to decompress after a stressful Erin experience.

The Peter Shore book never materialized, but a somewhat rambling version of a portion of Groucho's introduction has survived, due in part to my penchant for jotting down what was said at the lunch table. Although it lends new meaning to the term *non sequitur* and could hardly be called politically correct by today's unforgiving standards, Groucho's unique "conversation" with Hector shows that his mind still had some of the old playfulness to it as he approached eighty-five.

Groucho: "Peter Shore? I know his brother Sandy. He herded goats in Bulgaria and ran off to Savannah, Georgia, to marry a colored girl, but she wouldn't have him because he was white. By the way, he's the greatest decorator of houses I know. Most of them talk with their hands on their hips."

Hector: "Does Peter Shore do that?"

Groucho: "I don't know. You'll have to ask the goats. His first name is Peter because when he goes bathing, you can see it. He got rid of my furniture and my ex-wife. She called up and wanted me to take back the old furniture. I said, 'Over my dead body,' which isn't far off."

Erin: "How would you describe Peter's personality?"

Groucho: "It's fiery. Whenever he comes into a room, the place lights up—especially if you have a match."

Hector: "What's your favorite color?"

Groucho: "Black, like that girl from Savannah. She wasn't *all* black. She was true blue, which was all white with me. And I think that gives you a true picture of Peter Shore and his brother Sandy."

One can only imagine an editor trying to make sense of all that, had the book gotten the green light.

TWELVE

Although the Peter Shore book fell through, the relationship between Groucho, Erin and Hector was a promising one. As a result, plans were soon under way for Groucho and Hector to write a book about "You Bet Your Life," since the show had been enjoying a great deal of renewed interest nationwide due to its resyndication under the title "The Best of Groucho." Groucho would be given credit for authoring the book but the actual writing would be done by Hector, who worked with Groucho over a period of months organizing anecdotes, opinions and other pieces of information.

In addition to my ongoing secretarial and archival duties, I was recruited to provide two services in connection with the book, which would be published the following year under the title *The Secret Word Is Groucho*. One assignment was to accompany Hector as he interviewed people connected with the show and help out with questions Hector might otherwise have overlooked.

The other was to sit with Andy Marx in Groucho's den and screen reel after reel of "The Best of Groucho," jotting down memorable exchanges between Groucho and his contestants and making a separate list of actual questions and answers from the show for inclusion in an appendix Hector wanted to put at the end of the book. Once again, I felt fortunate to be spending hour after hour immersed in this material, and doubly fortunate to have been getting paid for it.

From time to time, Groucho would shuffle into the den and watch an episode or two—even though it was currently airing at eleven each night—enjoying the program all over again. He would sit on the couch, shouting out answers and making derisive comments about how stupid the contestants were for missing the questions. He also made it clear how much he appreciated his announcer-sidekick, George Fenneman, whom he referred to affectionately as "Feenamint," after the popular laxative of the same name.

As was the case at the Dorothy Chandler Pavilion during the

film clips, it was strange to watch Groucho watching himself decades earlier, although he didn't appear to be haunted by the sight of himself in younger days. On the contrary, watching his younger self on television was one of Groucho's favorite pastimes. In addition to "The Best of Groucho," if a Marx Brothers movie was going to be on he'd usually make a point of tuning in, regardless of how many times he'd seen it.

Even though he may have been his own biggest fan, Groucho was still a sharp enough critic to discern the good films from the not-so-good ones. One afternoon we were watching *The Big Store*, generally considered to be one of their lesser endeavors. Groucho seemed to be having a pleasant time watching the 1941 incarnation of himself, when suddenly the television screen was filled with the improbable image of the Ty-D-Bol man sitting in his little rowboat inside a toilet tank. I fully expected Groucho to bristle at this vulgar interruption, but rather than decry the intrusiveness of commercials, Groucho turned to me and said, "Y'know, this is funnier than the picture." He may have been right.

"The Best of Groucho" was first syndicated in 1962, after "You Bet Your Life" had finished its eleventh, and final, television season. There are some significant differences between watching an uncut episode of "You Bet Your Life" and watching a somewhat truncated "Best of Groucho." For starters, the original commercials for DeSoto and Plymouth cars were deleted since the sponsors of "Best of Groucho" would vary from city to city. Consequently, we are denied the pleasure of seeing Groucho sticking his head through a DeSoto-Plymouth "porthole" and uttering his trademark catchphrase, "Tell 'em *Groucho* sent you!" Another difference is more significant, and more annoying.

Some viewers assume that the reason the "Best of Groucho" shows appear so grainy and the camera seems to cut off the faces of Groucho and his contestants is because it is an old show from the early days of television, when production techniques were primitive. This is a logical hypothesis. It's also wrong.

The real reason the shows look that way is because a large DeSoto-Plymouth sign hung from the curtain in the background so that it could be easily seen throughout the show. Consequently, before the shows were syndicated, the film had to be optically blown up to the point where the sign was no longer visible. This resulted in the fuzzy picture quality and the seemingly bizarre composition of the shots.

Also, since "The Best of Groucho" would be airing on different stations, the "NBC" on Groucho's microphone had to be optically rubbed out, giving it a certain radioactive glow. If you ever get to see an original, uncut "You Bet Your Life" episode, you'll see that the picture is sharp, the people are properly framed and none of what is happening onstage is chopped off.

In the course of helping Hector with *The Secret Word Is Groucho*, I was given access to a wealth of trivia about "You Bet Your Life" that I might otherwise not have known. For instance, director Bob Dwan told us he would have Groucho wear the same sport coat on each program (a special jacket that was designed to look best while seated) so that he could have the option of splicing part of one show onto another.

In other words, if both pairs of contestants had proved less than captivating on one show, Dwan could edit in another pair of contestants from another show who might have come off more amusingly. Since Groucho looked the same each time, the home viewer would think it had all taken place on one show. In this way Dwan could virtually guarantee that at least half of every program would be entertaining.

I also learned the circumstances under which the show had switched from CBS to NBC when it went from radio to television in 1950. According to Groucho, both CBS and NBC were interested in carrying the show, so a meeting of executives was arranged at the house of Gummo Marx, who was Groucho's manager at the time. Initially Groucho was leaning toward staying with CBS, both because he was already with them and because, at the time, they had most of radio's biggest stars under contract. CBS Chairman William Paley showed up at Gummo's early to try and get the jump on the competition.

At one point, Groucho excused himself to go to the bathroom. Much to everyone's surprise, Paley got up and followed Groucho right into the bathroom, locking the door behind them. Then he approached Groucho, who was trying to take a leak, and said, "Look, you're a Jew and I'm a Jew. We should stick together. You can't afford to go with NBC."

Groucho was so put off by Paley's tactlessness in following him into the restroom and trying to turn the whole thing into a religious issue that he decided right then and there to go with NBC (which, by the way, was headed by David Sarnoff—also a Jew).

It was fun and interesting to meet the people behind the scenes. I even got to meet The Duck that used to drop down from the ceiling whenever a contestant would say the secret word. Head writer Bernie Smith had confiscated it after the show had run its course, probably rescuing it from an ignoble trip to the studio dumpster.

The secret word was the brainchild of producer John Guedel, an interesting man who had a huge, framed collage in his office made up entirely of the dozens and dozens of rejection slips he had received over the years. I figured either he had great self-confidence or he was a masochist. Guedel wore a rather obvious toupee, and it took great presence of mind to keep from staring at it while he was trying to tell Hector and me about his creative contributions to the show.

Guedel explained that when he was producing Art Linkletter's "People Are Funny" program for radio, they had a gimmick: Whenever an alarm clock would go off, someone in the audience would win money. He wanted something similar for "You Bet Your Life," something to create anticipation that would last throughout the show. He came up with the secret word. The duck, however, was Groucho's idea. He thought something should drop down from the ceiling when someone said the secret word, and he had always thought ducks were funny animals.

Guedel also took credit for bringing Groucho's daughter, Melinda, onto the show. He thought it would help give Groucho a warmer image than he'd had on-screen and that the audience would be more sympathetic to him, thus taking the edge off of some of the sharp comments he made to the contestants. Groucho ended up trotting out Melinda about once a year, usually to do a little song or dance, either with Groucho or with a celebrity guest.

Melinda later told us that she wanted nothing to do with show business and hated being pushed out into the spotlight like that. Groucho, on the other hand, was extremely proud of her, and can usually be seen beaming brightly while she's performing.

Another highlight of working on the book was spending time with George "Feenamint" Fenneman, a warm and friendly man whose deep, resonant announcer's voice seemed to fill his entire frame, even when all he said was "Hello." One thing about Fenneman I hadn't realized, but could certainly relate to, was that when he was hired to be Groucho's announcer it was a big thrill for him because Groucho had been *his* idol when *he* was a kid.

My friends and I had always envied Fenneman as someone who'd been lucky enough to have known Groucho "way back when," but in talking with him it was evident that Groucho was already something of a legend when he got the job. And that was back in 1947! Like me, Fenneman admitted to feeling a little guilty about getting paid to spend time with his hero.

Among the catchphrases most closely associated with the show is Fenneman's introduction: "And now, here he is, the one, the only, *Groucho!*" But that, I learned, wasn't the original wording. Initially the introduction was going to be, "And now, here he is, the funniest man in the world, Groucho Marx!" But Groucho had objected, saying that in the first place, he wasn't the funniest man in the world, and in the second place, even if he were, the audience's expectations would be way too high after hearing such a claim. So they scaled it down a bit and Fenneman's introduction became a part of broadcasting history.

Fenneman popularized another catchphrase around that time, but since it was done off-screen and since he received no credit for it, no one knew that it was George's dulcet tones. In the course of interviewing him for the book, Hector and I were startled to discover that it was none other than George Fenneman who uttered the immortal lines, "The story you are about to see is true. The names have been changed to protect the innocent," at the beginning of each episode of "Dragnet." Dum-de-dum-dum.

One of the elements of "You Bet Your Life" that may be misleading at first is the fact that the show had a writing staff, although they were never officially credited as such because the network wanted the viewers to think that Groucho came up with all his humorous remarks on the spot. Bernie Smith was the head writer, and under him were Howard Harris, Hy Friedman, Marion Pollock and Edwin Mills. When people hear that "You Bet Your Life" had writers, they are apt to feel betrayed somehow and leap to the conclusion that *everything* Groucho said on the show was scripted. This is both unfair and untrue.

Bob Dwan, who directed the show for its entire run, said that they would shoot about an hour's worth of footage and then edit it down to a half-hour for broadcast. Although the staff wrote many funny lines that were projected behind the contestants for Groucho to use at his discretion, much of what ended up in the final cut was, indeed, off the top of Groucho's head. The staff would interview the contestants well in advance of the show and then write up some humorous remarks, but Groucho insisted he not meet the guests ahead of time, just to add to the spontaneity.

The writers were enormously talented and of inestimable assistance, and they are to be saluted for having had to ply their trade in virtual anonymity. Indeed, after the show ended in 1961, many of them had difficulty finding further employment because people refused to believe that the show was even partially written.

But it would be a mistake to assume, simply because the show had writers, that anyone (say, Bill Cosby, just to pull a name out of a hat) could do what Groucho did, week after week, year after year, for eleven years—fourteen, if you count the radio days. In the end, it was Groucho's personality, wry commentary and interplay with the much-put-upon George Fenneman that made the show work. That, and the fact that the contestants were a tasty slice of middle-American pie.

Which leads to another bit of confusion that I'd like to attempt to clear up. You may have heard about a legendary line concerning a certain cigar that Groucho was alleged to have uttered during one program. Some say it never happened; others *swear* they've seen it on TV. As it turns out, the truth is somewhere in between.

One of the unexpected pleasures of spending time with the people behind the scenes was getting to the bottom of this infamous incident. For the record, it was Bernie Smith who provided us with the details. To our amazement, Bernie had kept a chart throughout the life of the show, in which he had meticulously recorded the names of the contestants, what the secret word was and how much they ended up winning.

There was, it seems, a sign painter named Mr. Story who lived in Bakersfield, California. He and his wife had what was reputed to be the largest family in America. Originally there were twenty-two children, but three had died. During the first season of "You Bet Your Life," when it was broadcast on radio only, the Story family was bused in from Bakersfield to be contestants on the show. After a bit of small talk, the conversation went like this:

Groucho: "How many children do you have?"

Mrs. Story: "Nineteen, Groucho."

Groucho: "Nineteen?! Why do you have so many children? It must be a terrible responsibility and a burden."

Mrs. Story: "Well, because I love children—and I think that's our purpose here on earth—and I love my husband."

Groucho: "I love my cigar, too, but I take it out of my mouth once in a while!"

The studio audience went wild, but director Bob Dwan ordered the exchange deleted before it could be aired because it was obviously too racy for 1947 sensibilities. So the Story story is true, but anyone who claims to have seen that program is either mistaken or lying because it occurred three years before the show's 1950 television debut and it was edited out of the radio show before anyone but the studio audience had a chance to hear it. Unfortunately, no copies of that legendary outtake are known to have survived.

Although the show aired on television from 1950 through 1961, "The Best of Groucho" contains only shows from late 1954 onward. I had wondered why this was, until Hector recruited me to help him interrogate the "You Bet Your Life" staff. As it turns out, it isn't because someone accidentally destroyed the earlier shows or because they were considered to be of inferior quality. The bottom line, as with so many things in life and television, was money.

One of the show's earliest writers was a former dentist named E.T. "Doc" Tyler. He left the show in early 1954, but when the program was about to be syndicated in 1962, he demanded a substantial sum of money—an amount much higher than any of the other writers had requested—or else no shows from that early period could be made a part of the package.

Whether or not he was merely trying to bluff producer John Guedel into coming up with more money is not known. What *is* known is that it was decided there were enough episodes from the later years to make up the package. So "Doc" Tyler never saw a nickel when "The Best of Groucho" was syndicated and we never saw an episode from the first four years.

A particularly memorable experience from working on *The Secret Word Is Groucho* was meeting Jerry Fielding. At the time, I recognized his name as the composer of the scores for several Sam Peckinpah films, including *The Wild Bunch* and *Straw Dogs*. What I didn't know was that, as a very young man, Fielding had been the bandleader on "You Bet Your Life" before being replaced by Jack Meakin. The reason he was replaced? He'd been blacklisted.

I'd never met an honest-to-goodness blacklist victim, although we'd certainly studied them in film class. Fielding was a fascinating character with a short, gray beard and moustache who lived in a rustic house out in a secluded, wooded area. He struck me as something of an aging beatnik, only instead of bongos he was surrounded by state-of-the-art recording equipment.

At one point I made a remark about all he'd been through as a result of the blacklist, and his reply surprised me: "Young people think of us as heroes or martyrs for standing up to the committee, but what we did was *nothing* compared to what kids are going through today—getting thrown in jail and beaten and killed, all because of their beliefs. Jesus, all we did was lose our jobs!" Fielding felt the blacklist period had been overromanticized by my generation and that the social and political changes that occurred in the sixties and seventies were much more significant than the relatively minor sacrifices he and his peers had made in the fifties.

Something else he said, which I'd never heard, was that when the House Un-American Activities Committee asked you a question and you chose not to answer under the Fifth Amendment, you then had to take the Fifth for each and every subsequent question; you couldn't pick and choose. So the committee could ask, "Are you now or have you ever been a member of the Communist party?" and you were entitled to take the Fifth. But if you were then asked, "Are you now or have you ever been a member of the American Nazi party? A drug dealer? A murderer?" you would have no choice but to take the Fifth in each of those cases, regardless of how evasive that might appear. According to Fielding, the committee took full advantage, inflicting as much damage as possible to the reputations of those who elected to exercise their Fifth Amendment rights. Democracy in action.

Even before the blacklist problem, Fielding had made a reputation for himself as something of a crusader. When he was serving as bandleader on "You Bet Your Life," none of the other West Coast radio orchestras had black musicians. Fielding felt this was wrong, so he hired jazz musician Buddy Collette, both because he admired his talent and to try and break the color barrier. Groucho agreed that discrimination was wrong and backed up the decision, but NBC told Fielding that he'd better not try anything like that again or they were going to "get" him.

Incidentally, speaking of Buddy Collette, there was a little joke that the "You Bet Your Life" band enjoyed playing on the studio audience before each show. The musicians would enter the studio single file, carrying their instruments. But instead of taking their seats, they would continue walking past the audience until they were out of view, then circle around back and enter again, making it appear as though there were dozens and dozens of band members. If not for the rather conspicuous Collette, the audience might never have caught on, but once they saw the same black man entering two or three times, they'd laugh at the joke that had been played on them and the musicians would finally take their seats.

Jerry Fielding's relationship with Groucho was an interesting one, and it didn't really get resolved until *The Secret Word Is Groucho* was published. Fielding said that just before Thanksgiving of 1953, someone from the House Un-American Activities Committee came right into the studio as he was about to strike up the band and handed him a subpoena. Instead of fighting it, he went into Groucho's office and told him he was quitting the show to save him the trouble of firing him. To his surprise and relief, Groucho told him he wasn't going to sit still for a political execution.

Fielding told the NBC executives that he intended to be an unfriendly witness and not give any information to the committee. The network brass were initially supportive, telling him he was a big talent and that it would all work out just fine. But Fielding had a sneaking suspicion that the committee was really after Groucho, who had been involved in several leftist organizations. What if they pressed him for information about Groucho's politics? The NBC execs hadn't really considered that possibility and they suddenly became extremely uncomfortable with the whole situation.

After that, Bob Dwan called Fielding and told him the sponsors were putting pressure on NBC and Groucho didn't want to fire him or anything like that, but maybe it would be a good idea if he didn't show up for the next program—just until things cooled off. So Fielding skipped the next program and, as it turned out, all the programs thereafter, although no one ever told him that he was officially fired.

He couldn't get Dwan on the phone. He couldn't get Groucho on the phone. The mere hint of a sponsor withdrawing valuable advertising dollars was all it had taken for everyone to head for the hills, leaving Fielding to twist in the breeze. As it happened, he wasn't out of a job for long and he soon found himself fronting a band in Las Vegas. But it was still a shabby way to treat a very talented man.

Fielding said he was angry at the time because the show was such a hit that he felt Groucho would have had enough clout to put up some sort of a fight on his behalf. After Hector and I went back to Groucho and informed him of Fielding's feelings about the situation, Groucho admitted, "Giving in to the sponsors' demands is probably one of the greatest regrets of my life."

They had rarely spoken since his firing. Although Groucho had gone to Las Vegas on several occasions to see and hear Fielding, all he got was the cold shoulder from his banished bandleader. But after nursing a grudge for over twenty years, Fielding agreed to attend the publication party for *The Secret Word Is Groucho.* Groucho was looking forward to the prospect of clearing the air, however belatedly.

As it turned out, once the two men were finally face-to-face in Groucho's living room, all Groucho could manage to say was "How are you?" But Fielding said it was the invitation that had meant a lot to him, if only as a gesture. He never realized Groucho had felt so badly about caving in to the sponsors and perhaps he had underestimated the man after all.

Another interview we conducted for the book turned out to be somewhat less rewarding. Arch Oboler was a prolific writer-director who is probably best remembered for his spooky "Lights Out" radio series. Although he had never really been a part of Groucho's circle, they had known each other at MGM and had both been in radio in the forties, so Hector felt Oboler might provide some insight and background material.

We went to Oboler's house, where he proudly showed off a poster for a film he'd directed called *Bwana Devil,* starring Robert Stack. "First movie ever shot in 3-D!" he boasted. Then he whetted our appetites by telling us that he had had the unforgettable experience of sitting next to Groucho at the writers' table in the MGM commissary on the very day after the Japanese had attacked Pearl Harbor in December of 1941.

Oboler said, "I will *never* forget that lunch as long as I live. Groucho ordered a fruit salad and for about an hour and a half, he kept us all in stitches by firing off one joke after another, tying in his fruit salad with the Japanese attack on Pearl Harbor!"

Hector and I looked at each other, puzzled as to how the two seemingly disparate subjects could ever be connected, and anticipated some heretofore unrecorded Grouchoisms from the day after that day of infamy. "What sort of jokes did Groucho come up with that would've incorporated both Pearl Harbor and his fruit salad?" I asked. It seemed like a logical request.

Oboler thought for a moment, then replied, "To tell you the truth, I can't remember a single one of them, but don't think I haven't tried. All I know is, I'll never forget how absolutely *hysterical* he was that day! Just brilliant!"

Thanks for sharing, Arch.

THIRTEEN

In early 1975 I took a screenwriting class given by a writer-producer named Bill Froug, who had produced the original "Twilight Zone" during its final season as well as "Bewitched" and numerous other television shows. I decided to write a script about a young writer who decides to do a story about a beloved, aging comedian. He soon discovers that the unfortunate entertainer is being taken advantage of by a ruthless younger woman, and he tries to make the old man see her for what she really is.

There's no accounting for how story ideas originate or where they come from. The brain is a strange and mysterious organ.

When Froug heard that I was working for Groucho, he said, "I sure hope you're keeping a diary!" The thought hadn't really occurred to me until he'd said it, but since I'd already been working there for about six months, I couldn't see the point in starting something up so late in the game. Had I known I was going to remain at Groucho's house for another two and a half years, I might have reconsidered.

In addition to being an excellent teacher ("Conflict is the heart of drama!"), Froug had written a book entitled *The Screenwriter Looks at the Screenwriter*, which was a series of interviews he'd conducted with various legendary Hollywood writers. Among them was Nunnally Johnson.

Apart from having been a driving creative force at 20th Century-Fox during Darryl Zanuck's heyday, Nunnally's friendship with Groucho went back many years. I was initially familiar with him as one of Groucho's pen pals in *The Groucho Letters,* a collection of Groucho's correspondence from the thirties through the mid-sixties.

Groucho's nickname for Nunnally was Lonely. Some years earlier, Nunnally had called Groucho on the phone and a newly hired maid had answered. He said, "Please tell Groucho that Nunnally Johnson called." Not being familiar with this unusual first name, she told Groucho that "a Mr. Lonely Johnson" had called. The nickname stuck.

In April Groucho was preparing to pay a call on Nunnally, something he did on a regular basis. Since Nunnally had long been suffering from emphysema, it was difficult for him to come to Groucho's, but Groucho didn't mind making the trip down the hill and always looked forward to Nunnally's company. Erin wasn't going to accompany him on this particular visit, so Robin, the weekend cook, was Groucho's escort. Robin asked me if I'd like to come along, insisting that Nunnally was a very nice man and that I'd probably enjoy it. Being an aspiring writer myself, I was more than a little in awe of Mr. Johnson, but I wasn't about to pass up the invitation, so I tagged along.

Nunnally lived in a big, comfortable house behind the Beverly Hills Hotel, across from Fred Astaire and down from Jack Lemmon. He was married to a warm, gracious woman named Dorris. Years earlier she had acted under her maiden name, Dorris Bowdon, and can be seen as a pioneer woman in *Drums Along the Mohawk* and, more memorably, as the pregnant Rosasharn in *The Grapes of Wrath*, for which Nunnally had adapted John Steinbeck's novel. They were wed after completing that film and remained happily married for more than thirty-five years. Although I was still a bit nervous, I felt an immediate sense of warmth and friendliness when the three of us entered the house.

Nunnally was seated in the den in an overstuffed easy chair. At his side was a huge jar filled with peanuts; probably a remnant of his Georgia roots. Behind him was a wall-to-wall bookcase containing, among other things, leather-bound volumes of the scripts he'd written, including *The Grapes of Wrath*, *How to Marry a Millionaire*, *The Three Faces of Eve* and *The Dirty Dozen*. It was truly humbling to see how much space those scripts took up on those shelves.

Dorris and Nunnally were congenial hosts and their Southern hospitality put me at ease. Due to his emphysema, Nunnally had to gasp for air after speaking and he said that even something as simple as crossing the room left him winded. I was reminded of Groucho's admonition on "The Merv Griffin Show" that every smoker should pay a visit to Nunnally to see where an addiction to cigarettes will lead.

In contrast to his limited physical capacity, Nunnally's mind was as sharp as an X-acto knife. As I sat there listening to him and

Groucho reminisce, I wondered which was worse: Having your mind intact and a body that refuses to cooperate, or being in relatively good physical condition and having a mind that's getting progressively foggier. I suppose an argument could be made for either case.

Generally speaking, Groucho didn't appear to be aware of his advancing haziness and, in that case, I would say that ignorance is definitely bliss. But on occasion, Groucho seemed to get crystal-clear glimpses of exactly how far he'd fallen, as though a darkened room were suddenly and briefly illuminated by a flash of lightning. Once, Erin blurted out, "Groucho, you're the funniest man in the world!" With a trace of sadness in his voice, Groucho quietly replied, "Not anymore I'm not." At times like that, I almost would have preferred that the room remain dark.

More often than not, however, Groucho didn't seem to feel like an old man. Once, when Erin asked him how old age was, Groucho replied, "I don't know. It isn't here yet." Another time Groucho and I were walking down the hallway when he decided to show me his impression of an old man. Frankly, I thought he made a rather convincing old man without any additional effort, but I was curious to see what he would do.

Slowly, Groucho bent forward, almost in a crouch. Then he let his jaw hang open and made his lips cover his teeth, giving him a toothless appearance. Finally, he made one of his hands tremble as though he had an uncontrollable palsy. Groucho had turned into a stereotypical old man before my very eyes. After a few moments, he shifted back into his normal demeanor and I had to admit that there was a difference between Groucho and an old man.

At the time of our visit to Nunnally's house, the biggest movie around was Irwin Allen's *The Towering Inferno*, an all-star disaster film that had been a joint effort of Fox and Warner Bros. At one point, Nunnally asked about my ambitions. I told him I was interested in being a writer, either for movies or for television. Pleased that I aspired to be something of a compatriot, he leaned toward me and said in his deep Southern drawl, "Tell me, Steve, does a little picture still have a chance in this town, or does it have to be one of those 'two-studio' jobs?"

I was somewhat taken aback that the man who had helped shape 20th Century-Fox was asking for my assessment of the motion-picture business, but I took a shot. "Well, I think if it's a good story—like *The Graduate* or *Alice Doesn't Live Here Anymore*—then a small picture can still get made. But big disaster movies *do* seem to be pretty popular these days." He seemed satisfied with my answer and I felt relieved just to have made sense.

When *The Towering Inferno* came up in conversation, Groucho said, "Irwin Allen knows how to make lousy pictures that people want to see." I mentioned that his next movie was supposed to be about insects. "Insects?" Groucho queried. "Then he must be starring in it!"

After some more reminiscing with Nunnally, Groucho seemed to be fading, so Robin and I prepared to take him home. As we were about to bid Dorris and Nunnally goodbye, I remembered something from Bill Froug's book. According to the interview, since Nunnally was no longer working, he'd had business cards printed up that said: RETIRED—No Business—No Phone—No Address—No Money.

I asked Nunnally if it would be possible for me to have one of them and he said, "I can't quite get to them right now, Steve, but if I find one, I'll send it along." I wasn't really sure if he meant it, but I got the impression he appreciated the fact that I'd heard about the cards and wanted one as a souvenir.

Two days later I went out to Groucho's mailbox and was startled to discover an envelope addressed, in blue ink, to "Mr. Steve Stoliar c/o Marx." Imagine that—top billing. Inside were five of Nunnally's business cards along with a note "From the Pickled Pine Desk of Nunnally Johnson," which read, "Steve—Maybe Grouch could use a couple of these. N.J." I was delighted to get the cards, and at the time I interpreted his note to mean that maybe Groucho might get a kick out of them. In retrospect I realize his note was an attempt to drop a not-so-subtle hint that it was way past time for Groucho to give up performing.

He never took the hint.

Groucho's own note-writing was of an extremely limited nature by 1975, although he would occasionally get the urge to dash one off. In May Groucho received a letter from a man who was writing a book about humorist Ring Lardner. He wanted to know if Groucho would mind sharing his memories of Lardner when they were both residents of Great Neck, Long Island, in the twenties. I had doubts that Groucho would feel like going to the trouble, but I brought the letter to his attention and, to my surprise, he was in the mood to comply with the request.

"Dear Mr. Friedman: I can tell you about Ring Lardner. During Prohibition, he came to my house to dinner. I had a matinee the next day, so around eleven o'clock at night I said, 'Ring, I'm going to bed.' He said, 'Have you got any whiskey?' So I brought out two bottles—probably bootleg. When I woke up the next morning, he was passed out on the floor, drunk. I called his wife to come take him home.

"I lived at 21 Lincoln Road, Great Neck. One day, my father decided to make some wine. Across from where we lived, there was a sewer and the rats used to come out of there and go into my cellar. After a while, when the wine was good and ready, it exploded and it killed all the rats in the cellar.

"I went back last year and visited Great Neck. The house is just the same, but they added a new kitchen. When I rang the bell at my old house, a man came to the door and ushered me in. He knew all about the Marx Brothers because he ran a projector in a theater. He knew as much about our movies as I did.

"Great Neck was full of stars, and I was one of the lesser ones. I give you this for what it's worth. Sincerely, Groucho Marx."

I have no idea if the book ever came out, but I'm fairly certain Mr. Friedman was a happy man the day he retrieved that particular envelope from his mailbox.

Although it may not have warranted publication in *The Groucho Letters*, I include it here as evidence that, as he approached eighty-five, despite the strokes and his increasingly foggy mental state, Groucho was still quite capable of dictating a friendly, interesting and sometimes humorous note.

On occasion, incoming mail was equally noteworthy. *The Cocoanuts* has the distinction of having been the only Irving Berlin musical from which not one hit emerged. In his defense, however, Berlin had written the song "Always" for that show, but George S. Kaufman had objected that it was too saccharine, so it was deleted. Apparently he didn't like the lyric, "I'll be loving you, always." He said he would've preferred "I'll be loving you, *Thursdays*" because it would have been more realistic. Berlin hung on to the song, put it in another show, and it went on to become a standard.

One day a Western Union messenger arrived at Groucho's with a telegram in hand. It said, "DEAR GROUCHO: CAUGHT *THE COCOANUTS* ON T.V. THE OTHER NIGHT AND I DON'T THINK 'ALWAYS' WOULD'VE MADE IT ANY FUNNIER. LOVE, IRVING." I found it interesting that this footnote in theatrical history continued to be something of a private joke between Groucho and Berlin, fifty years after the show had opened. And despite Groucho's own status as an entertainment legend, he was impressed enough to have gotten a telegram from Irving Berlin that he kept it out on the trophy table for all to admire.

Berlin, incidentally, was two years *older* than Groucho. If nothing else, coming into contact with so many active octogenarians helped me to see that all was not necessarily over at the traditional retirement age of sixty-five.

Fourteen

Since Martha Brooks had been driven to quit and Robin Heaney only worked weekends, Erin needed to hire a new weekday cook. After several interim chefs came and went, she settled on a permanent replacement for Martha. His name was John Ballow, and a sharper contrast to Martha Brooks would be difficult to imagine.

John was, I suppose, the first openly gay person I'd ever met. There had been certain students who were whispered about in high school, of course, but John was the first person I ever got to know who truly luxuriated in his own gayness. If John had ever been in the closet, it was only to pick out something truly wicked for a night on the town. He made no secret of his sexual orientation and, in those innocent pre-AIDS seventies, would burst into the house on Sunday morning proudly announcing, "I was *such* a *whore* last night!"

Where Martha tended to be discreet and unobtrusive, everything about John was loud and outrageous. His hair was always worn in tight blond curls, his eyes usually betrayed more than a trace of mascara, he maintained a thin, Cantinflas-style moustache, and his standard work outfit was a short black tuxedo jacket, a pair of tight black pants and a frilly white tuxedo shirt, daringly unbuttoned to the navel.

John was the only person I've ever known, before or since, whose song of choice was "That's the Way (Uh-Huh Uh-Huh) I Like It (Uh-Huh Uh-Huh)," which he would absently sing to himself while whipping up something for lunch. And if the kitchen radio was blaring a tune with a particularly catchy beat, he would occasionally drop everything and dance the Hustle with Linda Ponce, one of Groucho's younger nurses.

If John had been a Marx Brother, he would've been Disco.

Although not exactly a gourmet chef, John served up dependable fare and Groucho got a kick out of having such a colorful character around the house.

John: "Groucho, you haven't had your pears yet."

Groucho: "How many are there?"

John: "Two."

Groucho: "Well then they *must* be pairs. By the way, where'd you learn to cook?"

John: "From my mother. She's better than I am."

Groucho: "Different sex. (*After John exits*) Although I'm not so sure in *this* case."

Incidentally, I never felt that Groucho was homophobic; he was just blunt. One day he received a fan letter from a woman named Alexandra Woollcott Duncan. I asked Groucho if she might be a relative of Alexander Woollcott's, and he said, "Woollcott didn't have any children. He never married. He was a homo." Groucho meant nothing malicious or disrespectful by it; he was just expressing himself in his usual, direct manner. He believed that what two consenting adults did behind closed doors was *their* business and nobody else's.

Where I tried to be diplomatic when turning away fans at the door, John thought nothing of blurting out, "I can't let you in! Oh my God, if I did, that terrible woman would *kill* us!" One can only imagine what those poor tourists must have made of his rantings as they drove back down Hillcrest. Although I clearly had major complaints about Erin's behavior, some sixth sense of decorum kept me from divulging them to passersby.

In time John's sense of the dramatic—or melodramatic—would give him a certain fleeting notoriety during the bitter battle between Arthur and Erin over Groucho's conservatorship. John's testimony, as with everything else about him, was outrageously colorful and the media ate it up. But that was still a ways off. In the meantime, it was entertaining to have someone in the household who made Rip Taylor look demure by comparison.

Speaking of Rip Taylor, as difficult as this may be to wrap one's brain around, he once lunched at chez Groucho, courtesy of John. It was one thing to witness Groucho interacting with Burns or Jessel. But the contrast in styles between Rip Taylor and Groucho Marx was truly something to behold, and fortunately I was there to behold it.

When Mr. Taylor showed up, I introduced myself and showed him to the table, where we made small talk while awaiting the arrival of our host. Presently Groucho ambled into the dining room and took his seat. Rip seemed to be a very nice man and he was clearly humbled to be in the presence of someone he admired as much as Groucho.

Unfortunately, lunch wasn't exactly a mutual admiration society.

Rip: "How do you do, Groucho. My name is Rip Taylor."

Groucho: "That's your hard luck. What do you do?"

Rip: "I'm a comedian."

Groucho: "Well, you haven't said anything funny yet."

Rip: "Well, I open my act by coming out onstage in a robe that's covered with long silver tinsel and I say, 'Looks like they shot the Christmas tree!'"

Groucho: "And then what? You go home?"

A silence descended on the dining room shortly thereafter. Poor Rip. He never had a chance.

The lunch table continued to be the center of activity for the exchange of anecdotes, opinions and ideas at Groucho's house. One day, he sat down at the table with a particularly irritated look on his face. After a few moments, he blurted out, "Whatever made Buzzell think he could direct?" Although this query had some merit, it was just a shade on the tardy side.

Eddie Buzzell was a vaudeville song-and-dance man who had ended up a contract director at MGM, where he directed the Marx Brothers in *At the Circus* in 1939 and *Go West* in 1940, two films generally considered to be among the brothers' weaker endeavors. Groucho hadn't been watching either film on TV that day and I don't think I'll ever know what had made him come storming into the dining room questioning Buzzell's directing skills. It was almost as if he'd just come from the set after a particularly dispiriting day of shooting.

As a matter of fact, Groucho had written to his son, Arthur, during the filming of *Go West*, expressing his unhappiness: "My theatrical career has dwindled to being fitted once a week for a pair of early-American pants and having my hair dyed every three weeks. This is a fine comedown for a man who used to be the Toast of Broadway." But that was in 1940! I couldn't quite believe he'd remained upset for thirty-five years.

There wasn't any genuine animosity between Groucho and Buzzell. As a matter of fact, Groucho invited him to a party and he was happy to attend. Although I enjoyed meeting the dapper little man who'd directed those films, I ended up committing a faux pas that night that still causes me to wince.

Having recently become a fan of dancer Eleanor Powell after watching her impressive sequences in *That's Entertainment!*, I'd been seeking out her films at revival houses and on TV. One of them, 1942's *Ship Ahoy*, had been directed by Buzzell, but for some reason it was rarely shown. In striking up a conversation with Buzzell at the party, I mentioned *Ship Ahoy* and then said, "That's a hard picture to see." He smiled sheepishly and said, "Well, you know, audiences were different back when those pictures were made and I guess they might seem a little silly today."

To my horror, I realized that he thought I'd meant, "That's a hard picture to *watch*." I went out of my way to explain what I'd really meant, but it didn't wash away the feeling that I'd insulted the poor man's talents, however meager Groucho considered them to be.

One day Erin invited a rather stuffy, Margaret Dumontish friend of hers to lunch at Groucho's. She was a stage actress and was trying to drop not-so-subtle hints that Groucho should come and see her performance. He was less than enthusiastic about the idea.

Lady: "Do you ever go to the theater?"

Groucho: "No."

Lady: "Oh, well, you must've gone sometime. When was the last time you went to the theater?"

Groucho: "When Lincoln was shot. I was half-shot myself. Great man, Lincoln. They even named a penny after him. Now what were you saying?"

Lady: "Never mind. It wasn't important."

Sometimes the lunch-table conversation was light, sometimes not-so-light. One day Nat Perrin came to lunch with Red Buttons, who seemed to be in a somber mood. He explained that he'd just come from a nursing home where he'd been visiting Joe Smith of Smith and Dale, the once-popular vaudeville team that had been the basis for the two characters in *The Sunshine Boys*. Buttons had known the elderly Smith for years and had been visiting him for some time, but that day things had gone differently.

"He didn't know me," Buttons explained. "He kept playing this game from his childhood where he'd reach over and try to flip my zipper up and down. He was acting just like a little kid. I kept saying, 'Joe! It's me! Red Buttons, the comedian!' but he didn't recognize me. It's like he isn't there anymore."

There was a moment of silence and then Groucho looked up from his soup and muttered, "It's sad when that happens." Nat, Red and I turned to look in Groucho's direction as he returned to his soup and I knew, at that moment, that we all had the same thought: It sure is.

On another occasion, Adolph Zukor's name came up in conversation. Zukor had been the head of Paramount for many years, and in 1975 he was 102 years old. He'd become quite senile, but according to Groucho this was nothing new. Groucho said that in the forties, George Jessel had quipped, "Zukor considers the day a success if he can find his glasses by three in the afternoon." After quoting Jessel's line, Groucho thought a moment, then added, "I never want to get like Zukor." I didn't want him to get like Zukor either, but sadly, he was already well on his way.

One of Groucho's oldest friends was Arthur Sheekman, who had written for *Monkey Business*, *Duck Soup* and dozens of other comedies of the thirties and forties, often in partnership with Nat Perrin. Trivia buffs can spot Sheekman in *Horse Feathers* in the scene at the football game in which Groucho is in the sports announcer's booth. Sheekman is the thin fellow with the moustache, appropriately typing away in the background.

Additionally, according to Groucho, Sheekman had ghost-written Groucho's first two books, *Beds* and *Many Happy Returns.* Sheekman's wife, Gloria, came to lunch from time to time. If only I'd realized that Gloria Sheekman was also Gloria Stuart, who had costarred with Claude Rains in *The Invisible Man* and with Boris Karloff in *The Old Dark House*, I would've had more to talk with her about.

Arthur Sheekman suffered from arteriosclerosis, which had rendered him incapacitated both mentally and physically. Since he'd become too much for Gloria to handle by herself, she'd reluctantly put him in a nursing home so that he could be looked after properly. As with Nunnally Johnson, Groucho regularly visited Sheekman, who was obviously unable to come to Groucho's house. Gloria said that Groucho was the only one she allowed to see her frail husband, since they'd been such loyal friends for so many years.

Erin, not surprisingly, disapproved of Gloria's decision and for a time succeeded in convincing Groucho not to have her over to the house, in order to punish her for what she'd "done" to her husband. Once again, Erin was playing on Groucho's fear of being put in a home—the terrible fate that Erin insisted his son, Arthur, had in store for him if only he were given half a chance. Eventually Gloria was allowed back at Groucho's, but damage had already been done to their friendship, courtesy of Ms. Fleming. *Sic transit* Gloria Sheekman.

Groucho always took Sheekman a box of cookies and a bottle of whiskey. He would sit by his bedside and talk to him, never sure if any of what he was saying was getting through, and he always seemed depressed and depleted when he'd return home from his visit. Seeing his old friend in such a weakened state was rough on Groucho and, as with his comment about Joe Smith's condition, I knew just how he felt. Clearly Groucho was in much better shape than either Joe Smith or Arthur Sheekman, but as time marched on there were increasingly disturbing similarities.

Although there was still a lot of Groucho left in Julius Henry Marx, I would often get an "everything is relative" pang when I was with him. When I first saw him at the Dorothy Chandler Pavilion, it was a shock to discover that he was light years away from the man who had once hosted "You Bet Your Life." When I sat beside him at UCLA, I would've given anything for him to have been as sharp as he'd been at the Dorothy Chandler. And as I continued working in his house, I found myself wishing that he were in as good a shape as when I'd seen him at UCLA.

I could wish all I wanted, but it didn't seem to make much of a difference: Bit by bit, time would continue to exact its toll.

Fifteen

Although Groucho's television appearances were increasingly sporadic as he approached eighty-five, he was asked to be a presenter on the Emmy Awards in May. I was skeptical of Groucho's ability to handle cue cards and a large audience, but he was glad they wanted him to make an appearance, which counted for a lot in justifying the decision to go ahead with it.

Groucho was to be a copresenter with Lucille Ball, someone who had first worked with Groucho as a straight actress in the 1938 film *Room Service.* Although Groucho wasn't exactly a fan of Lucy, he didn't bear her any malice. One day at lunch he made an interesting assessment of her talent. He said Lucy was a good actress who handled comedy well, but she wasn't a particularly humorous person offstage. I don't suppose it matters. "I Love Lucy" continues to be one of the most enduring and endearing television comedies of all time, regardless of whether or not Lucy was an innately funny person in real life.

A few days before the Emmy Awards, one of the show's producers stopped by the house to discuss Groucho's role. As with so many occasions where a well-intentioned person tried to explain something serious to Groucho, not much progress was made, but it sure was fun to watch. After exchanging pleasantries, the producer took out a copy of the show's rundown sheet and began to look it over.

Groucho: "I didn't know you could read."

Producer: "OK. Lucy says, 'And now we present—'"

Groucho: "I don't like it."

Producer: "'—a man who needs no introduction.'"

Groucho: "That's what *you* think."

Producer: "If you want to add a little something, that's fine, but we're going to have to keep it reasonably tight."

Groucho: "I know *she* will be."

Producer: "Anyway, at six o'clock, we go live."

Groucho: "Live?"

Producer: "That's right."

Groucho: "Well, then, you'd better get somebody else."

The plan was for Groucho and Lucy to come out at the end of the show and present the Emmy for Best Comedy or Variety Series. They would trade off reading the nominees and then, courtesy of Bernie Smith, the original "You Bet Your Life" duck was going to drop down with an envelope containing the winner's name, which Groucho would reveal to the audience.

The telecast on May 17 didn't quite go as planned. For starters, Groucho's quip to the producer appeared to be a prophetic one: Lucy did seem a little on the tipsy side. Then, instead of trading off on reading the nominees, Lucy said, "If it's all right with you, Groucho, I'll read the nominees and you can read the winner." Groucho replied, "It's *not* all right with me." Lucy read the list of nominees anyway and then Groucho said, "Where is it? Where's the envelope?"

At that point, the duck dropped down with the envelope attached to its foot. But instead of letting Groucho open it, Lucy pushed him aside with her elbow, snatched the envelope and read the name of the winner. All Groucho could do was stand there looking bewildered and embarrassed. Incidentally, the winner was "The Carol Burnett Show." It was probably that sketch with the giant roll of toilet paper that clinched it.

Groucho felt he'd been treated shabbily by Miss Ball, commenting to me, "She was a horse's ass." Lucy released a statement to the press saying that just prior to going on the air she had received word that one of her children had been in an accident and she really didn't know what she was doing. Whether or not this was the case, a lot of people, not just Groucho fans, felt that Lucy's behavior was uncalled for.

One viewer sent a letter to Lucy and a copy of it to Groucho. It said, "We deplore your boorish treatment of Groucho Marx on the Emmy Show. If you learn to stand on your head and spit wooden nickels, we will see to it that no one of our acquaintance will spend dime one to see the performance. P.S. Groucho, you are a giant. The world loves you."

A short time after the Emmys, a dinner guest asked Groucho if he'd made any personal appearances lately. "Yeah," Groucho replied, with more than a trace of sarcasm in his voice, "I did 'The Lucille Ball Show' the other night!"

Another noteworthy springtime occurrence was Erin Fleming's conversion to Judaism. Lyn Erhard's hypothesis was that it came about as a result of Erin's search for "a contentment and feeling of peace in a troubled universe." Although this sounds like a noble purpose, most of us in the Marx household suspected an ulterior motive. Or two.

For starters, it was common knowledge around Groucho's that Erin had been seeing Marvin Hamlisch off and on for quite some time. No one circulated that idea more vigorously than Erin herself. She even had a naughty nickname for him with a distinctly Jewish flavor: "Matzoh Balls." Among Erin's various ambitions was a strong desire to become Mrs. Marvin Hamlisch.

Erin had a large antique painting in her living room showing a ballerina and an acrobat standing behind a sad-faced harlequin. I was looking at it one day when she came up behind me and said, "You know who they are, don't you?" I studied the faces but drew a blank. "Why, it's Groucho standing in front of Marvin and me!" she explained, as though any clod could see it.

From what I'd heard, Marvin, being a nice Jewish boy, never did anything of which his mother, Lilly, might disapprove. It was also my understanding that Lilly detested Erin. So perhaps Erin felt she might be more acceptable to Lilly if she renounced her Irish-Catholic upbringing and accepted Judaism.

Perhaps.

For some time, Erin had been attending Friday night services at Temple Emanuel in Beverly Hills and studying up on the laws and history of Judaism. Ten male sponsors were required for acceptance into the religion, so she drafted Elliott Gould and George Segal into service, among others. Erin purchased a sacred Jewish pendant called a *mezuzah,* which she took to wearing at all times. She labored diligently at the correct pronunciation of the various holiday blessings in their original Hebrew, as though she were running lines for an upcoming audition.

Despite months of hard work and Erin's eventual conversion to Judaism, she never did succeed in becoming Marvin Hamlisch's better half. Lilly remained the only Mrs. Hamlisch in Marvin's life for many years to come.

There was a second factor in Erin's conversion (third, if you count the contentment and feeling of peace in a troubled universe).

Sometime later, Hector Arce said to me, "You know, if Erin had simply married Groucho she could've avoided that big legal mess at the end, because she would've been his wife and she would've been entitled to the inheritance automatically." But Erin didn't marry Groucho, although they joked about it from time to time. In truth, Groucho encouraged Erin's interest in eligible young men because he knew he couldn't satisfy her in a physical way and he wanted her to be happy.

So the idea arose that if she wasn't going to be Groucho's wife, perhaps she could be his adopted daughter. This was apparently Erin's idea. As a matter of fact, Groucho had told Martha prior to her departure, "I already have two daughters. What do I want with another one?" He also pointed out that if he did adopt Erin, she would be his only officially Jewish daughter, since Miriam and Melinda were born of gentile mothers.

As with so many other things, Groucho acquiesced to Erin's wishes. Erin filed the necessary adoption papers in early 1975, but since such matters take time, it was months before any official decision would be made.

In the meantime, the court deemed it necessary for Groucho to undergo a psychological examination in order to establish that his intended adoption of Erin was being done of his own free will. Rather than leaving these things to chance, Erin spent a considerable amount of time drilling Groucho on how to answer the court-appointed psychiatrists' questions. But practicing for a psychological examination is about as useful as studying for a urine test.

Erin: "They're going to ask you if you're sane, Groucho. What are you going to tell them? Are you sane?"

Groucho: "No."

Erin: "How long has it been since you were sane?"

Groucho: "About thirty years."

Despite Groucho's humorous approach to the situation, the psychiatrists concluded that Groucho had grown too dependent on Erin to make decisions rationally and that his ability to answer questions had diminished to the point where they could not consider him to be of sound mind. Erin was furious at the doctors' conclusion and said that *they* were the ones who were incompetent, not Groucho. Groucho didn't quite know what to make of

Erin's fury, since he'd given it his best shot. Nevertheless, in the fall of 1975 Erin's request to become Groucho's adopted daughter was officially denied.

Erin did, however, remain Jewish. She described her experience at the temple's induction ceremony, or *mitzvah*, as "just like floating in outer space inside a spaceship." On the one hand, the temple's chapel *was* circular in design. On the other hand, I had a sneaking suspicion that Erin's feeling of floating in outer space inside a spaceship was not an infrequent sensation.

In May Erin and Groucho went to New York to catch a preview performance of a Broadway show for which Marvin Hamlisch had written the music. Upon their return Groucho decreed, "The show will run for years." Personally, I felt that Groucho's keen judgment had probably been impaired by a combination of Erin's infatuation with Hamlisch and the fact that they'd all become such good friends during Groucho's concert tour.

From what I could tell, the play didn't have much of a plot; just an assortment of characters taking turns talking about themselves. Additionally, Hamlisch had played a song from his soon-to-open musical during a party at Groucho's one night and it just didn't strike me as a particularly memorable tune. The song was "What I Did for Love," the show was *A Chorus Line*, and it went on to become the longest-running musical in Broadway history. Now you know not to ask my advice if your show is ever in the midst of out-of-town tryouts. Who knows—I might've wanted to take "Always" out of *The Cocoanuts*, too.

Sixteen

Today, Father, is Father's Day
And we're giving you a tie.
It's not much, we know,
It is just our way of showing you
We think you're a regular guy.
You say that it was nice of us to bother,
But it really was a pleasure to fuss.
For according to our mother, you're our father,
And that's good enough for us.
Yes, that's good enough for us.

"Father's Day"—Harry Ruby

Father's Day of 1975 was fast approaching and I *didn't* want to give mine a tie. I suppose I was like a lot of children who hunger for their father's pride and approval but find it in somewhat short supply. Many was the time I'd tried to impress him with something I'd accomplished, only to receive a well-intentioned yet tepid acknowledgment. Dad was notoriously difficult to buy gifts for, and when asked what he wanted, he usually said something like, "I just want everybody to be healthy." That was fine, except it was a little hard to wrap.

I was sorry that my mom hadn't lived to see me get the job at Groucho's. She used to get so excited when she'd see a celebrity—*any* celebrity—at the grocery store, that I know she would have been proud of my good fortune. But I still had my dad and since he had been a big Marx Brothers fan when he was growing up, I decided to make arrangements for him to have lunch at Groucho's as my Father's Day gift. If nothing else, I knew he couldn't exchange it for a different color.

I checked with Erin and with Groucho, who said it was OK, and then picked the weekend closest to Father's Day so that Dad could get the added benefit of being served by the lithe and leggy Robin Heaney. (Somehow I didn't think John Ballow, with his mascara and plunging neckline, would've been Dad's style.)

I typed up an invitation on Groucho's stationery, put it in an envelope, stuck a bow on top, and presented it to Dad, who was clearly surprised. He wanted to know if I was serious. I was. Apparently my idea had some merit. Robin asked if my dad liked soup, which he did, so she decided to make homemade chicken noodle soup in his honor.

I think I was probably as nervous as I'd ever been while awaiting the arrival of a noted guest for lunch at Groucho's. Since it was a special occasion, I wanted everything to go just right. I'd already been at work a few hours when the doorbell rang, causing my heart to pound. I let Dad in and showed him a few items of interest in the front part of the house, then led him into the dining room. It was a strange feeling, seeing someone as familiar as my dad in these surroundings. It seemed so incongruous, like running into a teacher at the supermarket.

Erin and Robin were quite friendly, but Groucho, between his age and his general lack of interest in sales managers from St. Louis, was rather perfunctory. He wasn't rude; he just tended to give "yes" and "no" answers to Dad's questions. After some small talk, Robin brought out her special chicken noodle soup, which we proceeded to ingest. Erin and Groucho discussed my finer points, which was flattering to hear, especially in Dad's presence.

And then, after the soup, Dad decided it was time to tell one of his jokes.

I suddenly had the urge to dash under the table or excuse myself and sprint down the hallway, back to the safety of my office. I felt this way for two reasons: One, Dad tended to tell corny, overly long jokes. Two, Groucho almost never told jokes per se, and never felt any obligation to humor those who did with polite laughter. If you think about it, Groucho is best known for the remarks he made in his films and for his off-the-cuff comments in the course of normal conversation. But it was rare that Groucho was ever partial enough to an actual *joke* to bother telling it.

There were a few exceptions. Although most of his lunchtime humor was spontaneous, Groucho was fond of two jokes in particular, and he would tell them to guests from time to time. One was: "A woman's husband dies so she has him cremated. She puts his ashes in a vase and keeps it on her living room table where everybody can see it. Every time someone comes over, they put their cigarette ashes into the vase. One day a man comes over and says, 'Say, your husband looks like he's putting on a little weight.'" As jokes go, it's fairly amusing.

The other one Groucho liked was also, apparently, one of Chico's favorites. It went as follows: "A man gets lost in the woods without food, water or female companionship. He finally comes across a cabin that has a very inviting knothole in the front door. Unable to control himself, he drops his pants, sticks his thing in the knothole and goes to work. A short while later, the owner of the cabin opens the door from the inside and says, "Excuse me, but would you mind coming *in* and fucking *out?* We just sat down to dinner."

Unfortunately, the joke my father elected to tell that day was not on par with either of these. It was one of his long, drawn-out stories, this one concerning a man who ends up falling off a mountain. To make a very long story short, the man thinks he's going to die when all of a sudden a giant Buddha appears and catches the man in his huge, outstretched hands. "Thank God!" the man exclaims, and the Buddha squashes him.

Groucho didn't laugh either.

Dad started to explain it to him, figuring the absence of laughter could have been due only to his faulty hearing or advanced years, but Groucho interrupted and said, "He should've thanked Buddha." I have a Frank Modell *New Yorker* cartoon in my office, the caption to which is: "Just because I'm not laughing, it doesn't mean I don't get it." I think Groucho subscribed to the same philosophy when it came to people trying to tell him jokes.

After lunch, Groucho shook my father's hand, then excused himself and went back to his room. Dad remained to chat with Erin, Robin and me. I took him on a brief tour of the rest of the house, and after a while, he decided it was time to head back to Tarzana. I walked him to his car and asked what he thought of Groucho. "He's quite old," was his response. I asked him how he liked the soup. "It was very oily and could've used a little seasoning," was his answer. Finally I said, "Did you like Robin?" "She's so thin. Nothing but skin and bones," he replied. Then he thanked me for arranging everything and drove off.

Between the awkwardness at the table and his less-than-enthusiastic review, I felt that I'd completely blown it. Yet when I returned home later that day, Dad said, "Well, I guess that was one of the three biggest thrills of my life, along with standing next to Lou Gehrig and touching the *Spirit of St. Louis*!" Apparently I'd done all right after all. He may not have been the most demonstrative man in the world, but when all was said and done, it really *was* a pleasure to fuss.

July marked a year since I'd first shown up on Groucho's doorstep. On the one hand, it was hard to believe an entire year had gone by. On the other hand, I'd experienced such a rich and varied parade of events in and around Groucho's house that, in a sense, it seemed like I'd been there a lot longer. Erin surprised me by upping my salary from three dollars an hour to five. I hadn't asked for the raise and I still felt that three bucks an hour was more than adequate pay for me to be able to hang out at Groucho's house, but I was happy to get the increase just the same.

I hadn't been putting in as much time on the fan mail and memorabilia as when I'd begun. Once all those boxes of clippings, letters, scripts and photographs had been organized and put in some sort of order and once the fan mail had been brought up to date, my duties were more along the lines of keeping everything maintained. Special projects, such as going over the Anobile transcripts and helping Hector Arce with *The Secret Word Is Groucho*, allowed me to put in more hours.

Although some of the bloom was off the rose in terms of my initial euphoria over getting the job, I still never took any of it for granted and I wasn't in any hurry to leave. A lot of people have asked me why I didn't do something about Erin's irrational behavior or why I chose to keep working there under such stressful conditions.

In the first instance, it didn't seem to me that there was any sort of action I could take. After the Connie August fiasco I believed that Groucho had, as those psychiatrists concluded, grown far too dependent on Erin. Attempting to convince others to have her removed would probably have been futile, and possibly harmful to Groucho as well. I felt that it would be like kicking a crutch out from under him and that, for all her faults, Erin had become vital to Groucho's existence.

And to whom would I have complained? The obvious choice, I suppose, would have been Arthur Marx, whom I'd met only once or twice and who had been portrayed as a heartless villain—by Erin

Fleming, of course. Also, as I've said before, Erin could be an absolute pleasure if she so desired and Groucho clearly derived a considerable amount of emotional nourishment from having her around. So the situation was more complex than it might have appeared to others.

As for my reasons for continuing to work there, I suppose if I'd been sufficiently irritated by Erin's behavior I could have kept my pride intact, announced that I didn't need to subject myself to any more of this craziness and walked out the same door I'd entered so naively a year earlier. But regardless of the fact that the true glory days might have passed, it was without question still compelling to be a part of that world. For the same reason Daryl and I had stayed at Groucho's eighty-fourth birthday party until after Jack Lemmon had driven off, I just didn't want to *miss* anything.

Regardless of Erin's mercurial temperament, my feelings of affection and devotion toward Groucho never diminished. If anything, they'd grown stronger as I came to understand exactly what he was up against, between Erin's behavior and his gradually weakening condition. And although compliments from Groucho were hardly plentiful, they occurred just often enough for me to feel appreciated.

About this time, I found a portrait of Groucho from *Animal Crackers* at a Hollywood bookstore. As far as I was concerned, it was screaming to be inscribed. It had been a year since Groucho had written, "To Steve—A great secretary," on that other photo, and although part of my job involved being almost elbow-deep in Groucho autographs, I still had a strong urge to have him sign a number of things to me before time—mine or his—ran out.

So I gave the picture to Groucho, who uncapped his black Sharpie and wrote, "To Steve—A valuable man—from Groucho." He accidentally crossed the first *l* in *valuable*, which caused him to comment, "It looks like it says, 'To Steve—the vegetable man,' but *you* know what I mean." I did and I appreciated it.

I made the decision to stick it out at Groucho's regardless of how hazy he got or how crazy Erin got, all the while assuming that either Groucho was going to fail to wake up one day or, when I least expected it, Erin was going to can me without a moment's warning and without any reason other than that she'd gotten tired of looking at my face.

During lunch one day, Groucho turned to Erin and said, "What's the matter, don't you feel well?" Erin said she felt fine and wanted to know why Groucho had asked. "Because you haven't fired anyone today!" was his response. He was nobody's fool.

If life at Groucho's sometimes felt like a Robert Altman film, especially with Elliott Gould, Sally Kellerman, George Segal and Bud Cort wandering around (and later, Shelley Duvall and Warren Berlinger), there was also the night I attended the showing of an *actual* Altman film along with Groucho, Erin and Robin Heaney. It was an advance screening of *Nashville*, held at Altman's Lion's Gate Studios in Westwood.

Groucho enjoyed the film, although I don't think he made it all the way through. The highlight of the evening for him seemed to be running into Goldie Hawn. Altman was at the front of the screening room introducing the film, but his speech was punctuated by Groucho's cries of "Goldie! Goldie! Over here!" Goldie made her way over to Groucho, gave him a kiss that perked him up considerably, and then the soon-to-be-released *Nashville* unspooled. I thought the film was extremely well made and highly entertaining but perhaps a bit long, although that may have been due to the fact that it was an early cut and somewhat longer than the version that was officially released.

Another notable occasion was the night in late July when Mae West came up and saw Groucho. This particular rendezvous had been arranged by Hector Arce through his friend, producer Stanley Musgrove, who was a close friend of West's. Shortly before her visit, I mentioned to Groucho that *Animal Crackers* was being paired with *My Little Chickadee* at a local revival house. Hector and I talked about how West and her costar, W.C. Fields, allegedly had so detested each other during the shooting of *My Little Chickadee* that they preferred passing notes around the set rather than speaking to each other. Hector continued on the subject of Miss West.

Hector: "Groucho, did you know she has a mirrored ceiling in her bedroom?"

Groucho: "She doesn't need those mirrors anymore. I once saw her in Vegas and she had six strongmen in her act. I asked her how they were and she said, 'What a waste of manpower—they're all homos!'"

I guess that meant they couldn't possibly have been related to Alexander Woollcott.

Groucho and Mae West didn't really know each other well, despite the fact that they'd both been working on Broadway in the twenties and at Paramount in the thirties. There's a common misconception that everyone in Hollywood knows everyone else—and everything *about* everyone else. One example of this is a story Groucho told about how, when he'd been pulled over for speeding one day, the cop handed him a ticket and asked, "How come there aren't more Laurel and Hardy movies on TV?" How should *Groucho* know?

Although their paths had certainly crossed over the years, Groucho and Mae West tended to travel in different social circles. Groucho admitted that she had a lot of talent, writing and performing her own material, but said that he personally found her style to be "vulgar."

Nevertheless, the agreed-upon night arrived. Erin was extremely nervous. Although it was only going to be a brief, after-dinner visit, she felt that Mae West was Hollywood royalty, and she wanted everything to go off without a hitch. She admonished Groucho to be on his best behavior. He said he was always on his best behavior. Hector and I showed up a little early in case any last-minute things needed doing, and Harpo's son, Billy, was also on hand in case anyone felt like singing. But no one *really* knew what to expect.

Eventually the doorbell rang and in came Stanley Musgrove; Paul Novak, who was Mae's right-hand man; and, in the flesh, Mae West. She was wearing a white pantsuit, her suspiciously long, suspiciously blond hair piled high atop her head. I was immediately struck by two things: how marble-white her skin appeared and how incredibly short she was.

With regard to my first observation, Hector said Mae never went out in the daytime, only leaving her all-white Hollywood apartment building after the sun went down. As for her height, Hector said that she stood, believe it or not, four-foot-eleven. Granted, she had probably shrunken somewhat over the years, but the fact remains that she was much shorter in person than she appeared on-screen—a testament to her strong cinematic presence and to how she allowed herself to be photographed.

Although her mind seemed to be in top form, West required some assistance in walking across a room or going down even a few steps. Hector explained that due to an inner-ear problem she had trouble with depth perception, which meant she couldn't measure distances accurately and needed a little help getting around. Otherwise, for a woman in her mid-eighties she was remarkably well preserved—a deliberate choice of words since, with her doughy, alabaster skin, she gave the appearance of someone who'd been stored in a bottle of formaldehyde for a considerable length of time.

The books said that she'd been born in 1892, but Hector confided that she'd actually been born in 1888, making her two years older than Groucho. Frankly, I would've thought that when you got to be that age and still looked that good, you'd *want* to boast about how old you were. But with Mae West vanity prevailed, and she chose to maintain the illusion that she was a few years younger than she actually was.

Once she was comfortably situated on the couch, Groucho came down the hall and immediately greeted her with, "Hiya, Mae! What do you hear from Bill Fields?" Erin glared at Groucho for his lack of decorum in bringing up such a sore subject, but Mae simply snapped back, "In your dreams, Groucho, in your dreams!" Her voice still had the sassy nasality that had become her trademark.

No sooner had Groucho finished asking about Fields than he launched into another sensitive query: "Say, didn't they throw you into the pokey once?" Again, Erin was dying inside over Groucho's lack of tact. He was referring to the time in 1926 when the New York police had closed down her play, *Sex*, for alleged indecency, and had thrown her in jail. Mae smiled at Groucho's question and said, "Yeah, they did, but I always manage to wiggle out of tight situations like that." And she wiggled her shoulders a little as she spoke.

It was as if someone were doing a Mae West impersonation, except it was really Mae West! I just sat there, watching these two dinosaurs converse. It was different than Groucho and Burns or Groucho and Fenneman. To me, they were the king and queen of screen comedy in the thirties.

A footnote on that subject: Although the college crowd of the late sixties and early seventies had come to embrace the Marx Brothers, Mae West and W.C. Fields as the last word in comedy immortals, the most popular screen comedians during the early thirties, from a box-office standpoint, were, surprisingly, Eddie Cantor, Will Rogers and Joe E. Brown—three people who probably didn't have a dozen young fans between them by the mid-seventies. It just goes to show how tastes change.

After some polite conversation, Billy Marx took his place at the piano and Groucho treated Mae to a few of his old standbys, which she seemed to appreciate. Then Billy asked if she'd honor us with a song. There was some awkward whispering between Mae, Stanley Musgrove and Paul Novak, with Mae finally explaining to us that she really didn't feel comfortable singing without her records as backup and she hadn't thought to bring them with her that night. As a compromise, she offered to "do a little recitin'."

I watched as she rose, walked over to the piano, and steadied herself with one hand. To create the proper mood, Billy softly played a honky-tonk version of "Frankie and Johnny," which she acknowledged with a warm smile and a wink. And then Mae West did her "recitin'." It was a poem entitled "Pleasure Man," all about a certain gentleman and his romantic exploits. It had come from a play of the same name, which Mae had written, and which, like *Sex*, had also run into problems with the more puritanical members of New York society in the twenties.

What a remarkable tableau: Mae West, all in white from head to toe, standing by a baby grand piano on which "Frankie and Johnny" was being played, reciting a bawdy poem she'd written decades earlier about a man she'd loved and lost. If I'd squinted I would almost have believed I was back at Paramount on the set of *She Done Him Wrong*.

After her performance, Erin embarrassed me by introducing me to Mae as someone "who knows every line from every single one of your movies!" I didn't even know the *titles* of every one of her movies, much less the lines. I prayed she wouldn't quiz me or ask for a demonstration as I shook her hand. To my relief, she never pressed the point. Later, she signed a copy of one of her books, "To Steve, Sin–cerely, Mae West."

She was truly an original. A few days later, Groucho received a letter from her thanking him for an enjoyable evening and mentioning how much fun it had been in the Paramount projection rooms way back when, watching his rushes while she awaited her own. She closed the note, of course, with an invitation for Groucho to come up and see her sometime.

He never took her up on it.

In August, plans were under way for a tribute to Groucho at USC, to be held shortly after his eighty-fifth birthday. The subject came up in conversation one day when Andy Marx stayed for lunch.

Andy: "I understand USC is gonna have a testimonial for you."

Groucho: "Yeah. I'll get up and say a few insincere words."

Andy: "When is it?"

Me: "October 12."

Andy: "That's right around your birthday."

Groucho: "I can wait. They're coming fast now."

Andy: "What do you want for your birthday?"

Groucho: "Last year."

Why couldn't he have said "a new camera," as he'd done the year before? Groucho's mortality was something that always hung in the air, whether it was acknowledged or not.

As September was drawing to a close, Erin reminded Groucho of another birthday that loomed large on the horizon:
"Groucho, did you know it's Steve's birthday this Tuesday?"

Groucho: "Is it? Well, we'll have to give him something, even if it's only his discharge."

At least I knew that *Groucho* was kidding. If Erin had said it, I might not have been so sure. As it turned out, I wasn't given my discharge. Neither was I given my own cake. This time around, everybody's focus was on Groucho. But being able to take part in that particular celebration was enough of a present, so I hardly felt slighted.

After all the hoopla of "Groucho at Eighty-five" which had dogged him throughout the year, the actual date had *finally* arrived.

Seventeen

The day before his birthday, a large envelope arrived containing an elaborate, official-looking document proclaiming October 2, 1975, as Groucho Marx Day. It was even signed by L.A. mayor Tom Bradley. Although banks and schools remained open and there was regular mail delivery that day, it was still considered an honor. In addition to the proclamation, a telegram arrived from Woody Allen saying, "HAPPY 85TH BIRTHDAY. NOW YOU OWE ME A WIRE ON MINE."

That year I gave Groucho a new biography of his old friend Irving Berlin, which he devoured almost in one sitting. He even cut out some of the pictures from the book and set them out on the trophy table. As a bibliophile, I'm usually against the slicing up of books, but I was flattered that he wanted to display pictures from one that I'd given him.

Although Groucho had a small gathering of friends over to the house on October 2, the elaborate, official party was held on Sunday the fifth so that more of the two hundred invited guests could attend. Erin was so concerned that everything be done just right, she hired Peter Shore to advise her on flowers, furniture configurations and table settings. Not that any of that mattered to the guest of honor.

On Sunday morning Daryl and I arrived early so that we could help Erin and Groucho's young publicist, Tom Wilhite, festoon the house and backyard with helium "Happy Birthday GROUCHO" balloons. By the time we'd finished, the place was bursting with birthday balloons. Tom, incidentally, had a story that bore some similarities to my own.

While he was still a student at Iowa State University in 1972, Tom had, in effect, "produced" the first *Evening with Groucho* show, prior to Carnegie Hall. Like me, Tom had been a big Groucho fan for a number of years and was delighted when Groucho accepted his invitation to come and speak on campus. Erin and Groucho had decided to try out the show at Tom's university, figuring that if you bomb in Ames, Iowa, who's gonna notice?

But the show had gone well, and as a result Tom was rewarded with a publicity job at the public relations firm of Rogers & Cowan in Beverly Hills upon his graduation in 1974. Although he was only two years older than I was, Tom always seemed serious and mature beyond his years. While I tried to have as good a time as I could while I was at Groucho's, Tom always gave the impression of someone who was preparing to brief the press on the president's new budget or some similarly weighty matter. Even filling balloons with helium seemed a heavy task.

A few years later, Tom became one of the highest-ranking executives at Disney Studios and, after that, a successful motion-picture producer. I guess there *is* something to be said for developing a businesslike demeanor at an early age, although I still prefer being serious whenever necessary and not whenever possible.

In mid-afternoon, Groucho took his seat of honor in the living room and prepared to greet his guests. The first to arrive were Zeppo and Gummo, fresh from Palm Springs. As usual, Zeppo brought some cans of tuna that he claimed to have caught himself (but I knew better). Also as usual, Zeppo reminded Gummo that Zeppo and I had dated the same girl but that I'd gotten further with her than he had.

As a birthday present to Groucho, Hector Arce had hired a professional photographer to take pictures of the proceedings. Although it was certainly a newsworthy occasion, it was still considered a private affair and thus officially off limits to other photographers. So on October 5, 1975, what turned out to be the last photos of the three surviving Marx Brothers were taken in Groucho's living room. A reporter from the *New York Times* took notes for the official press coverage of the event.

Eventually the other guests, stylishly late, drifted in. Slowly the house began to fill up with familiar faces. Among them was Steve Allen, whom I'd admired for years. Before Johnny Carson and long before David Letterman, Steve Allen was spreading late-night silliness across the nation. Although I didn't get much of a chance to spend time with him on this particular occasion, I found him to be quite affable and pleasant. Toward the end of Groucho's life, I would have a much more memorable experience with Steverino.

Also present was Peter Sellers, whom I'd enjoyed as Dr. Strangelove as well as Inspector Clouseau. Like Groucho in his pre-

TV days, Sellers' appearance was drastically altered without his moustache. He seemed shy and unassuming that night. "Just to sit there and realize you are in the same room with Groucho Marx is a delightful experience," he commented. That night, he was just another fan.

Sellers tended to stay in the background, observing the action from a distance. I had heard that when he wasn't in character for a film he was almost invisible, and that was the impression he made on me. I almost forgot that he was there, except that he's clearly visible in some of the photographs from that evening. Appropriately, he's standing in the background.

Milton Berle was there as well, and although I respected his status as Mr. Television from his phenomenal success in the fifties, the only thing I remember about him that night was that he kept butting into the conversation I was trying to have with Hal and Doris Kanter. Later, Berle asked Groucho how he felt. "Clever," Groucho responded.

Red Buttons, Nat Perrin, Morrie Ryskind, Carl Reiner, Irwin Allen, Edie Adams and Jack Lemmon helped round out the long-time friends, while Erin's contingent of newer friends, including Elliott Gould, Sally Kellerman and Bud Cort, were there as well.

Carroll O'Connor and Sally Struthers also took part in the festivities, and it was strange to see Archie Bunker and Gloria Stivic under a different roof, out of character. Struthers was quite nice, and we spent some time running through a list of everyone we could think of who had the same "S.S." initials as we did. Groucho, incidentally, was a big fan of "All in the Family." He did say, however, that he didn't feel he was watching a real family—just a group of actors reciting dialogue. Nevertheless, he rarely missed an episode.

The feeling that I'd opened the door and walked into Oz was rekindled by the arrival of the husband-and-wife team of Liza Minnelli and Jack Haley Jr., the children of Dorothy and the Tin Man, respectively. Also present was Judy Garland's other daughter, Lorna Luft. Some of the pictures from that evening made it into *People* magazine, and I was startled to discover a shot of Daryl and me sitting right behind Jack and Liza, listening attentively to Groucho singing. It was odd to think that our picture was on magazine stands all over America, and naturally, I bought a number of extra copies as souvenirs.

I may have become more comfortable around celebrities by the time this party rolled around, since I'd been spending time at Groucho's for over a year, but I can't say that I ever really got *used* to it. For Daryl and me, it would always be "us" and "them."

Hector and Groucho had just finished up the manuscript of *The Secret Word Is Groucho*, so some of the "You Bet Your Life" gang were there as well, including Bernie Smith, Bob Dwan and George "Feenamint" Fenneman. It was nice to see them again after having spent time with them during the interviewing process some months earlier and they seemed to enjoy seeing their old employer once again, despite his frail appearance.

Although the place was filled with well-wishing friends and acquaintances, Groucho's relatives were not particularly abundant. In addition to Zeppo and Gummo, Andy Marx was there, plus Andy's mother, Irene, and his grandmother, Grace Kahn. Conspicuous by their absence were Arthur, Miriam, Melinda and Melinda's children. The fact that Erin had drawn up the guest list must've been just a coincidence.

Once most of the guests had arrived, Groucho's strawberry birthday cake was brought out. It was impressive, if not downright dangerous, to see eighty-five candles blazing away, illuminating the Groucho caricature that took up most of the massive cake's surface. With some assistance, Groucho blew out the candles and then remarked, "Eighty-five is a funny age. I'm still in perfect health, except mentally."

After cake and coffee were consumed, Groucho strolled over to the piano and steadied himself, while Billy Marx sat down at the keyboard. The various conversations in the room came to a halt almost simultaneously as we sat down on the living-room floor and waited to be entertained. Even though I had heard Groucho run through his repertoire of "greatest hits" on a number of occasions, I never tired of listening to them, and since the audience had a number of new faces in it there was a different feel to the experience that night.

Groucho warbled such favorites as "Father's Day," "Show Me a Rose" and "Oh, How That Woman Could Cook" (which had been written by Grace and Gus Kahn), and then Bob Hope entered the room in a black tuxedo. I thought he was a little too formally dressed until I learned that he was en route to a Friar's roast in honor of Danny Thomas.

Although Hope's Vietnam hawkishness had been a little off-putting and I hadn't found much to laugh at in his recent television specials, I was a big fan of his radio and Paramount days, when he made the *Road* pictures with Bing Crosby as well as numerous other delightful comedies, including *My Favorite Brunette* and *Monsieur Beaucaire*.

Even if their recent work left something to be desired, I could always appreciate celebrities for what they had once accomplished. In Europe, an artist is considered as good as his greatest achievement. In America, he's only as good as his latest achievement. Personally, I prefer the European approach.

Hope listened to Groucho's singing and quipped, "Are you cutting an album or something?" Although Groucho had been the center of attention, Hope's powerful presence created an immediate shift in the focus of the room. Bob Hope is truly one of those larger-than-lifers. As a result, Groucho briefly relinquished the spotlight and invited Hope to take his place near the piano.

Groucho: "One of the best comedians of our time has just come in. This is a man who has made *me* laugh. Why don't you say a few words, Bob?"

Hope: "You don't have to say those things just because I'm here."

Groucho: "If you weren't here, I wouldn't have said them!"

Hope: "This has been going on for forty years. I've never been able to top you."

I figured Hope would launch into some humorous comments about Groucho, either by way of reminiscence or affectionate ribbing. After all, they'd known each other since the thirties and had worked together in radio, television and personal appearances during World War II. As a matter of fact, they had toured on the same train for months during the Hollywood Victory Caravan, along with such luminaries as Cary Grant, Bing Crosby, James Cagney and Laurel and Hardy.

Instead, Hope smiled and said, "You know, that Danny Thomas is so religious, he even has stained-glass bifocals!" I couldn't believe it. Here was Bob Hope, standing in Groucho Marx's living room, surrounded by a colorful array of Hollywood personalities, and who does he talk about? Someone who wasn't even there. He was using us to try out his material for the Thomas roast later that evening! People used to say that Hope was lost without his writers, and it appeared to be true. At least he didn't ask for *cue cards* to be held up in the middle of the living room, butIwannatellya.

After Hope finished testing his Danny Thomas material, Groucho resumed his singing. Accompanied by Erin and Robin Heaney, he ended with a curious ditty known as "The Peasy Weasy Song." It was a relic from the Marx Brothers' vaudeville days and consisted of a number of clever, tongue-twisting verses, such as:

A humpback went to see a football game.
The game was called on account of the rain.
The humpback asked the halfback for his quarter back.
So the halfback kicked the hump off the humpback's back.

As always, it was a crowd pleaser, and some of the newer guests seemed surprised that Groucho could handle such intricate lyrics given his diminished capacity. Us "regulars," however, knew that Groucho was a trouper and would do whatever it took to make it through each song so that he could bask in the enthusiastic applause that invariably followed.

A little later, Billy Marx tried to coax Liza Minnelli into singing by playing the introduction to "Cabaret," but she wasn't of a mind to pick up on his cue. Like most of us, she was only there to listen and enjoy. As a consolation, Sally Kellerman gave out with a smoky rendition of "When Sunny Gets Blue," and then Bud Cort sang something called "I've Got to Find My Place in the Sun," at the conclusion of which he keeled over backward. Intentionally.

After the performances Groucho decided it was time to retire, so he retreated to his room, changed into his pajamas and bade his guests farewell from the comfort of his bed. As Carroll O'Connor and Sally Struthers were leaving, they were coaxed into posing for a photo in bed with Groucho. That one made it into *People* as well.

As usual, Daryl and I stuck around to help clean up, fearful of missing out on even one memorable moment. Although we'd been to his birthday party the year before (and although that one had included a small nod to me), it was still a special evening. And it was evident to those who'd attended that Groucho may have had the best time of all.

EIGHTEEN

A week after his eighty-fifth birthday, another significant event occurred at Groucho's house. It was the arrival of S.J. Perelman, fresh from one of his legendary junkets to faraway lands. Although to some it may not have appeared to be a particularly noteworthy event—after all, Groucho made a habit of keeping in touch with his former writers—I knew better.

Their relationship went back to 1929, when Sidney Joseph Perelman had met Groucho Marx after a performance of *Animal Crackers* on Broadway. It had been a case of mutual admiration. Perelman had admired Groucho's comic style and Groucho had been amused by Perelman's unique wordplay, which could be seen in the humorous cartoons he'd drawn and comic pieces he'd written for *Judge* and *College Humor* magazines.

When Perelman's first collection of humor, *Dawn Ginsbergh's Revenge*, was published the same year, Groucho dashed off a blurb for the dust jacket: "From the moment I picked up your book until I put it down, I was convulsed with laughter. Someday I intend reading it." That book has become quite valuable, with or without the dust jacket. Groucho's own copy, a gift from Perelman, had a green flocked cover that made it even scarcer.

After having filmed *The Cocoanuts* and *Animal Crackers* in New York, the Marx Brothers moved to California in 1931. Groucho hired Perelman to work on their first true "Hollywood" film. Although Perelman had never written a script before, Groucho was very reassuring and told him he had every confidence that he would have a big career out west.

So, in search of some of that legendary Hollywood money that movie executives seemed to be throwing at transplanted Manhattan literati in the thirties, Perelman and his wife, Laura, came out to sunny California. There, he and cowriter Will Johnstone (who also had no script experience) set to work creating material for the Marx Brothers' next motion picture.

Perelman's account of the first reading of the script is enough to discourage any budding screenwriter from putting pen to paper. According to Perelman, after he'd spent hours reading the entire script out loud in front of the Four Marx Brothers, their wives and various production executives, Chico had said to Groucho, "Well, what do you think?" to which Groucho had replied, "It stinks," at which point the Marxes and their entourage left the room. Decades later, Perelman told friends that he'd never really gotten over the cruelty of Groucho's reaction that night.

After a considerable amount of rewriting, including additional dialogue from Nat Perrin and Arthur Sheekman, *Monkey Business* emerged and Groucho and Perelman's relationship improved somewhat. Following *Monkey Business*, Perelman was asked to work on *Horse Feathers*. More than sixty years later, these two films remain at or near the top of the list of the Marx Brothers' funniest films.

Perelman went on to work on a number of other screenplays, in the process earning an Academy Award for his work on *Around the World in 80 Days*. He continued to write humorous pieces, mostly for *The New Yorker*, which would be collected in book form every few years. Eventually his humorous prose filled nineteen volumes, not counting the plays *One Touch of Venus* and *The Beauty Part*.

Despite his prolific output and despite having been considered one of the greatest humorists of the twentieth century—right up there with Robert Benchley and James Thurber—Perelman was forever haunted by people who saw him only as a former gag writer for the Marx Brothers. Wherever he went, the only question journalists seemed to ask was, "What was it like writing for Groucho?" This was the equivalent of the public seeing F. Scott Fitzgerald only as someone who'd written dialogue for Joan Crawford at MGM, while completely overlooking *The Great Gatsby*. Not surprisingly, this produced a certain amount of friction between Groucho and Perelman over the years.

To make matters worse, Perelman was sometimes credited with having created Groucho's persona, despite the fact that *Monkey Business* occurred after three Broadway shows and two motion pictures in which Groucho's character had been already fully developed. Given Groucho's ego, it's unlikely he was pleased to see Perelman being given credit for having "invented" his on-screen self.

Groucho was almost always complimentary when it came to discussing Perelman's talent, however. Indeed, Perelman's name was included in the list of six humorists to whom Groucho dedicated his 1959 memoir, *Groucho and Me.* He did feel, though, that some of Perelman's movie work was too literary for Hollywood.

Whenever interviewers would try and pry loose humorous anecdotes from Perelman, he would make statements such as, "I'm bored to tears with the subject of the Marx Brothers," or, "I'd rather be chained to a galley oar and lashed at ten-minute intervals than work for those sons-of-bitches again." There's even a book about Perelman entitled *Don't Mention the Marx Brothers.*

Groucho, in turn, felt betrayed by the man to whom he'd given such a big break back in 1931. In later years, he would be quoted in print as saying that Perelman's writing wasn't what it used to be and that few things were less interesting than a humorist who wasn't funny anymore. On and on it went, back and forth.

In the late sixties Groucho and Perelman happened to both be in London at the same time, and the two of them appeared on a talk show along with playwright and critic Kenneth Tynan. According to Groucho it was a dull affair, with he and Perelman each trying to top the other, leading to the dreariest of results.

Thrown into this stew was Erin's contention that at a dinner party in the fifties when Groucho had been between wives, Perelman had made a pass at Groucho's dinner companion. Erin said Groucho had never forgiven him for that. It didn't seem likely that Groucho would have nursed a grudge for twenty years over something like flirtation, and in retrospect I must carefully scrutinize almost everything that Erin ever told me, but I include this tidbit of information in the event that there is some truth to it.

Suffice it to say that things were not particularly warm and cozy between Groucho and Perelman by 1975.

The man who had won an Oscar for *Around the World in 80 Days* was, at seventy-one, returning to the States after having gone around the world in *180* days, visiting England, Scotland, France, Russia, Greece, Israel, Iran, Thailand, Malaysia, Singapore, Borneo, Java, Australia and Tahiti, among other exotic locales. The adventures he experienced on this trip would eventually appear in book form under the title *Eastward Ha!,* which was to be the last collection of Perelman's essays published during his lifetime.

His final stop before returning to New York was Hollywood. Despite whatever awkwardness there may have been over the years, arrangements had been made for Perelman to come to dinner at Groucho's. Since this was going to be a quiet dinner and not a party, I assumed I'd be departing for my room at UCLA long before Perelman arrived. To my surprise, as I was preparing to leave, Erin matter-of-factly said, "Don't you want to stay and meet Sid?" Gulp.

In addition to my concern over his strained relationship with Groucho, the truth was that I was in no hurry to meet someone whom I had understood to be something of a misanthrope. My image of Perelman was one of a wily old curmudgeon who rarely left his Manhattan lair except to visit mysterious faraway lands. In terms of interpersonal relationships, I imagined him to be a rather bitter man who had zero patience for the average public, especially members of my generation.

To make matters worse, I understood Perelman to be particularly fastidious when it came to bedecking himself in sartorial splendor—and I was in my usual work regalia of T-shirt, blue jeans and tennis shoes. Old tennis shoes, at that.

So I thanked Erin and proceeded to bow out, explaining, "I'm hardly dressed for the occasion." She laughed and said, "Oh, don't be silly. Sid won't mind!" Then she went back to her place to change into something more appropriate. Keeping in mind Erin's dismissal of my clothing concerns and not really wanting to miss this reunion, I decided to stick around.

At seven o'clock the doorbell rang. Erin, having changed into an extremely formal dress with a plunging neckline, answered it. In strode the most dapper-looking fellow I'd ever seen, sporting wire-rim spectacles, a neatly trimmed moustache and a natty three-piece suit. Among his entourage were several begowned, bejeweled and befurred ladies, plus veteran character actor Andrew Duggan, who had appeared in a sketch entitled "Malice in Wonderland," which Perelman had written for television in the late fifties.

If I'd had any doubts about the inappropriateness of my drab clothing before, they were more than confirmed by the entrance of this elegantly attired group. As Perelman came into the living room, I tentatively made my way over to him and said, "Mr. Perelman, it's an honor to meet you." He smiled politely and shook my hand, but all I could think was, *Oh sure. He can see by my faded jeans and dirty tennies just how much of an honor this must be for me.*

Groucho came into the dining room and Perelman greeted his old compatriot warmly. I detected no bitterness between them, and from the look on Perelman's face, he seemed a little saddened at the degree to which Groucho had deteriorated from the last time they'd seen each other. Since I saw Groucho several times a week, I sometimes lost sight of the fact that people who had never seen him in person, or who hadn't seen him in a while, needed time to adjust to his current condition.

Dinner was served, during which Perelman regaled those assembled with some of the trials and tribulations of his recent jaunt, mixed in with gossip about East and West Coast personalities. He had a soft, velvety voice with a slight New England accent, and he sounded as though he were just getting over a chest cold.

While coffee was being served, Perelman said, "Do you mind if I smoke?" "I don't care if you *burn*," Groucho replied. Lighting a cigarette, Perelman said, "That was good. Now let's try it for time," and I felt that, for one brief moment, we were all back at the studio watching the two of them work out a scene.

After dinner everyone adjourned to the living room for quiet conversation. Although I'd taken a semiactive role in other gatherings at Groucho's, I was sufficiently intimidated by this group—and by my lack of formal wear—so I stayed in the background as a more or less silent observer. At one point, talk turned to Marx Brothers movies. I knew this wasn't exactly Perelman's favorite subject, but he didn't seem too annoyed this time around. After all, he was in Groucho Marx's living room. Some of the guests were trying to recall specific lines that Perelman had written.

"I shot an elephant in my pajamas!" one woman exclaimed. "That was yours, wasn't it, Sid?" "No," he replied quietly.

"Vaccinated with a phonograph needle!" another woman interjected. "You wrote that, didn't you, Sid? The one about being vaccinated with a phonograph needle?" Again, Perelman politely replied, "No."

"The dean is waxing roth," I quietly stated. Perelman's bushy eyebrows elevated slightly. He smiled at me and said, "Yes. That was one of mine." The others in the room seemed startled that this kid in faded blue jeans was more familiar with their friend's work than they were, but I took their reaction to be more appreciation than resentment.

A short while later, I withdrew to my office to fish out an early draft of *Horse Feathers,* which I'd uncovered during some of the recent excavations in Groucho's closet. While I was digging it out, Perelman excused himself to go to the restroom down the hall. On his return trip, I collared him and asked if he'd seen that particular version of *Horse Feathers* recently.

Intrigued, he entered my tiny office and proceeded to thumb through the stapled stack of old onion-skin pages. He seemed to enjoy rereading his work after more than forty years. Perelman, incidentally, was slightly wall-eyed—as was Groucho—so that when he was looking at you, it was only with one eye at a time; the other was looking slightly past you. Despite this bit of optical awkwardness, we began to talk.

Since I knew they'd been good friends, I told him that I'd recently become a big fan of Robert Benchley's, and then mentioned one of my favorite Benchley essays about a children's Christmas pageant. Perelman recalled the piece, and we discussed Benchley's fondness for giving people quaint names, such as "Mr. Murney" and "Miss McNulty." "Oh yes," Perelman said, "Benchley used 'Mr. Murney' quite often." I told him that my father had recommended Benchley to me some years earlier, but since parents rarely had the same tastes as their children, I'd steered clear of him, only to discover his work on Groucho's shelves and fall in love with it immediately.

Perelman asked what I wanted to do and I told him that I was interested in being a writer, probably for television since it appeared to be the best way to balance writing and earning money at the same time. He seemed a little disheartened by my response and advised me to write plays instead because they were a purer form of writing, not quite as given to being rewritten by dozens of other hands. I respected his wisdom but had doubts about the likelihood of actually making a living by writing plays in the latter part of the twentieth century.

I glanced at my watch and realized that twenty minutes had elapsed since I'd invited him in to look at the *Horse Feathers* script. Suddenly I began to hear cries of "Where's Sid?" "What happened to Sid?" "I hope he's all right!" drifting in from the living room.

Where was Sid? He was in Steve's office, chatting about Benchley and the Algonquin Round Table and writing, that's where he was. I felt that even if I hadn't made much of a first impression in the living room, our conversation in my office had more than compensated for my lack of taste in evening wear.

Before he went back to rejoin his entourage, I asked him if it would be possible for him to inscribe a copy of his latest collection, *Vinegar Puss*, for me. I had not brought it along, but he said he'd be happy to do it and that I should leave it at the front desk of the Chateau Marmont, where he was staying.

The gathering broke up shortly after Perelman returned to the living room. After everyone had gone, I thanked Erin for letting me stick around. Driving back to the co-op, I was in a state of near elation because I'd actually succeeded in engaging the cantankerous S.J. Perelman in a twenty-minute conversation. Back at the co-op, Daryl wasn't in yet, and I was bursting to tell someone—anyone—about my evening.

I realized that many of my friends and acquaintances would have trouble placing the name. Half my generation wouldn't have known the difference between S.J. Perelman and Itzhak Perlman (and the other half wouldn't have heard of either one of them). Explaining who he was just wouldn't do: I needed to tell someone who could appreciate my experience instantly.

So I thought of Dad, who would certainly know who Perelman was and who would, in turn, be proud of his boy. Since it wasn't too late in the evening, I dialed his number. When he answered, I proudly announced, "I have just had dinner with Groucho Marx and S.J. Perelman." His response? "Well, I just hope you're not neglecting your studies."

Bang! Once again, the balloon had popped. I suddenly remembered our Father's Day lunch and the disparity between how I'd envisioned it going and how it had gone. He hoped I wasn't neglecting my studies.

What he didn't realize was, those *were* my studies.

The next day, I drove my copy of *Vinegar Puss* over to the Chateau Marmont. At the time, the Marmont was synonymous with Old World charm and elegance: Garbo stayed there whenever she came to town. It would be years before the hotel would forever be intertwined with the sobering image of John Belushi's bloated body being wheeled away on a gurney. When I handed the bag to the concierge, I announced, perhaps a bit too loudly, "This is for Mr. Perelman. He's expecting it."

I called the hotel the next day and the clerk informed me that my package was ready. I sped down Sunset Boulevard, leapt into the lobby and retrieved my prize. En route to the car, I tore open the bag and carefully opened the cover of the book, revealing, in black ink, "For Steve Stoliar, with very cordial wishes for his ultimate success as a writer. S.J. Perelman."

I've often thought that that inscription was one of the main reasons I decided to become a writer. After all, had I become a plumber, people wouldn't have known what to make of Perelman's unique dedication, so what choice did I have in the matter?

NINETEEN

On October 12, the USC Friends of the Libraries held their tribute to Groucho Marx. It had been arranged by Hector Arce through Stanley Musgrove, who was a board member of the USC Libraries organization. Since it was to be a literary luncheon, Hector selected excerpts from Groucho's books, based on Groucho's own suggestions, and arranged for them to be read aloud by special guests Jack Lemmon, Lynn Redgrave and Roddy McDowall.

In light of the afternoon's collegiate setting, the luncheon began with the screening of a clip from *Horse Feathers* featuring Groucho, dressed in cap and gown, teasing elderly college professors while singing and dancing to Harry Ruby's "Whatever It Is, I'm Against It." Once again, the chasm between the brash young man flying around up on the screen and the frail old man sitting beside me was considerable.

George Fenneman was the amiable and effective moderator for this tribute to his erstwhile employer. In addition to the book excerpts, questions from audience members were also read. When the luncheon began, Groucho seemed a little tired and distracted, and there was some concern as to whether or not it had been wise for him to have attended at all. But once the question-and-answer session started, he began to perk up.

At one point, Lemmon read a particularly serpentine question about why, if Groucho had written several books and numerous articles, had he not taken credit as a writer on the Marx Brothers' films when, in fact, he was known to have contributed material to them. As soon as Lemmon had finished reading the question, Groucho gave his answer: "You know, I'm crazy about your wife!" This broke everybody up and put the whole place in a lighter mood.

The audience was extremely responsive to the readings and laughed heartily in all the right places, which obviously made Groucho feel good. Afterward, with Billy Marx at the piano, he sang a few of his favorite tunes. Having never heard them sung before—at least not in person—the audience devoured them. Although he was a little weaker than usual that afternoon, nobody seemed disappointed, including Groucho. And Hector deserved his own round of applause for having so deftly choreographed all the elements that went into making that afternoon such a success.

That same week, I'd noticed a "Broom Hilda" cartoon in the *L.A. Times* that featured a reference to the South American pampas, "where all the romantic Grouchos roam." To illustrate the pun on *gauchos*, the cartoonist, Russell Myers, had drawn a bunch of serape-attired Grouchos puffing on cigars as they passed one another on a vast plain. I showed it to Groucho, who got a kick out of it and said he wanted to invite Myers to lunch.

Groucho dictated a quick note extolling the virtues of Myers' handiwork and, as a result, a lunch was arranged. Russell was a friendly, unassuming midwesterner who was absolutely floored to have received a fan letter from Groucho Marx. By way of thanks, he brought along the original pen-and-ink of the cartoon, which Groucho promptly added to the trophy table.

I went out to Groucho's mailbox the following week and found a small cardboard "can" addressed to me. Inside was another original cartoon, rolled up for mailing, and a note from Russell apologizing for the fact that he didn't have any cartoons about "romantic Steve Stoliars roaming the South American pampas," but that he hoped I'd accept the cartoon as a thank-you for having arranged lunch. It now hangs proudly on my living-room wall.

Around this time, Lyn Erhard fell out of favor with Erin. It was certainly not a unique occurrence, and it meant, of course, that she'd fallen out of favor with Groucho as well. This effectively ended Groucho's official sanction of and participation in Lyn's book, for which she had been steadily gathering information for nearly two years.

What caused the rift? Hector had had lunch with Lyn one day when she happened to mention that her agreement with Doubleday & Co. was thus far only verbal. Hector in turn brought the subject up with Erin. Erin asked Hector's literary agent, who had once worked at Doubleday, to check it out. Word came back that, indeed, Lyn Erhard had no written agreement with Doubleday to do a Groucho biography. As a matter of fact, no one could even confirm that there had been an *oral* agreement. Furious, Erin tossed Lyn out and Groucho took to referring to her as "an impostor."

It's up to one's individual taste whether that's better or worse than being called a pipsqueak.

When Lyn was booted out, Groucho suddenly took a disparaging attitude toward the work he and Lyn had done together. Hector later confessed that he'd felt terrible about having stirred everything up. He'd accepted Lyn's claim that she'd had that verbal agreement with one of the myriad editors at Doubleday, and it had really only been Erin's suspicious nature that had led to her dismissal. In retrospect, it seems a little disingenuous of Hector to have been surprised at Erin's reaction. Regardless of the circumstances, Groucho never spoke to Lyn Erhard again.

She continued working on her book just the same, and it was published after Groucho's death under the title *Hello, I Must Be Going: Groucho and His Friends.* Since Lyn was a curious woman, it stands to reason that she would write a curious book. The dust jacket features a drawing by trendy artist Leroy Neiman, whose greatest contribution to pop culture was probably the tiny naked lady who decorates the pages of *Playboy's Party Jokes.* It shows Lyn conversing with a slightly scowling Groucho at the lunch table—just the two of them.

Much of the book is composed of verbatim transcripts of tape recordings she made at Groucho's house, as well as separate interviews with Erin, Zeppo, Morrie Ryskind and others, especially the new wave of Erin's celebrity friends. Despite the enormous value of these interviews as well as the considerable amount of historical information and infrequently encountered photographs, it remains a frustrating book.

For starters, it has no index. If the reader desires to read about *A Night at the Opera,* he or she must skip and skim through 568 pages in hopes of a chance encounter with that particular subject. To add to the confusion, the book is not in chronological (or any discernible) order, so that once one locates the period one wishes to read about, there's almost no telling what might follow. One chapter ends with Gummo discussing leaving the Marx Brothers' vaudeville act during World War I, and the next chapter begins with a discussion of Groucho's rising popularity with college kids in the early seventies. Consequently, it is almost impossible to find anything except by accident.

Then, in addition to dwelling on superfluously tony minutiae such as the name of the exclusive *patisserie* that whipped up Groucho's birthday marzipan or the ritzy Beverly Hills clothier who provided his elegant Bordeaux sweater, Lyn implies a close friendship with Groucho that I, for one, did not see. Granted, I was not there before July of 1974 and I did not accompany them to New York, but from where I was sitting on a daily basis I would not describe them as *friends*, although they were certainly on pleasant terms. Lyn appeared simply to be someone who was working on Groucho's biography and who had a flair for staying out of people's way in the course of doing her research.

The most troubling item in the book is a reproduction of a handwritten inscription. It reads, "To Charlotte—Best from Groucho," and the *G* has been turned into a caricature of a cigar-smoking, eyebrow-raising Groucho. First of all, Groucho never referred to Ms. Erhard by her nom de plume, Charlotte. He only called her Lyn or One Cheer, because she had received exactly that from the crowd as she exited her car at the 1974 Oscars. Worse, not one letter of the inscription looks anything like Groucho's handwriting. And I'm unaware that he ever made such a deft self-caricature out of the capital *G*, even in his younger days. In addition to taking up an entire page within the book, this spurious creation is also reproduced on the front cloth cover.

My final problem with the book is that Lyn tends to be an Erin apologist, arguing at one point that people simply misunderstood Ms. Fleming; that maybe a man who was hard of hearing *needed* to be screamed at; that maybe a man who was becoming mentally hazy might be "jerked back into reality" by Erin's verbal and physical behavior. Although there are some positive things to be said about Erin Fleming, I don't believe that these are among them.

Since Lyn was out of the loop during the last two years of Groucho's life, she might be forgiven her rationalization of Erin's behavior. It's conceivable that she never really saw Erin in full fury, even when she was tossed out. But in those last two years, when Lyn was no longer around, Erin's irrational outbursts and harsh treatment of Groucho and others escalated sharply. In view of that, her behavior becomes indefensible.

Sometimes I think of Lyn's book as the way I would *like* things to have been: Groucho, endearing and irascible, living out his final days in quiet comfort surrounded by celebrity friends, a devoted woman and gourmet food. Unfortunately, Lyn's rather naive account showed only one facet of what life was really like inside Groucho's house during his last years.

TWENTY

If Lyn Erhard was on the outs in late 1975, the gods were still smiling on Hector Arce. Since his collaboration with Groucho on *The Secret Word Is Groucho* had gone so smoothly, another project popped up. This one was less ambitious but no less significant. It was an updated reissue of Groucho's first book, *Beds*.

The original edition of *Beds* was a compilation of short, humorous essays about sleeping habits, which originally had been written for *College Humor* magazine. In his later years, Groucho gave Arthur Sheekman credit for having written it in its entirety, although it seems likely that Groucho made certain contributions, at least in terms of concept and editing. In addition to the essays there were several photos of Groucho preparing to turn in for the night and lying in bed with attractive young ladies—tastefully rendered, of course.

Regardless of its actual authorship, *Beds* came out as a slim hardcover book in 1930. There was only one printing. Consequently, when the Marx Brothers were rediscovered in the sixties and seventies, the book became a sought-after collector's item. By 1975 it tended to sell for around a hundred dollars.

Over the years, fans had urged Groucho to make *Beds* more readily available, so Hector made arrangements with Bobbs-Merrill Publishers to come out with a paperback reprint containing a new introduction by Groucho (with Hector's assistance) as well as some new photos of him in bed with various celebrities. These included Burt Reynolds, Lynn Redgrave, Valerie Perrine, Elliott Gould and Phyllis Diller, who had been a contestant on "You Bet Your Life" and whom Hector had interviewed earlier in the year. The new version also contained the photo of Groucho in bed with Sally Struthers and Carroll O'Connor that had been taken at his eighty-fifth birthday party. To round out the illustrations, I managed to dig up a few shots of Groucho in and around beds from his film career.

One other photo stands out in my mind. It showed Groucho in bed with Robin Heaney. Standing beside the bed are Barbara Odum (one of Groucho's nurses), Tom Wilhite, Hector Arce and me.

Behind us, a partially obscured Erin Fleming watches over everything. To me, it's an interesting shot because of the people in it and how they are arranged. Hector felt he looked too fat, so it wasn't published, which was a great frustration at the time. After twenty years, my disappointment has finally been assuaged by its inclusion in this book.

The *Beds* reprint came out in the spring of 1976 with a cover photo of Groucho standing in front of a dozen mattresses, which had been taken at an Ortho showroom. Several boxes of books arrived at Groucho's house, and when Erin opened one to check them out she hit the roof. I'd certainly seen her angry on a number of occasions, but I'd never gotten used to the sheer force of her fury. Her voice could slice right through fine leaded crystal. Erin screamed bloody murder and hurled one of the books clear across the living room. As was often the case, Hector and I had no idea what had set her off.

Erin was furious because the cover photo had been printed in black and white instead of color. She said it looked cheap and made Groucho look cheap (although I doubt Ansel Adams or Richard Avedon would've agreed with her conclusion). She insisted that the cover had always been envisioned in color—and she demanded that the entire printing of black-and-white books be recalled and a new batch printed up featuring a full-color cover.

That she got her way is a testament to Erin's ability to intimidate people into giving her what she wanted. I don't know that Bobbs-Merrill ever thought *Beds* was going to be a big seller, which is probably why it was a paperback to begin with, but recalling an entire printing and doing it all over again almost certainly canceled out any hopes of a profit.

The purpose of the reprint had been to make *Beds* available to the general public and not just to book collectors with a lot of money. In the process, however, another scarce collectible was inadvertently created. The first "second edition," with the black-and-white cover, is now a certified collector's item because it was recalled. It isn't as valuable as the original 1930 edition, but it still sells for fifteen or twenty dollars—substantially more than the two-dollar cover price and considerably more than the subsequent edition with the color cover.

After the work on *Beds* had been completed, Bobbs-Merrill

came up with an offer for Hector and Groucho to put together a picture book of Groucho's life, inspired by Charlie Chaplin's book, *My Life in Pictures*, which had come out the previous year. It was envisioned as the ultimate collection of Groucho photographs and memorabilia and would include well-known poses from his films as well as behind-the-scenes shots and rare family photos. The book, which was called *The GrouchoPhile*, would eventually be published in November of 1976.

The process by which the book was assembled was as follows: I would work with Hector on the selection of the photos—over seven hundred of them by the time we'd finished—and put them into chronological order. Hector would bring the photos into Groucho's room and jot down his comments about them. This commentary became the captions to the photographs.

Sometimes Groucho wouldn't say anything more elaborate than, "That's me and Danny Kaye." More often than not, however, he would have an interesting comment or anecdote to accompany the picture. When he was shown a shot of himself and cartoonist Rube Goldberg, it prompted him to recall that he'd been at a New Year's Eve party at Goldberg's one year when James Thurber had gotten drunk and tried to hit him over the head with a beer bottle. We never knew what sort of story from Groucho's past would surface as a result of the photos. And neither did Groucho.

Occasionally a piece of memorabilia would trigger a truly startling bit of information. Since we wanted to establish once and for all that Groucho had been born in 1890 and not 1895 as some books claimed, Hector arranged for a copy of Groucho's birth certificate to be sent from New York. When it arrived I looked it over, intrigued by such a unique and personal artifact from Groucho's past. As I was handing it back to Hector, I noticed something peculiar: Where it said, "Number of Previous Children," a "3" had been written. And where it said, "How Many Now Living (in all)," it also said "3."

I thought that perhaps an error had been made. Chico and Harpo were older than Groucho, having been born in 1887 and 1888 respectively. I assumed that whomever had put a "3" next to "Number of Previous Children" had inadvertently included Groucho, who had, as presumed, been born in 1890.

Just to be on the safe side, Hector and I took the birth certificate in to Groucho, who was reading a book. He looked up, wanting to know what we'd unearthed *this* time. Hector asked Groucho if his parents, Sam and Minnie, had had any other children besides Chico and Harpo, who had been born before him. Very matter-of-factly, Groucho said, "Yes. Their first son was Manfred. He died before I was born, when he was three years old."

Hector and I exchanged a startled look: Manfred? "What did he die of?" Hector wanted to know. "Old age," Groucho quipped, and then returned to his book. Hector and I went back to my office where we proceeded to discuss the ramifications of this astonishing revelation.

If the average moviegoer were to be asked how many Marx Brothers there were, the answer would probably be three: Groucho, Harpo and Chico. Film buffs knew that Zeppo had made it a quartet, at least until 1933. And devout Marx fans were aware of the fact that there had been a fifth brother, Gummo, who had left the act during World War I. But no one of our acquaintance—not even Erin—had ever heard of a *sixth* Marx Brother until that day.

Who knows what Manfred might have gone on to achieve as the senior member of the Marx Brothers? Alas, we'll never know. But I sure was glad I'd given that birth certificate such a thorough going over. Incidentally, that same piece of paper also revealed that Groucho's father wasn't really "Sam" at all. His actual name was Simon. Sam was a nickname, which was used whenever he wasn't referred to as Frenchy. Got that?

After the captions were recorded and the photos organized by year and subject, such as Vaudeville or *Duck Soup*, I would provide Hector with an appropriate Groucho quote from that particular period, which would be used as the header to each chapter. Work on *The GrouchoPhile*, which was obviously a fascinating project for me to be involved with, began in late 1975 and lasted through much of 1976.

Hector was curious to know why Groucho's collection of memorabilia had been earmarked for the Smithsonian Institution, of all places. I told him that, as with so many other things, it had been Erin's idea. Occasionally offers would come in from smaller institutions eager to display Groucho's personal memorabilia.

I recall one letter from a small eastern college that already had the donated papers of notables along the lines of George S.

Kaufman, Moss Hart and Robert Benchley. I thought that Groucho's things might have felt more at home amid the belongings of those other kindred spirits, and I had grave doubts that the Smithsonian was intending to put the *Spirit of St. Louis* in mothballs just to make room for Groucho's pith helmet.

I favored a smaller place that might pay more attention to the material and not just tag it and stick it in the basement. Erin listened to my argument and said she'd consider a smaller place, but nothing was ever done about it. She had made up her mind. She liked the prestige of saying it was going to the Smithsonian Institution, and so that was that.

In November, Erin added to her medical credentials by appearing in a small role on "Marcus Welby, M.D." She had only a few lines, but it marked one of her rare acting gigs during this period when Groucho's personal and business affairs were taking up more and more of her time.

Toward the end of the year, I accompanied Groucho to a performance of the play *The Royal Family* at the Huntington Hartford Theater. It had been written by two of Groucho's Algonquinite friends, George S. Kaufman and Edna Ferber, and was a thinly disguised parody of the Barrymore family. The star of this particular revival was Eva LeGallienne, one of the legitimate theater's most enduring leading ladies.

It was interesting seeing this with Groucho, both because he'd known the playwrights (not to mention the Barrymores) and because he'd seen the original production on Broadway back in 1927, so he was able to compare the two. Also in the cast that evening was character actor Sam Levene as a fast-talking theatrical agent. According to Groucho, they had built up the role as a showcase for Levene, because "the part of the comedian wasn't in the original." Once again, I appreciated Groucho both for who he was and as a living witness to a bygone era.

For Christmas of 1975 I was given a check for fifty dollars—half of what I'd received the year before. I didn't really attach much significance to the reduced amount. I got the impression that I wasn't being singled out and that, for whatever reason, bonuses were being slashed across the board.

Certainly Groucho hadn't cooled toward me. Neither had we really grown closer. Although I'd been there for over a year, I was battling against time in terms of my rapport with Groucho. With another person, the passage of time would most likely lead to a more intimate understanding between the two of us. But for Groucho, the passage of time represented the loss of some small fragment of his mind and personality. His gradual deterioration wasn't really noticeable except in retrospect, when I would realize that he had been ever-so-slightly sharper a few months earlier.

Since I wasn't putting in as many hours at the house as I had at the beginning, it was, literally, out of sight, out of mind. So it was difficult to carve out any deeper a foothold in Groucho's consciousness than I'd already managed to do. But if that was as far as things were destined to go, I could certainly live with that. It was so much more than most people would ever have, and that included other members of the household.

Christmas also marked a run-in with one of Erin's entourage, Bud Cort. Perennially short of money, Bud had been staying in Melinda's old room off and on for some time, usually sleeping in until around noon. As I said earlier, I was a big fan of *Harold & Maude*. I once asked Bud if he had an opinion as to why the film hadn't done well when it had first been released, yet had gone on to become a cult classic only a couple of years later. Bud put his index finger to his lips and whispered, "Never complain; never explain," and then wandered off. As I also said earlier, Erin's circle tended to be a bit on the offbeat side.

In addition to his general quirkiness, Bud also had a certain childlike quality that extended beyond his baby face and big eyes. I remember one day when I was working on fan mail in my office. Bud came racing in and asked if I was planning on going to the post office that day. He had a letter he wanted me to mail. I checked my watch and told him, "No, but I don't think the mailman's been here yet. You can check and see."

It was obvious from the perplexed look on his face that Bud didn't understand what one thing had to do with the other, so I explained, "Why don't you put your letter in the mailbox and put the flag up? The mailman will take it when he delivers the mail." Bud's eyes turned into huge saucers. "You mean you can *do* that?" he asked in disbelief. "Yeah," I answered, continuing, "then you can tell when the mail's here, because the mailman puts the flag down."

"Oh wow!" Bud exclaimed. "Oh *wow!*" he exclaimed again, this time retreating down the hallway, running his fingers through his hair, still unable to fully accept the idea that one can put outgoing mail in one's own mailbox. Had he been six years old I might've understood his wide-eyed naivete, but at the time Bud was about twenty-five.

Bud decided to throw a Christmas party for about fifty of his closest friends and acquaintances. He informed them that the festivities were going to be held at the home of the one, the only, Groucho Marx. But for some reason he neglected to inform Groucho. Or Erin.

Given Erin's mercurial temperament and suspicious nature, one might assume that she would have blown her stack upon finding out that such a thing was being planned behind her back. But in addition to being mercurial and suspicious, she was also impossible to predict. Bud, being one of her favorite hangers-on and ersatz children, got no grief at all from Erin.

Groucho, however, was another story. When he heard about the party Bud had planned, he summoned him into his room and said, "Do you know the meaning of the word *chutzpah?*" Bud was humbled somewhat but begged Groucho to let him go through with the party so that he wouldn't be made to appear foolish in front of his friends by having to call it off on such short notice.

Not really wanting to punish Bud, Groucho agreed to let him have his Christmas party. According to Hector, it was populated by "underground movie makers, Sunset Strip hustlers and drug freaks"—not exactly Groucho's crowd.

In later years Bud, like Lyn Erhard, would give in to the temptation to inflate his friendship with Groucho. It's true that Groucho often got a kick out of Bud and his antics. But Bud was decidedly one of *Erin's* friends. Most of the household took turns accompanying Groucho on his daily walks, and it was almost always an enjoyable task watching Groucho taking in the sunshine and delighting startled passersby. But Bud would almost have to be lassoed into going along on the few occasions when he was asked, while he thought nothing of making Melinda's old room his home for weeks at a time until better offers came along.

Apparently, he *didn't* know the meaning of the word *chutzpah*.

There was, however, a sweet note to the holiday season. It was the arrival of Melinda and her two children, Miles and Jade, on

December 30. Once again, I'd been on my guard after hearing Erin's less-than-flattering comments about Melinda and her family. And once again, my own experience was at odds with Erin's opinion.

I found Melinda to be sweet, thoughtful and attentive, both as a mother and as a daughter. She had grown from the precocious little girl who'd been trotted out annually on "You Bet Your Life" into an attractive young woman. Additionally, I found her children to be absolutely adorable and well behaved, especially given the fact that they were ages five and one.

I remember one afternoon when Melinda played the violin for Groucho. She was quite good and it was obvious from his beaming face how proud Groucho was of his daughter and how happy he was to see her and his grandchildren again. All of Erin's venomous railings about Melinda's indifference and greed went right out the window the minute she and her children entered the house.

It was also obvious how uncomfortable Erin and Melinda felt around each other, so Ms. Fleming announced that she would not be coming by the house until Melinda had gone. Thank God. After all, Melinda had arrived with two small children, something Erin desperately coveted. And we can't lose sight of the fact that Erin had only recently been turned down as Groucho's adopted daughter. How must Melinda have felt while *that* plan was in the works? No, it was just as well they steered clear of each other.

There was an initial awkwardness between Melinda and Groucho, which, I assume, was a combination of his advancing age, the natural growing apart of father and child and the divisive acrimony which had almost personified Erin's position in Groucho's life. When all was said and done, however, theirs was a happy, touching reunion, and Groucho told Melinda he didn't want her to go. Sadly, after three days of visiting the time came for her to leave for Mendocino.

Before she left, Melinda vowed to return. As things turned out, that would not occur for quite some time.

TWENTY ONE

Nineteen seventy-six began with a bad case of syphilis.

Before you jump to any conclusions, I should probably say that this did not involve anyone I've written about thus far. Erin had hired a new maid several months earlier who had come from Guatemala. Although her English was quite limited, she was a pleasant woman who did an efficient job of keeping the place neat and tidy. Then one day, she complained of a high fever and an uncomfortable rash.

To her credit, Erin was genuinely concerned about the maid's condition. Rather than having her visit some sort of free clinic, she insisted on taking her to see her personal physician in Beverly Hills and picking up the tab herself. The maid was enormously relieved to discover that Erin was coming to her rescue. Erin's sympathy ended abruptly, however, when the doctor diagnosed the maid's illness as syphilis.

The maid tried as best she could to explain to Erin that she must've gotten it from her husband, whom she had visited in Guatemala during the recent holiday season. Since she hadn't been sleeping with anyone else, it *had* to have been him. Now she didn't know where to turn for help.

Erin was no longer in any mood to be compassionate. Instead, she flew into one of her more ferocious rages, screaming at the maid, calling her a "filthy whore," and damning her to hell for her selfishness in exposing Groucho and the rest of us to her "disgusting disease." The maid promptly burst into tears. After all, she was living in a strange place; her husband, who had been unfaithful to her, was several countries away; she was ill; and now she was being called a whore by her employer.

As if that weren't enough, Erin immediately ordered the maid and all of her belongings thrown out of the house and onto the driveway. Since she'd been living in the servant's room at Groucho's, she had no other home this side of Guatemala. Had it not been for the compassion of one of Groucho's nurses who was on her way out anyway, she might still be sitting there, huddled on the curb, sobbing uncontrollably. The nurse gave her a lift to the bus stop so that she could at least get back to the employment agency and try to figure out where to go from there.

Despite the fact that this was a venereal disease, passed on in the usual way, in her hysteria Erin was terrified that Groucho was somehow going to contract syphilis by touching a chair that the maid had cleaned. "What would happen if Groucho came down with syphilis?" Erin asked Hector. "James Bacon might run the item," Hector quipped, referring to the noted Hollywood columnist. Erin stared daggers at Hector, seeing not the slightest trace of humor in the situation. As far as Erin was concerned, a serious syphilis epidemic at 1083 Hillcrest had been narrowly averted by her quick action in tossing the maid and everything she owned out the front door.

Years later, when I heard people talking about how harshly Leona Helmsley had treated her employees, I wondered what all the fuss was about.

Needless to say, Groucho did not contract syphilis nor any other venereal diseases during his final two years. But he could hardly be said to have been in good health. As the new year dawned, Groucho continued his gradual decline. One of the more tangible examples of his deterioration was in his signature. For fifty years, Groucho had been signing his first name with a very distinctive *G* that had remained remarkably consistent. Suddenly, in early 1976, he began changing the *G* into almost a *Y* shape, so that his name read "Yroucho."

It wasn't difficult for me to fix the signatures by adding a slight curve to the top of the *Y* with my trusty Sharpie after taking the signed pictures back to my office. I doubt that many fans scrutinized the signatures closely enough to detect the alteration. I'd often been called upon to clean up the occasional flub in an inscription, but he was making this error on each and every photo, letter and check that was placed before him. As a matter of fact, the bank eventually asked for a fresh sample of his signature just to ensure that the checks which were coming through had actually been signed by the man himself.

Groucho continued signing "Yroucho" for several months and then, just as mysteriously, he shifted back into "Groucho," although the new *G* looked a little different than it had before.

Then, to make matters worse, for a few weeks he took to adding two curved marks, almost like parentheses, above his signature for no apparent reason. This presented more of a challenge, as I tried to form the first mark into a *t* in "Best," and the second mark into a sort of comma before Groucho's signature. It looked a little strange, and I hoped the recipients would simply write it off as a side effect of Groucho's advanced age. They wouldn't have been off by much.

The exact meaning of this shift in the way Groucho signed his name could probably best be explained by a psychologist—or a graphologist—specializing in the elderly. What it meant to me, aside from having to doctor up a lot of photographs, was that Groucho was continuing his slow fade.

Nevertheless, Groucho's sense of playfulness was still in evidence at the lunch table. In January I went to a revival house to catch a couple of old favorites. I decided to tell Groucho about it.

Me: "I saw a couple of great pictures last night."

Groucho: "Yeah? Which ones?"

Me: "*Monkey Business* and *Horse Feathers*."

Groucho: "Oh? I've never seen them."

Me: "They were pretty good. I can't remember who was in them. The Ritz Brothers, I think."

Groucho: "When Miriam was ten years old, she came home from the theater. I said, 'What'd you see?' and she said, 'The Ritz Brothers. Now they're *really* funny!'"

Later that month my friend, Jim Bell, who was attending the University of California at Santa Barbara, informed me that S.J. Perelman was going to be an honorary professor in residence at the university for the month of February and that he'd be doing a public reading of some of his writings in the campus auditorium. The date of his appearance was February 4.

I figured this was a rare opportunity to see Perelman again and since I'd recently unearthed an original edition of *Dawn Ginsbergh's Revenge* for the criminally low price of $6.50, I thought it might be nice to have him sign it in the event it was possible to see him after his talk.

On February 4, I carefully placed the old book on the passenger seat of my trusty Pinto and headed up from Westwood toward Santa Barbara, in eager anticipation of an enjoyable evening. Halfway there, my car belched out a cloud of blue smoke and promptly died. I had it towed to a nearby service station, where the mechanic determined that the car had blown a head gasket and a piston ring.

Using the dipstick, he showed me that there was no longer any oil in the car. I told him that I never kept oil in my car because I didn't want to get the dipstick dirty. He gave me one of those "What, are you serious?" looks that taught me it was rarely worth trying to kid around with garage mechanics.

I called Jim from the service station to come fetch me and we made it to campus just in time to catch Perelman's appearance. He was warmly received by the youthful crowd and it was enjoyable listening to him read his own words the way he wanted them read.

After he'd finished and the applause had died down, I went up to the podium and reintroduced myself. He remembered me from Groucho's house and said it was nice to see me again. I gave him Groucho's love—a precious commodity given their history—which Groucho had said to be sure and give him. Then, as I had hoped, he inscribed my copy of his first book. But it was no longer the bargain it had once been. The book may have cost me only $6.50, but getting it signed had run me another $275 in automotive repairs.

A few days later, Groucho asked me how the evening had gone.

Me: "I thoroughly enjoyed Mr. Perelman's talk, but my car broke down on the way up there and a friend had to pick me up and take me the rest of the way."

Groucho: "The car I sold you?"

Me: "Yes."

Groucho: "Why don't you sue me?"

Jim sent me a copy of the article about Perelman's talk that appeared in the UCSB school paper. The headline read: "Perelman Personifies Gap Between Author and Works." Apparently the reviewer didn't think Perelman had been a particularly entertaining speaker. He had assumed that someone who had once been "a gag writer for the Marx Brothers" would have come off much funnier.

I was furious. Here Perelman agrees to appear at the school as a personal favor to one of the deans, and then some young whippersnapper has the gall to pan his "performance" because he wasn't very funny. He'd never tried to pass himself off as a funny speaker, only a funny writer. Had I been Perelman, I would've caught the next plane to New York right then and there. As it was, he honored his commitment to stay on campus for the remainder of the month of February.

That same week, I got a lesson in determining the accuracy of firsthand recollections. One day at lunch, while Hector was still gathering information for the lengthy captions in *The GrouchoPhile*, Groucho told us about how the Marx Brothers had gone from being a singing act to a comedy act after a donkey had run past the theater in the small Texas town in which they were appearing, causing the audience to ignore the Marx Brothers and run out to watch the runaway donkey. This had irked Groucho, prompting him to unleash upon the audience a string of ad-libbed insults, which seemed to go over better than the songs.

Hector said, "According to Harpo's book, that story about the donkey took place in Oklahoma, not Texas. Who's right?"

Groucho said, "I am, because I'm alive and he's not."

That settled that.

Also in February, Groucho was asked to be a part of a Bob Hope special entitled "Joys." This was to be a parody of *Jaws*, wherein a ferocious land shark is on the loose, devouring famous comedians one at a time. It was a curiously morbid premise for a Bob Hope special, but it was timely and the format allowed for a large number of comedians, spanning various eras, to come in and tape a short portion that could then be edited together into a ninety-minute show.

The sequence in which Groucho was to appear wasn't going to be taped in front of a studio audience, but since we'd gotten to be friends with Hal Kanter, who was producing the show, Daryl and I were allowed to hang out around the NBC studio where it was all taking place. Groucho had a brief routine with George Burns about whether or not they were too old to still be flicking their Bics, and then diminutive actor Billy Barty came by dressed as the young Groucho. Groucho was also supposed to wave and say hello to composer Sammy Cahn, who wasn't present the day Groucho's sequences were taped.

Personally, I thought Groucho did a pretty good job of perking up and conversing with Burns, reacting to Barty and pretending to be saying hello to an absent Sammy Cahn. After all, this called for genuine *acting*, complete with remembering lines and reacting to what was being said. It was a far cry from relating a humorous anecdote over lunch or singing "Show Me a Rose" in the relaxed comfort of his living room.

Later I sent Hal a note thanking him for allowing us to come and watch, and telling him that I thought Groucho had come off surprisingly well, all things considered. Hal sent me a note in response, saying that if I thought Groucho had come off well, I must never have seen him at his best. He confessed that he'd shed many a tear in the editing room fighting tooth and nail to keep even those precious few moments in the final edit.

Once again I had lost sight of how far Groucho had fallen. I'd grown so accustomed to seeing him at the house, making humorous remarks and sharing interesting stories, that I'd almost forgotten how much of a shock it could be for the average person to see him in his present condition. He may have done a better job of acting than I'd anticipated for an eighty-five-year-old Groucho, but compared to most of the other guests on that show he was little more than a poignant reminder of his former greatness.

Even Groucho, when he saw the show on television the following month, didn't think he was very funny.

The other thing that stays with me from that particular afternoon was watching Bob Hope work. He would read most of his lines off strategically placed cue cards, and after each take he would stride over to a video monitor to see how he'd presented himself. He never did two takes in a row without first checking the monitor; he had to evaluate his appearance after every few lines.

After one particular take he suddenly flew into a rage, convinced that his hair looked bad. He made the engineer run the piece of videotape back and forth, while he carefully scrutinized his hair. It looked all right to Daryl and me, the same way Bob Hope's hair had looked for some time: thinning and suspiciously dark, yet neatly groomed. But for a reason unknown to anyone who was watching the monitor, Hope thought his hair looked awful.

He screamed for his hairdresser to come out and watch the videotaped replay of the previous take. "Jesus Christ! Look at that!" Hope demanded, giving the hairdresser a dressing down. "Look at my hair! What the hell's going on? Do you know what you're *doing?*"

The hapless hairdresser stared vacantly at the monitor. It was obvious from his bewildered expression that he had no idea what

Hope was ranting about. Of course, there was no way for him to have satisfactorily answered the question, because if he'd said he *did* know what he was doing, Hope would've said, "Then why does my hair look so lousy?" and if he'd said he *didn't* know what he was doing, Hope would've thrown him out.

As I recall, the hairdresser just stood there looking sheepish until Hope had finished tearing into him, then he was allowed to slink back into his corner. It was a side of Hope I'd heard about but had never seen—not in Groucho's living room and certainly not in front of a studio audience. I'm sure it was because he was only in front of cast and crew that he felt he could let his hair down, so to speak, without danger of damaging his reputation with the general public.

Around this time I decided to reread *The Groucho Letters* for the first time in several years. It was interesting to read about Groucho's correspondents now that I'd met some of them—for instance, Nunnally Johnson, Nat Perrin and S.J. Perelman—in person. I was discussing the book with Terrie McCord, an extremely pleasant and efficient nurse who had recently been added to the staff, and I made an offhand remark that it seemed unlikely I would ever be getting an official "Groucho letter" since I worked down the hall and Groucho could more easily communicate with me in person. And besides, any letters that Groucho wanted to send were dictated to *me* in the first place.

The following week I came into my office and found an envelope on my desk with my name on it. I opened it up and there, on Groucho's stationery and in his own hand, was the following note, dated February 13, 1976: "Dear Steve—I am glad you work for me. You are loyal and intelligent. Groucho." Or, to be precise, "Yroucho." It wasn't elaborate or humorous and would hardly be considered one of Groucho's better letters, but it sure meant a lot to me and I was grateful to Terrie for having prevailed upon Groucho to take a moment and pen the note.

Groucho's regular correspondence, although it had certainly dwindled, was still something in which he would occasionally indulge. One day, after he'd been rereading a James Thurber book and had been particularly charmed by one of his whimsical drawings, he called me into his room and proceeded to dictate a letter to Thurber's widow.

"Dear Helen: I'm still reading Thurber. I've never stopped. He did a cartoon on p. 102 of 'Credos & Curios' showing a dog, a mouse and an owl in front of a fireplace. I wonder if it's possible for me to get the original of that. I think you know my address. You can tell me whether or not you can arrange this. Cordially yours, Groucho."

Mrs. Thurber wrote back, explaining that she was sorry but that all of his drawings had been donated to a university so that the public could admire them and use them for research purposes, so she was unable to comply with his request. Oh well. At least they weren't buried at the Smithsonian.

On the same day he dictated the Helen Thurber letter, Groucho also sent one to *New York Times* columnist Israel Shenker, who had penned a piece about Groucho that had been included in an anthology of Shenker's writing. The publisher had contacted most of the people Shenker had written about and asked if they would take a moment to send a note, which would then be bound into a single volume and presented to the author.

"Dear Shenker: I see other people have praised you. I guess they should. I don't want to be any different. It's a wonderful piece you wrote about me in your book. You certainly have plenty on the ball. Which one, I don't know. Sincerely yours as of June 5, 1894, Groucho."

For the record, the letter was written March 6, 1976.

A few days later, Groucho attended the American Film Institute dinner saluting director William Wyler. One of the people paying tribute to Wyler that night was Audrey Hepburn, who had appeared in *Roman Holiday*. After telling an amusing anecdote about working with Wyler, she launched into a lengthy list of reasons why she was indebted to the veteran director: "If it wasn't for Willy, I wouldn't have met my husband. If it wasn't for Willy, I wouldn't have had a *Roman Holiday*. If it wasn't for Willy, I wouldn't have won the Oscar," and so forth. In the midst of her litany, Groucho blurted out, "If it wasn't for Willy, I'd be home in bed watching my show!"

For some reason, the AFI never got around to saluting Groucho.

A week or so later, George Jessel returned for another lunch. He was filled with more reminiscences about vaudeville and old Hollywood. I had recently found a piece of sheet music to a song entitled “And She’d Say Oo-La-La Oui-Oui.” The composers of this obscure ditty were Harry Ruby and George Jessel. I showed it to Jessel, who told me that it had sold a million copies in 1919, at ten cents apiece. Unfortunately he hadn’t held onto that money, and one of the reasons he would stop by Groucho’s periodically was to “borrow” some funds. For old time’s sake, Groucho would usually give him a check for a thousand dollars or so.

The next day a Passover dinner, or *seder,* was held at Groucho’s. Since it was Erin who was the more passionate about Judaism, all Groucho wanted to know was, “When do we eat?” and “When do I get to sing?” Jessel led the service and afterward sang a couple of songs, including his old trademark, “My Mother’s Eyes.” Although he had gotten a little creaky, his voice was still strong and expressive, and it was easy to picture him on Broadway playing a cantor’s son in *The Jazz Singer.* It made me wonder all the more what might have happened to his career had he not turned down the film version.

The following week Hector and I were invited to Jessel’s house out in Reseda, an older section of the San Fernando Valley. Hector’s literary agent had thought that there might be a *GrouchoPhile* type book in Jessel’s collection of memorabilia, so we drove out there to look things over.

As with Jessel himself, there was a certain sense of sadness to the house. The place was indeed crammed with decades of memorabilia, but it was in total disarray. There were medals of recognition from different heads of state lying around on top of a bureau where one might have expected to find car keys or sunglasses. And when he handed me a silver box that was sitting on a coffee table, I opened it up to find letters from Harry Truman, Judy Garland and John F. Kennedy jammed inside, as though they were old Christmas cards. A story went with every item, sometimes interesting, sometimes not.

As it turned out, Hector’s agent had overestimated the publishing world’s interest in *The GeorgiePhile,* or whatever it might have been called. Although this news didn’t surprise me, it did disappoint me: Hector had promised that, had the deal gone through, he would have stepped aside and let *me* cowrite the book with Jessel.

Oh well.

Author's collection

A classic portrait from 1939. When I asked him to write something personal, Groucho said, "What do you want me to say? 'I love you?'" This was *almost* as good. (Note how his moustache is made entirely of greasepaint.)

Above: Chico, Groucho, Harpo and Margaret Dumont during one of the more sedate moments in *Animal Crackers,* 1930. My efforts resulted in both the re-release of this nearly lost film and a dream-come-true job working for my idol.

Above right: the arrival of Captain Spaulding in the same film, with Zeppo, Lou Sorin, Groucho and Margaret Dumont.

Right: Zeppo, Chico, Harpo and Groucho horsing around on a Paramount soundstage in 1932.

All photos: © Universal Pictures

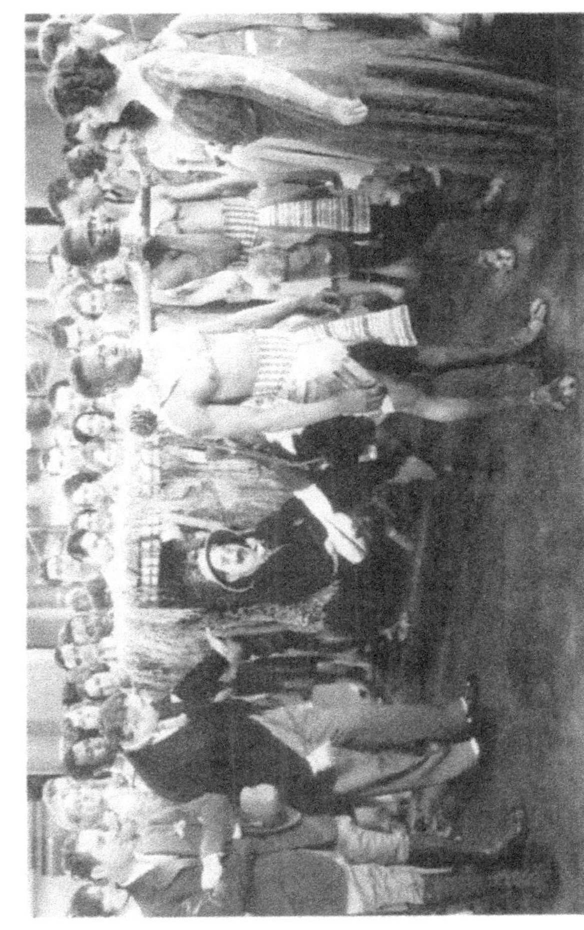

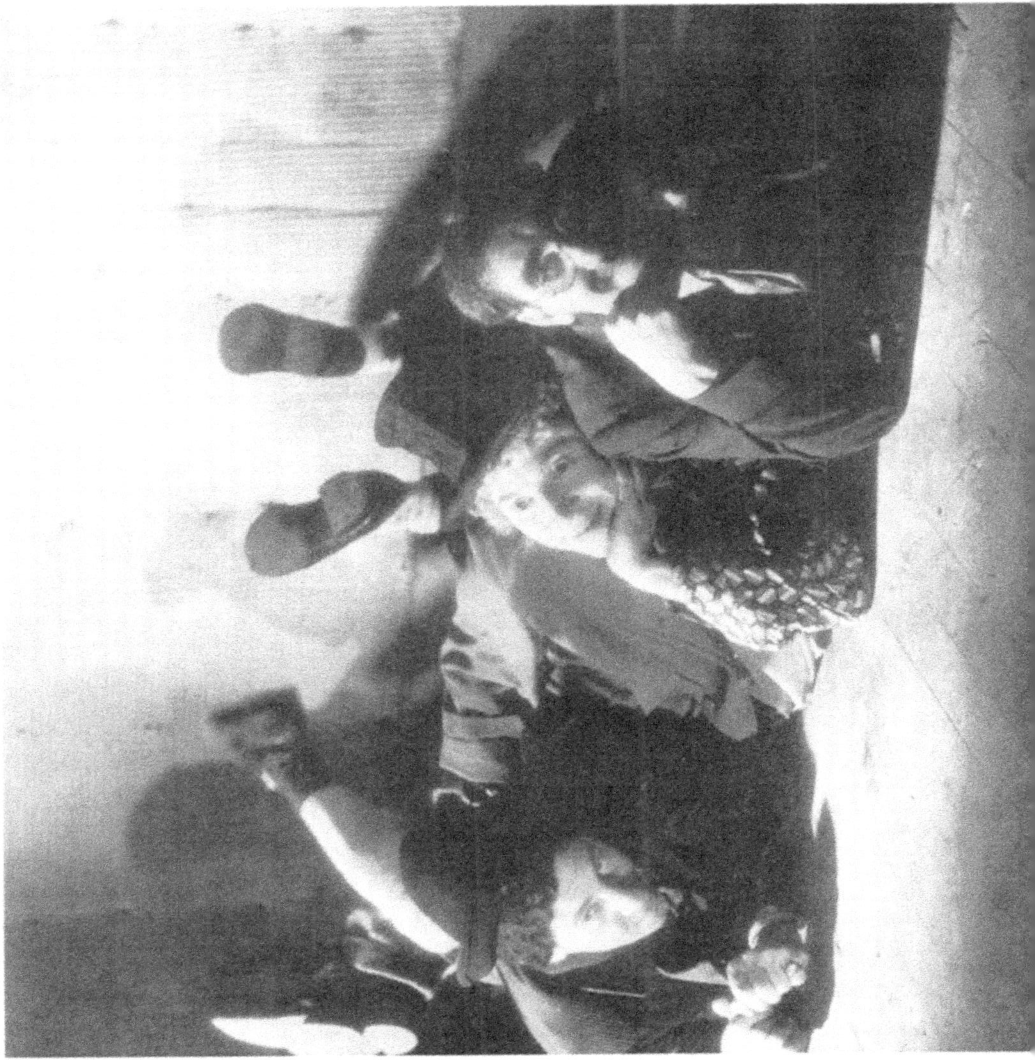

Author's collection

Left: Groucho, Zeppo, Harpo, Chico and Gummo on the set of *Duck Soup*, 1933. Gummo, low man on the totem pole, had left the act years earlier and this would be Zeppo's last film before retiring to become an agent.

Above: Groucho masquerading as Julius Henry Marx, early 1930s. He was unrecognizable without a moustache, be it greasepaint or home-grown.

Right: a late fifties portrait of Groucho from his "You Bet Your Life" days.

Elmer Holloway, NBC

Left: At UCLA during the campaign to re-release *Animal Crackers* in February of 1974. I couldn't believe I was actually sitting next to Groucho Marx.

Steve Reich

AP Wirephoto

Right: Groucho talks with students and reporters while I hang on his every word and my roommate, Daryl Busby, tries to hold back the crowd. This AP wirephoto appeared in newspapers around the world.

Above right: Groucho and Erin Fleming at UCLA. At the time, I thought he was extremely fortunate to have such a woman in his life. I would later revise that assessment.

UCLA Daily Bruin

Robin Heaney

Above: I felt as though I were posing next to a prized marlin I'd just landed when this shot of Groucho and me was taken in his backyard in October of 1974.

Below: He indulges in a quick tango with his cook, Robin Heaney. This photo was taken by nurse Connie August, who would launch an unsuccessful attempt to overthrow Erin Fleming the following month.

Connie August

Above: In the fall of 1974, Groucho let me tape a short video documentary on him for a TV-production class. Daryl operated the camera while I conducted the interview.

Above right: Next, Groucho and Erin harmonize. Off camera, things were somewhat more discordant.

Above and left: Also from my documentary, Groucho sings "Show Me a Rose," then dons a Mickey Mouse cap for our amusement. (Note the Hirschfeld-inspired shirt, which was one of his favorites.)

All photos by Irwin Hale

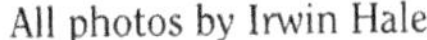

The photos on these two pages were taken at Groucho's 85th birthday bash in October of 1975. Left, a pensive portrait taken before many of the guests had arrived. At bottom left, Groucho sings while Harpo's son, Bill, provides piano accompaniment.

All photos by Frank Diernhammer

The two photos at the right show Chita Rivera's daughter, Lisa Mordente; Liza Minnelli; Jack Haley, Jr.; Lorna Luft; John Hillerman, Daryl and me listening attentively as Groucho sings. Behind Groucho stand screenwriter Morrie Ryskind and Peter Sellers.

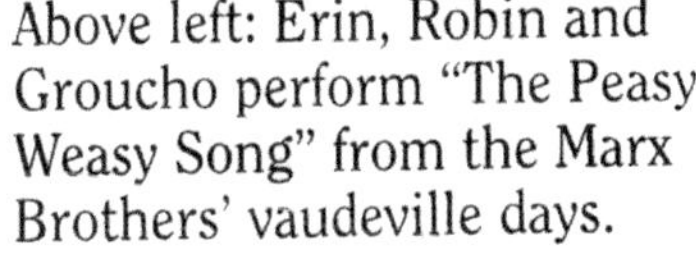

Above left: Erin, Robin and Groucho perform "The Peasy Weasy Song" from the Marx Brothers' vaudeville days.

Above right: Bob Hope exchanges quips with Groucho.

Right: the last photo of the extant Marx Brothers: Zeppo, Groucho and Gummo.

Frank Diernhammer

Above: Groucho in bed with "All in the Family" stars Sally Struthers and Carroll O'Connor at the conclusion of his 85th birthday party.

Right: Groucho and Mae West at Columbia Studios in 1975. On the left is Paul Novak, a former body-builder in Mae's nightclub act who became her right-hand man.

© 1975 Columbia Pictures

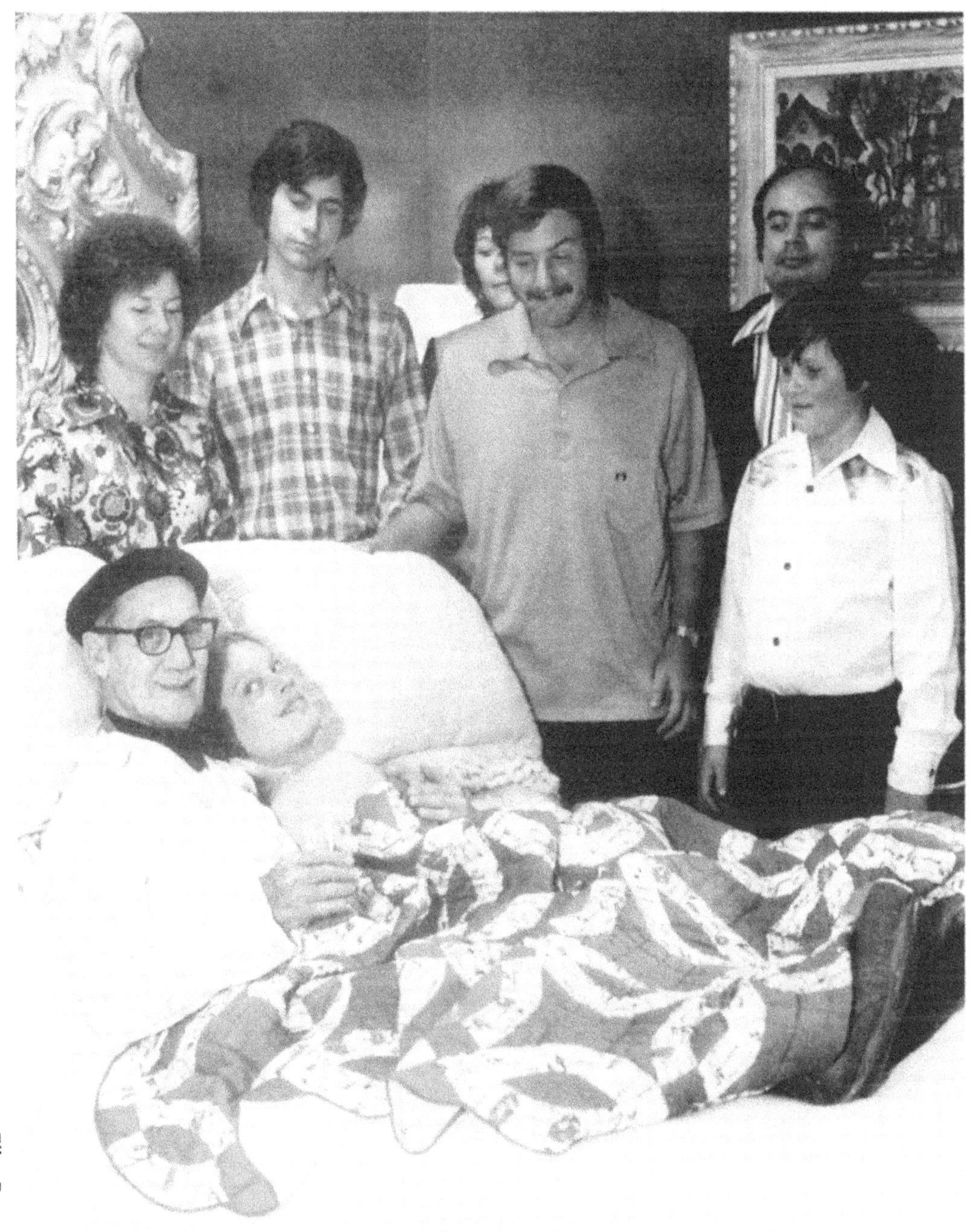

Ellen Berman

This shot of Groucho snuggling with Robin had been intended for the 1976 reprint of Groucho's first book *Beds*, but was ultimately pulled. Looking on are, from left to right: Barbara Odum, one of Groucho's nurses; Tom Wilhite, Groucho's publicist; me; Groucho's biographer, Hector Arce; and Barbara's son. Watching over everyone and everything–as usual–is Erin Fleming (rear).

Stan Adams

Left: one of my favorite pictures and a scene I often encountered: Groucho relaxing in his pajamas, enjoying a good book.

Above: Jack Lemmon and Groucho discuss the finer points of cigar smoking at a 1976 charity event while George Jessel looks on (or off) sporting his usual, infectious grin.

Right: George Burns, Bob Hope and Groucho kid around during a break in the taping of a 1976 Hope special.

Richard Berman

NBC

One of the last pictures ever taken of Groucho, early in 1977. Groucho poses in his yard beneath a Hirschfeld-inspired sign, which had been used as set dressing during a guest shot on Bill Cosby's variety show in 1973. Not long after this picture was taken, Groucho would be hospitalized for a broken hip, which would ultimately lead to his death on August 19th at the age of 86.

Twenty Two

One of Groucho's longtime friends was author Sidney Sheldon. Although he's known primarily as a writer of popular fiction, Sheldon had a lengthy career as a screenwriter, winning an Oscar for his script to the 1947 Cary Grant comedy, *The Bachelor and the Bobby Soxer* (and beating out Ruth Gordon and Garson Kanin for *A Double Life* and Charlie Chaplin for *Monsieur Verdoux*). It was only in later years that he came to be known as someone who specialized in somewhat trashy—but highly successful—novels.

In March of 1976, Sheldon came out with a novel entitled *A Stranger in the Mirror.* It's the story of a veteran comedian who is taken in by a vain, ambitious younger woman who tries to use the aging entertainer as a stepping stone to stardom. Since her movie career never quite takes off, she becomes the comedian's dutiful wife. In the process she alienates the comic's family and friends and exacts revenge on those whom she feels have wronged her. When the actor has a crippling stroke, she gains respect for her unswerving attentiveness to his every need.

Sound familiar? Yep, it's just like that script I'd started to write for Bill Froug's screenwriting class—but *besides* that. Lest you consider the resemblance to Groucho and Erin purely coincidental, here is the dedication at the beginning of *A Stranger in the Mirror*:

"The art of making others laugh is surely a wondrous gift from the gods. I affectionately dedicate this book to the comedians, the men and women who have that gift and share it with us. And to one of them in particular: my daughter's godfather, Groucho."

Kinda hard to ignore the connection, once you read something like that. Obviously the book doesn't purport to be any sort of accurate depiction of Erin and Groucho—and Sheldon denied that it had been based on them—but the inspiration is readily apparent. There are, however, a number of differences between the characters in *A Stranger in the Mirror* and those at 1083 Hillcrest.

For one, the fictional comedian, Toby Temple, is known primarily for playing nightclubs, which was something Groucho never did. For another, Temple is famous for being well endowed, which seems to have been a physical trait borrowed from Milton Berle if we can believe Hollywood lore. And finally, when Temple has a second stroke, his ambitious wife, Jill Castle, pushes him into the pool in his wheelchair rather than continuing to look after him. Temple drowns and the death is ruled an accident.

Startlingly, that last incident has its genesis in an actual Erin/Groucho encounter that took place in March of 1974, shortly after his appearance at UCLA. Groucho was swimming out to one end of his pool, but when he started to swim back he became exhausted and began to sink. Erin dived in and pulled him out of the pool, thus saving his life. It's interesting to note that Sheldon seems to have taken what had in reality been one of Erin Fleming's rare acts of genuine heroism and turned it into an act of murderous villainy.

If Sheldon's book, with its unmistakable dedication, was meant to be a wake-up call to Groucho, it fell on deaf eyes: Groucho never read it. One might assume that Erin would have flown into an uncontrollable rage upon the book's publication, hired a team of high-priced lawyers, and attempted to sue Sidney Sheldon for every cent he had, claiming she'd been libeled. The fact that her suit would've been virtually groundless would never have stood in her way if she wanted to go after Sheldon. Instead she shrugged it off, commenting, "It's just a novel." Once again there was no second-guessing Erin's response to a situation.

On March 23, only a few days after *A Stranger in the Mirror* began appearing in bookstores, Groucho was given the Sunair Humanitarian Award in the International Ballroom of the Beverly Hilton Hotel. As fate would have it, I happened to be seated at the same table as Sidney Sheldon and his wife, Jorja. When Erin came around to our table, Sheldon asked her what she'd thought of the book. All she said was, "I'm sorry, Sidney, but I just haven't had a chance to read it yet."

Also at our table were Hector Arce; Arthur Whitelaw, who had produced the play *Minnie's Boys* on Broadway; Carol Kane, who had just been nominated for Best Actress for her performance in *Hester Street*; and Groucho's personal physician, Dr. Morley Kert, who would gain a certain measure of notoriety the following year during the bitter conservatorship battle between Erin and Arthur.

The toastmaster for this fund-raising dinner was, inevitably, George Jessel.The dais of celebrities who had agreed to say a few words on Groucho's behalf included Irwin Allen, Red Buttons, George Fenneman, Jane Fonda, Redd Foxx, Sally Kellerman, Jack Lemmon, Zeppo Marx, Rosalind Russell and columnist Earl Wilson (substituting, ironically, for another Wilson—Flip—who had to cancel).

Jessel started things off on an inadvertently humorous note by referring to Groucho's devoted manager-companion as *Erin Flynn*. Most people didn't seem to notice, but his flub caused a visible clenching of Erin's teeth as she forced herself to smile during Jessel's "tribute" to her efforts. Then Jessel put everyone else in an uncomfortable mood by pulling a tattered piece of paper out of his tuxedo jacket and reading a lengthy poem he'd written about the American flag, entitled "It's Only a Scrap of Cloth." The gist of his poem was that, yes, it may only be a scrap of cloth, yet he would gladly lay down his life for it.

I'm sure it must've been the high point of the evening for Jane Fonda.

Most of the testimonials resembled stand-up routines rather than personal thoughts on Groucho, but Hector assisted in the preparation of some of the commentary, which kept things reasonably appropriate. Red Buttons did his famous "never had a testimonial dinner" bit, which went over nicely.

As was the case at the USC tribute, Groucho seemed weak and somewhat distracted, but he appeared to be enjoying himself, basking in the glow of all the kind words. I was beginning to get the feeling that each of these honorary dinners was certain to be his last and that we'd better make the best of it. Of course, I'd felt the same way after witnessing *An Evening with Groucho* at the Dorothy Chandler Pavilion—and that had been three and a half years earlier!

In the spring, both *Beds* and *The Secret Word Is Groucho* were published. I've already detailed Erin's displeasure over the cover of *Beds*, but the arrival of *The Secret Word Is Groucho* was a much happier occasion. It was decided that there would be an official publication party at Groucho's, attended by the former "You Bet Your Life" staff as well as other celebrities and members of the press.

This was the party at which Groucho could only bring himself to ask Jerry Fielding how he was. George Fenneman, Bernie Smith, Bob Dwan, Jack Meakin and Howard Harris also attended, and before departing everyone was given a copy of the new book, personally inscribed by Groucho and Hector. It was a kick to see my name in the acknowledgments: Groucho offered "special thanks" for my contributions and referred to me as the "keeper of the Groucho Marx Archives."

I also had the pleasure of meeting Edgar Bergen at this party. I was a little disappointed, though not surprised, that he'd decided to leave Charlie McCarthy and Mortimer Snerd behind. Although Bergen had once appeared on "You Bet Your Life" alongside his awkwardly adolescent daughter, Candice, his main contribution to the book had been sharing his thoughts on "Do You Trust Your Wife?"—a game show Bergen had hosted that had been directly inspired by the success of "You Bet Your Life."

The show had been designed to humorously test how well two couples knew their spouses. Although "Do You Trust Your Wife?" only lasted from 1956 through early 1957 with Edgar Bergen as host, it was revived in late 1957 and lasted through 1962, with a new title—"Who Do You Trust?"—and a new host, Johnny Carson.

Also in attendance that evening was director Vincente Minnelli, whose memoirs Hector had cowritten two years earlier. I happened to have been walking past Minnelli when one of the partygoers asked him a predictable question: "So how's Liza?" Without hesitation, Minnelli answered, "Well, as you may know, she has a very painful menstrual cycle." Understandably, this left the questioner nonplussed; all he could do was smile and wander off to strike up another, presumably less awkward conversation. Minnelli's remark remains one of the strangest comments I've ever heard a father make about a daughter.

Groucho was pleased with how *The Secret Word Is Groucho* had turned out, and he took to handing out copies to whichever friends of his happened to be dropping by the house. As a result, Erin put the remaining carton of books on my desk along with a typically peculiar note that read, "Steve—Please *hide* books from Julius. He has a tendency to give them to mosquitoes and gnats. E." I didn't realize Groucho's friends could be classified as mosquitoes and gnats (except perhaps Mr. Perrin, who spelled his first name somewhat differently).

Another book was published in the spring of 1976, although its significance here has nothing to do with its subject matter. It was called *Goldwyn* and it was written by Arthur Marx. In the course of publicizing the book, Arthur had given an interview in which he mentioned how Groucho hadn't wanted Totie Fields to play Minnie in *Minnie's Boys* because she appeared "too Jewish" to be their mother (eventually, Minnie was played by Shelley Winters). In the same interview, Arthur had commented, "I'm out of the will and, as far as I know, so are my sisters, Melinda and Miriam. She brainwashed Groucho. We all got along great until Erin came into the picture."

In another interview, this time with columnist James Bacon, Arthur kidded that since Groucho had deemed Totie Fields to be too Jewish to have played Minnie Marx, he must be anti-Semitic.

Infuriated by the one-two punch of Arthur's comments about her and about Groucho's alleged anti-Semitism, Erin summoned Bacon to lunch one day along with Arthur Whitelaw, who had produced *Minnie's Boys* on Broadway. Whitelaw explained to Bacon how beneficial Erin had been to Groucho, and Erin added some choice words about what a rotten son Arthur had been.

At one point Groucho began to weep, commenting, "He's no good." Erin beseeched Groucho not to cry: "You'll make me cry, too!" As usual, Groucho took his cue from Erin and stopped crying for the time being, although from that point on he would occasionally begin to cry for no *apparent* reason.

In truth Arthur had not been taken out of the will at all, although his presumption almost became a self-fulfilling prophecy. Shortly after the James Bacon lunch, Groucho sent his attorney a letter indicating that he was going to be changing his will so that Arthur's portion of the inheritance would instead go to the United Jewish Appeal. He'd show his son just how anti-Semitic *he* was. Groucho never did get around to putting this change into effect, but it underscores just how acrimonious the Erin/Arthur/Groucho situation had gotten by 1976.

While we're on the subject of *Minnie's Boys* and Erin's influence, I want to bring up a point. There is a common perception that by 1971 Groucho was virtually unhireable, the Marx Brothers were totally forgotten and that Erin single-handedly restored Groucho and his brothers to the nation's consciousness. This is not entirely accurate.

Minnie's Boys, which concerns the Marx family in their early vaudeville days, had been in the planning stages as far back as 1968 and had been written by Arthur Marx and his partner, Robert Fisher, in 1969. There had been numerous pre-Broadway problems involving cast and script. As a matter of fact, S.J. Perelman had been called in to help during out-of-town tryouts. As Perelman commented in a letter to his friend, the great theatrical caricaturist Al Hirschfeld, "Night before last, I was sped by Rolls-Royce and uniformed chauffeur to the bedside of a sick musical called *Minnie's Boys.* Plot there was none, and laughter less."

The play opened in March of 1970, and although it folded after several months it has continued to be performed in amateur productions ever since. The point is, there was clearly enough interest in the Marx Brothers more than a year before Erin had even *met* Groucho to mount a full-blown Broadway musical about them, regardless of its lack of success.

Also, in going through Groucho's film collection, I ran across a print of his appearance on "The Dick Cavett Show" from September of 1969, two years before Erin made her debut in Groucho's life. At one point on the show Groucho comments, "I understand there's quite a renaissance of the Marx Brothers' movies around the country now." This is met with enthusiastic applause. Then, after some witty repartee with Cavett, Groucho says, "This is a song from a picture called *A Day at the Circus,* which we did at MGM. I sang this in a Pullman car."

At that point an enormous noise erupts from the obviously youthful audience—a cacophony of screaming, whistling and wild applause. Over all the noise Groucho says, "Now why are you applauding a Pullman car? There *aren't* any more Pullman cars!"

All Groucho had to do was mention a song from *At the Circus,* which he always referred to by its shooting title, *A Day at the Circus,* and the overly enthusiastic crowd immediately knew he was referring to "Lydia the Tattooed Lady." How did they know about this obscure ditty, which had come from a film that had been released before most of them were even born?

The anti-establishment college crowd of the sixties had clearly taken the iconoclastic Groucho to its heart some years before Erin had entered the picture. Although *Animal Crackers* wouldn't be seen again until after our committee triggered its rerelease in 1974, the other dozen Marx Brothers films were frequently run in revival houses and film classes from the late sixties on. Also, the picture book *Why a Duck?* had been in the works for more than a year before Erin had come to work as Groucho's secretary. It had sold extremely well, which had nothing whatsoever to do with any efforts on Erin Fleming's part.

It's true that Erin contributed mightily to Groucho's popularity and that he might never have received his French medal or honorary Oscar had it not been for her persistence, for better or for worse, in pushing Groucho back into the limelight. But what I discovered as I continued to assemble his archives was that the elements of Groucho's "renaissance" were firmly in place long before Erin appeared on the scene. She didn't *create* the tidal wave of recognition that Groucho was enjoying, but she certainly rode it with great skill.

On May 24, Groucho appeared on a Merv Griffin show that had been designed as a salute to the late Ernie Kovacs. The other guests included Edie Adams, Milton Berle and Mickey Rooney. On it, Groucho sang a couple of songs and said a few words about what a talented man Kovacs had been.

Although no one knew it at the time, Groucho had just made his last full-fledged television appearance.

TWENTY THREE

Shortly before graduating, I decided to pay one last visit to the UCLA Research Library and perhaps give in to the temptation to swipe that 1932 *Time* magazine with the Marx Brothers on the cover. When I'd seen it a few years earlier, I'd resisted the urge to snatch it because I felt it should remain in place to satisfy future generations of Marx Brothers fans. But with some strange, twisted sense that I was somehow entitled to it, and since it was so difficult to locate another one, I intended to commit this small crime and be done with it.

I entered the library trying to act nonchalant, located the bound volumes of *Time,* and flipped to the 1932 issues. To my shock and disappointment, the magazine was there but the cover had been crudely sliced off and was now missing. Someone had gotten to it before me!

I've always felt that there was a moral to this story. I'm just not certain what it is.

In June of 1976 I graduated from UCLA's Motion Picture/Television department with a Bachelor of Arts degree. To be honest, the sheer magnitude of what I had experienced and was continuing to experience at Groucho's had eclipsed most of whatever it was I'd been trying to accomplish at school. I had officially let go of History and now, after two years in the MP/TV department and two years of working in Groucho's house, I was firmly convinced that my future lay in the entertainment field, most logically as a writer. My degree, however, did not entitle me to any sort of entree into the motion picture or television industry. It didn't even entitle me to a discount at the U.A. Westwood.

I moved back to the family house in Tarzana and began to contemplate what exactly I was going to do with the remainder of my life now that I was a college grad. Going to school, regardless of its drawbacks, had been a source of safety for me for sixteen years (seventeen, if you count kindergarten). The grade levels may have changed and the schools shifted location, but it was still the same basic process of going from class to class, doing the work, getting graded and moving on to the next level. It didn't require a great deal of thinking ahead, except in terms of what I was going to do for summer vacation until school started up again in the fall.

Since I saw no point in pursuing a master's degree and since it was unlikely that my part-time work at Groucho's was suddenly going to mushroom into full-time work again, I knew I had to start thinking about a job. Even if I hadn't come to that conclusion on my own, my father would've come to it *for* me. He was pressuring me big time, suggesting at one point that I go to work at a nearby tire store simply because he'd seen a Help Wanted sign out front. That's why I spent four years at a major university: to sell tires.

In truth, it was unrealistic to think that I was going to be magically hired to write for some TV show simply because I was reasonably intelligent, had graduated from UCLA and hung out with Groucho Marx. No, there was no getting around it: I was going to have to get a *job*-job.

As if that realization weren't stressful enough, shortly after I'd moved back into the comfort of our home Dad informed me that since Penny's two daughters were out on their own, he and Penny were going to be putting the house up for sale and moving into a condominium in Beverly Hills. Consequently, I would have to find my own apartment. And pay for it all by myself. And take Patches the cat, now a stately thirteen, with me. I had only just begun to feel how good it was to be back home and now I was going to have to move out and find a job in order to support myself? I felt miserably ill-equipped to handle that much responsibility that soon.

As it turned out, the house wouldn't be sold for several months, so I was able to enjoy my final "summer vacation" at home before adulthood kicked in for good. Daryl and I spent a lot of time in our swimming pool plotting our assault on the entertainment industry, and I continued to work at Groucho's during part of the week and on weekends, just as I had when school had been in session.

Groucho was still spouting Grouchoisms, to be sure, although they were getting fewer and farther between. One day he was talking about women and aging. At one point he expressed his philosophy: "You're only as young as the girl you feel." In discussing one young lady in particular, Groucho said, "She had hair all the way down her back. None on her head, just down her back." Hector asked Groucho if his wives had had any common traits. Groucho said, "I married my wives for their beauty. None of them had anything upstairs, except another man from time to time."

That year, a new brand of cigarettes called Tramps appeared on the market. Rather than featuring pictures of famous hookers, the package showed Charlie Chaplin in his traditional baggy-pants outfit. One of Groucho's nurses was reading a magazine that featured an ad for Tramps on the back cover. Groucho noticed it and said, "Chaplin once told me, 'I wish I could talk like you,' because when he started talking on-screen he wasn't funny anymore. Now he's making cigarettes." A sad commentary on the fickleness of fame.

Groucho was still being asked to make public appearances, although with much less frequency. One of them was at the Student Academy Awards ceremony in late June. As usual, Groucho wasn't particularly interested in sitting quietly while someone else was trying to be serious:

Speaker: "On behalf of the Academy, each winner will receive a thousand dollars."

Groucho: *"Cash?"*

Speaker: "Er. . . now then, these young filmmakers—"

Groucho: "Hey, what about the *old* filmmakers?"

Speaker: "—will take their place—"

Groucho: "They're not gonna take *my* place!"

Speaker (*exasperated*): "Nobody wants to, Groucho."

Well, if you're going to invite Groucho Marx to be your guest of honor, you're going to have to expect that kind of behavior.

Around this time, two new faces were added to the Marx household. John Ballow was still preparing the meals during the week, but since Robin Heaney had left earlier in the year to pursue other dreams—one of the few employees to have left on good terms and of her own volition—a weekend cook was needed. After a few interim chefs, Erin settled on Jules Plourde, a jovial French-Canadian with an infectious laugh and a weakness for Johnny Ray songs. As a sort of counterpoint to John Ballow's disco interpretations, Jules would launch into all-out, gut-wrenching renditions of "Cry" and "The Little White Cloud That Cried" while he was preparing meals.

The other new member of the household staff was a young Cal Arts student named Henry Golas. Since Henry was familiar with the mechanics of film and projectors, he had been hired to clean and sort Groucho's movies as well as screen them in the den from time to time when Groucho wanted to watch something or show it to friends. Andy Marx had handled such matters before then, but he was moving on to other things and had been spending less and less time at his grandfather's house. I could barely thread a needle, much less a projector, so I welcomed the addition of someone who could handle the technical end of things.

Although Henry became a semiregular around the house in the summer of 1976, he had done a few jobs for Erin since 1975, when he had audaciously sent Groucho a telegram telling him he was a sincere admirer and asking if it would be possible to have dinner with him. Not having gotten a response, Henry simply showed up on the doorstep one day when Erin was conveniently out of town and told John Ballow that he was a friend of Groucho's.

John, with his usual lack of discretion, immediately provided Henry with Groucho's phone number. Armed with that prize, Henry called Groucho's house, talked his way past the nurse, chatted briefly with Groucho and actually managed to wrangle a dinner invitation. Although I didn't necessarily approve of his tactics, I could certainly relate to his strong desire to meet Groucho.

By the time the dinner arrangements had been made, Erin had returned from her trip. Astonishingly, she didn't cancel the rendezvous or even question Henry's credentials. Instead she allowed him to come to dinner at Groucho's, where she learned of his familiarity with the vagaries of motion-picture equipment. Soon she began setting aside certain technical tasks for him.

In the summer Henry began working at Groucho's more regularly. He was also working part-time at Disneyland as a safari guide on the Jungle Cruise, navigating boats through dangerous, crocodile-infested waters. Depending on the atmosphere at Groucho's house on any given day, it was very likely a toss-up which setting was the more colorful. On occasion, they may actually have been interchangeable.

Although Henry and I became good friends almost immediately, I began to worry that Erin might be grooming him to replace me. After two years of working there, I reasoned, the novelty of having me around the house had worn off, and now Henry was the fair-haired kid. I'd seen so many others come and go at Erin's discretion (or lack of it), it was only a matter of time until my number was up. Then I started to worry that Erin's rampant paranoia was somehow catching. After all, there had been no outward signs of dissatisfaction with my work. Of course, since when had that been a prerequisite for dismissal at Groucho's house?

As it turned out, my instincts hadn't betrayed me. Since I wasn't working very often at Groucho's and since I needed to start pulling in some more money, I asked Erin if it would be possible to get a raise. I was still performing the same duties I always had, I reminded her. Why should I earn less money simply because I'd gotten more efficient? Erin told me that she'd check with Groucho's accountant to see if such a thing was possible. Instead, as Henry later confided in me, Erin had gone straight to Henry and offered to show him how to do my job. Out of respect and friendship for me, Henry had told her that he really didn't have the knowledge or the time for it, what with going to school and working and all. For turning down Erin's offer and for other things, I'm grateful to Henry.

I retained my status as Groucho's secretary and archivist, but Erin said there was no way they could afford a raise. Hector later told me that Erin's rationale for turning down the raise had been to prod me into trying out my wings now that I was a college graduate. According to Hector, Erin said she had done it for my own good.

Hector didn't buy it either.

As Erin became more irrational and Groucho less lucid, the house took on an increasingly uncomfortable atmosphere. Nevertheless, after two years it was still a fascinating place to be and I didn't really want to have to leave for any reason short of Groucho's death. I was handcuffed to this roller coaster and determined to ride it out to the bitter end.

Henry, Hector and I became a sort of poor man's Three Musketeers, hanging out together and conferring with one another both at the house and away from it, about all things Marxian, Flemish and otherwise. We kept in continuous touch about what was happening so that if only one of us was at the house when something noteworthy took place, the others learned of it almost immediately. I was glad to have both of them to help me sort things out. It took someone who was a part of that strange world to fully understand the complexities of life at Groucho's.

Also during the summer of 1976, I met my pen pal, Diane

Szasz, in person. Our correspondence had continued at a feverish pace and we had also taken to calling each other on the phone from time to time. Now, with my having graduated and with her in the midst of summer vacation, she thought it might be nice to come out to California from Ohio and meet me.

I shan't bore you with the lurid details. Suffice it to say that we hit it off in person just as smashingly as we had through the mail, and our friendship blossomed into what would have to be, for the time being, a long-distance romance. Although Diane had to return to Ohio after a week or so, we made plans for her to return to L.A. in November, time and money permitting. I was sorry to see her go but encouraged that we'd be seeing each other in a few months. Beyond that, it was anybody's guess. This was certainly an interesting fringe benefit of working as Groucho's secretary: A simple fan letter had resulted in romance.

This time, however, I was not going to let Zeppo anywhere near her.

Twenty Four

In August of 1976 I finally got up the nerve to write Dick Cavett a letter. He had been out to L.A. in the spring to shoot a special about Hollywood's back lots and had stopped by Groucho's to have dinner. To my frustration, it had been on a day when I hadn't been working there. I so wanted the opportunity of telling him how much my friends and I had enjoyed *Cavett.*

I was trying to think of what to put in the letter to distinguish me from other fans. Obviously the fact that I worked for Groucho set me apart from most, but it wasn't enough. I was thumbing through my copy of *Cavett* when I came to the part where he talked about meeting Groucho for the first time, after George S. Kaufman's funeral in 1961. Cavett wrote that he'd scribbled down some short notes to remind himself of the funny things Groucho had said to him that day, but that much to his frustration he could no longer remember what the cryptic notes meant.

According to Cavett's book, one note said, "Harry Ruby's envelopes" and another said, "Kaufman and seduction in car." I wasn't positive that I knew what he'd meant by them either, but having worked for Groucho and heard so many stories from the master himself, I thought I might have some good possibilities. So I drafted a letter to the noted talk-show host and took a stab at deciphering his long-lost Groucho notes.

In collating Groucho's correspondence, I'd noticed that Harry Ruby had a large number of rubber stamps that he would use liberally in the margins of letters and on the fronts and backs of envelopes. One of them said, "PARDON MY TYPING." Another said, "...AND MY SPELLING." And a third said, "NO ANSWER REQUIRED!" I offered that as my theory as to what "Harry Ruby's envelopes" meant.

With regard to "Kaufman and seduction in car," I had heard Groucho tell a rather earthy story about Kaufman, some of which took place in the backseat of a car. With some concern that I was being a little vulgar in my inaugural letter, I offered Groucho's story: "Many years ago, Kaufman was fooling around with an actress named Natalie Schaefer. One day, she and Kaufman had lunch out and she ordered a club sandwich, while he ordered cream of tomato soup. During lunch, she reached over and, without asking, stole a spoonful of his soup. Kaufman was annoyed, so he ordered a whole new bowl for himself. After lunch, she and Kaufman got into a limousine. No sooner did he have both arms—and legs—around her, than she said, 'George, dear, you're considerably nicer now than you were at lunch,' to which Kaufman replied, 'There's a big difference between fucking and cream of tomato soup.'"

Yes, this was the same Natalie Schaefer who went on to play Mrs. Howell on "Gilligan's Island" some years later.

Warily, I put my letter into an envelope and sent it off to the Manhattan address I'd copied out of Groucho's address book.

A few weeks later I received an ivory-colored envelope with a New York postmark and "DICK CAVETT" embossed on the back. Inside I did *not* find my letter returned with red-inked corrections, as I'd feared. Instead there was a note that read, "Dear Steve, You were uncannily on-the-nose with your two guesses. Leaving for London in two hours, so this is hastily contrived. Write again, and I will answer again and better. Yours, Dick."

Thus began our correspondence.

In fairness to the reader (and to Dick Cavett), I should say a few words about what he represented back then. He has taken a considerable amount of kidding and criticism over the years, some of it deserved, for his tendency to name-drop and his penchant for stopping a guest's narrative in order to interject a witticism or an incident from his own experience. There are some people who simply cannot stand to watch Dick Cavett under any circumstances. To each his gout, as the French say.

I view Cavett's shows more as conversations than as interviews, and I prefer that he do more than just ask questions and listen to answers. I am genuinely interested in hearing what *he* has to say, whether it's a funny remark or an obscure piece of information that has some bearing on the topic of conversation. I would not have the same interest in hearing what, say, Merv or Arsenio or Conan had to add under the same circumstances.

Pressure was put on Cavett early on to soft-pedal his comparatively intellectual approach to guest selection and conversational topics in order to reach a broader audience, since on occasion he had actually gotten higher Nielsen ratings than Johnny Carson. But Cavett made the conscious decision to remain true to his own tastes, assuming that those who felt similarly would gravitate toward him. He refused to sell out just to attract more viewers, and in so doing he sacrificed being a bigger success in television, in order to be able to continue doing things the way he wanted to do them.

Nevertheless, from 1968 until 1975, Cavett's ABC show was the last word in hip, topical conversation, much as Letterman's is today. (Carson and Griffin were seen as appealing more to older, middle-class Americans.) As a result of Cavett's favorable reputation and obvious intelligence—S.J. Perelman said Cavett was probably the only talk-show host who actually *read* the books his guests had written—he attracted an eclectic assortment of personalities who might otherwise have shied away from the talk-show circuit. These included Marlon Brando, Katharine Hepburn, Woody Allen, Gore Vidal, Noel Coward, John Lennon, Norman Mailer, Janis Joplin, Fred Astaire, Salvador Dali, Laurence Olivier and Jimi Hendrix, just to name a dozen.

Groucho's admiration for Cavett caused his stock to rise considerably in my mind. Groucho had taken something of a paternal interest in the young man from Nebraska during Cavett's initial efforts as a nightclub comic and early-morning talk-show host. If Groucho thought so much of him, there must be something that set him apart from other names in his profession.

So, long before the Rick Moranis parodies and the AT&T commercials, Dick Cavett represented to a great many viewers something of a classy, intelligent oasis in a sea of television mediocrity. Once again, I prefer to side with the European point of view which states that an artist is as good as the best work he ever accomplished, not just the most recent.

At the time our correspondence began, his ABC show had ended and his PBS show had not yet begun. I was initially conservative in the things I divulged in my letters, since I did not know his personal feelings about Erin Fleming or the questionable wisdom in allowing Groucho to continue making public appearances. Cavett wrote me that I "may speak freely" about such matters, so gradually I felt more comfortable in discussing what might otherwise have been considered delicate issues.

In September the Tarzana house was officially put on the market and the clock started ticking on getting a job and finding an apartment. Hal Kanter arranged for Daryl and me to meet with producer James Komack, with whom Hal was working on "Chico and the Man." Komack had a writer's apprenticeship program and there was a chance he might hire us.

We went to Komack's office armed with a variety of writing samples, but he only wanted to see sitcom scripts. The closest thing we had were those Carol Burnett sketches. As it turned out, there were only two slots open in the program and we didn't get either of them, but it was exciting to have actually "taken a meeting" with a famous television producer.

Eventually Hector came to my rescue on the job front. His friend, Stanley Musgrove, had an office at Universal and said that if I filled out an employment application he'd see to it that it was given special attention. I filled it out and was told that there was a year-long waiting list for the mailroom—the job Hector and I figured would be a good starting-off point.

The only position available was in the steno pool, which required taking a typing test. Hector didn't see how working in the typing pool was going to help me, but I was desperate for a job and figured it was worth a try. I wasn't sure if I'd be able to pass the fifty-five words-per-minute requirement, but somehow I managed. As a result I was hired to work in the Universal typing pool from eleven in the morning until eight at night, Monday through Friday. Some "special attention."

And I almost didn't get the job.

The woman in charge, Muriel Gregory, had been working in steno since 1938, when Boris Karloff and W.C. Fields were still making movies on the lot. When it came time for my interview, I stressed how in addition to having been Groucho's secretary I had also helped out on three books: *The Secret Word Is Groucho*, *Beds* and *The GrouchoPhile*, which was due out in a couple of months. Rather than clinching the deal, it led Muriel to conclude that I was—that horrid word—"overqualified," so I actually had to fight to be given the chance to sit there and type all day.

Despite the monotony of typing scripts for "Columbo," "Kojak" and "The Bionic Woman" every day, it was fascinating to be working on an actual studio lot. Instead of gabbing with other typists during lunch breaks, I tried to do as much exploring as I could without getting into trouble. One of my favorite places to hang out was inside *The Phantom of the Opera* stage, which still had the removable balcony seats that had been constructed for the 1925 Lon Chaney film.

In addition to television episodes, certain feature scripts would come our way. It was fun to try and second-guess which would be hits and which would be misses on the basis of a portion of the script. I had a fairly good eye for spotting winners and knew from page one that *Animal House* would be a big hit. Conversely, when a script about Howard Hughes getting into a stranger's car and singing "Santa's Souped-Up Sleigh" came my way, I smelled a stinker. *Melvin and Howard* went on to win an Oscar for Best Screenplay, so I guess my *Chorus Line* instincts were still around.

It struck me, as I typed scripts from eleven to eight each day, that some of them were very poorly written. This was both discouraging and encouraging—discouraging because it meant they were paying out hundreds of thousands of dollars for true mediocrity, and encouraging because it meant you didn't have to be George S. Kaufman in order to sell a script. I filed this revelation away for future reference.

While I often saw current television stars on the lot—Lindsay Wagner, Telly Savalas, Lee Majors and Robert Blake, to name a few—it never really rang my chimes since they weren't veterans of the Golden Age of Hollywood that I so revered. Occasionally, however, an older actor or actress would guest star on a series, and I'd have the opportunity of glimpsing, or if I was lucky, meeting them.

I was able to meet Lauren Bacall when she appeared on "The Rockford Files" and Fred Astaire—one of my idols—when he guest starred on, of all the unlikely programs, "Battlestar Galactica." And one afternoon I was walking past the commissary when the side door flew open and a tan, fit Cary Grant strode out, beaming a smile right at me. I felt like a middle-aged housewife in curlers: "Gosh, Cary Grant *smiled* at me!"

When I started at Universal, Alfred Hitchcock still had an office on the lot. I would often see him cruising through the main gate in his chauffeur-driven, dark green Lincoln at precisely 11:20 each morning. He was rumored to be in preproduction on a film called *A Short Night*, but most people assumed that, at his age and in his fading condition, it was probably never going to happen. Nevertheless he came into his office almost every day, rain or shine, put in a couple of hours of work and correspondence, and consumed a catered lunch before heading homeward.

On the apartment front, I was terrified that I was going to be in over my head rent-wise. Daryl and I had initially planned on getting a place together, but since he was unsure of his finances he didn't feel compelled to get his own place just yet. So I found the top half of a crumbling duplex in North Hollywood for $150 a month. The good news was that they'd let me keep Patches and it was only a few blocks away from the house that Hector was renting, so I didn't feel as stranded as I'd feared. But it was still a big adjustment.

I was working at Universal from Monday through Friday and at Groucho's on weekends, still managing to keep up with the fan mail and memorabilia. The latter would be added to from time to time as Erin authorized the acquisition of additional photographs and posters from some of the Hollywood bookstores. It was a strange feeling, going from the anonymous, cog-in-a-wheel atmosphere of the Universal steno pool during the week to Groucho's spacious Beverly Hills home on weekends. If nothing else, it meant I'd be able to handle my rent each month without fear of bankruptcy.

In September Groucho was set to make an appearance on, of all things, "The Donny and Marie Show." I don't think Erin gave much thought to the occasional offers that came Groucho's way. If it was legitimate and the money was good, she tended to OK it. I don't believe she stopped to assess whether or not the appearance was an appropriate one for Groucho. And by the fall of 1976, it's unlikely that he should've been making *any* television appearances at all.

For production reasons the finale was taped first, with Groucho participating. Then Erin became upset with how the show was going and told Groucho that they were leaving right then and there, before his solo spots could be taped. Consequently, when the show aired he appeared only in the finale, probably to the confusion of the viewing public. Whether their about-face was perceived as a reflection of Groucho's haziness or of Erin's fickleness, it didn't look good for either of them that they walked out in the middle of taping a popular prime-time variety show.

While Groucho's television work was becoming increasingly iffy, he could still be counted on for interesting dining-room conversation. In early September Groucho was discussing a bear act he'd seen in vaudeville.

Erin: "What sort of tricks did it do?"

Groucho: "You know, *bear* tricks. If they didn't do 'em, they fired the bears."

Erin: "Yes, but what *kinds* of tricks?"

Groucho: "Haven't you ever seen bears in a zoo?"

Erin: "Yes, but they didn't do any tricks."

Groucho: "Then they were lousy bears."

Around this time I met Maxine Marx, Chico's only daughter, who was visiting from New York. She bore a striking resemblance to her late father, and every so often she would get a certain crooked smile on her face that was positively uncanny. Maxine could be a little off-putting at first because she was very highly opinionated, but I liked her and enjoyed listening to her stories and her well-informed view on different aspects of Groucho's life.

Maxine had some harsh things to say about her uncle. She blamed Groucho for the breakup of the Marx Brothers in 1946 because, according to her, Groucho had listened to those around him who told him he should go solo. Maxine also said that growing up around Groucho could be very trying. Whenever she would wince at one of his puns he would snap at her, "How much do *you* make a week?!"

Maxine also had some interesting things to say about Groucho's older daughter, Miriam. According to Maxine, after Groucho and his first wife, Ruth, had divorced in 1942, Miriam had become the lady of the house. It had been Miriam who had introduced Groucho to one of her schoolmates, Kay, who would soon become Groucho's second wife. Miriam's "replacement" by Kay had been stressful enough, since she had to compete with her friend for her father's attention. But when baby Melinda was born to Kay and Groucho in 1946, Miriam more or less snapped, spiraling downward into a morass of drinking, expulsion from college and a host of other psychological and emotional problems.

Such was Maxine's assessment.

Shortly before Groucho's eighty-sixth birthday, a reporter came by to do yet another profile of the aging entertainer.

Accompanying us at the lunch table, as usual, was one of Groucho's young nurses.

Reporter: "Groucho, do you enjoy insulting people?"

Groucho: "I never insulted anyone. Just Hitler."

Reporter: "What did you say to him?"

Groucho: "I can't tell you in mixed company. So if you gentlemen will leave, I'll tell *her!*"

Unfortunately, the dining-room table was also the setting for many of Erin's fits of rage, which were occurring with greater frequency. And Groucho, sadly, was often the recipient of her fury. I remember an incident around this time, when Erin asked Groucho to tell some dinner guests a few funny anecdotes about the making of *A Night at the Opera.* Groucho thought for a moment, then said he couldn't come up with any.

Instead of shrugging it off and changing the subject, Erin flew into a rage, screaming at Groucho at the top of her lungs, "You stupid, senile old *bastard!*" Just because he couldn't think of some funny things that happened during *A Night at the Opera.* Everyone at the table was embarrassed for him. But above all, we just wished she'd stop doing things like that to the poor man.

Another time, Groucho began coughing at the table, because the strokes had made it difficult for him to swallow. Instead of being understanding of his condition and perhaps patting him on the back, she yelled, "Oh, *stop* that, Methuselah! You know I can't stand it when you do that!" She then told us to ignore him, that he was only doing it to get our attention.

Sure. Like that stroke he'd had on her birthday two years earlier.

The nurses told me that Erin's rantings caused Groucho's blood pressure to shoot up dangerously high and that he would sometimes become incontinent after a particularly upsetting incident. And then, as if it weren't heartbreaking enough to see her laying into him, Groucho would want to know what he could do to smooth things over. Whatever unkindnesses Groucho may have done to family and friends over the years, he didn't deserve to be treated this way, and it cut into me like knives whenever Erin would lose her temper and scream at him.

Groucho's eighty-sixth birthday party was a much less heralded affair than the one he'd had the year before, and it was probably just as well. He seemed to be getting weaker and foggier with each passing month. His walks were getting shorter, while his naps were getting longer. The party featured the usual odd blending of Groucho's old friends and Erin's new buddies, more the latter than the former by now. Ryan O'Neal was there along with his Oscar-winning daughter, Tatum. Groucho sang a few tunes from his repertoire, once again with Billy Marx at the keys, but his voice was barely above a whisper and there was clearly a more somber mood to the room than at his last birthday party.

Part of the evening's entertainment consisted of a lengthy magic act by The Great Amazo, the thirteen-year-old son of celebrity photographer Steve Schapiro—another of Erin's entourage. For one of his tricks, he asked a guest to pick a card, any card. After shuffling the deck, the chosen card appeared: the nine of clubs. People were starting to get fidgety by this point, especially the guest of honor himself. But The Great Amazo pushed onward, this time shredding a newspaper and then wadding it up in order to make it appear whole again. As he started to unfold the paper he exclaimed, "Well, what do you think we'll find?" A bored Groucho said, "The nine of clubs," effectively upstaging the magician and putting an end to his act.

It reminded me of a story Groucho told about when Houdini had been appearing at the Winter Garden Theater in New York in the twenties. Houdini did a trick that consisted of putting some needles and thread into his mouth and then spitting them out, strung together. Houdini would always select someone from the audience to come up and attest to the fact that there was nothing suspicious going on. Since Groucho was virtually unrecognizable without his greasepaint moustache, Houdini had picked him as his stooge, thinking him an average theatergoer. With great panache, Houdini announced, "Look into my mouth and tell me what you see!" Groucho looked inside and said, "Pyorrhea!" thus stealing the thunder from the legendary magician.

For me the highlight of Groucho's eighty-sixth birthday party was Carroll O'Connor, whom I had never really spent much time with at earlier get-togethers. Since there wasn't anyplace else to sit, he ended up taking the empty seat next to me. We spent considerable time discussing television, "All in the Family" and how certain shows can get away with more controversial topics if they're a hit in the ratings. As he was walking out the door, O'Connor turned and said to me, "By the way, it was nice having dinner with you." Likewise.

Also in October, after the finished manuscript of *The GrouchoPhile* had been submitted to the publisher, Hector was asked by his agent if he'd be interested in writing Groucho's official biography. He was hesitant to say yes. After all, Groucho's previous collaborators had been dismissed as pipsqueaks and impostors. Plus, Hector had never intended to make a career of writing books about the Marx Brothers. He'd just stopped by, a year and a half earlier, to jot down some of Groucho's thoughts on interior decorator Peter Shore. Three books later he was faced with the prospect of writing Groucho's life story.

It was impressed upon Hector what a unique perspective he had since he'd been in and around Groucho's house for so long. So, almost reluctantly, he agreed to begin work on Groucho's authorized biography. Although he would be handling most of the writing chores himself, Hector told me he could use my help in keeping the facts straight and in interviewing some of the people in Groucho's life when the time came for their input. I looked forward to working with Hector on yet another volume.

On October 31, a tribute to symphony conductor Zubin Mehta was held at the Ambassador Hotel. Lenny Atkins, who had married Irene Kahn after Arthur Marx had divorced her, was chairman of the event. Amid the artists on the program that night was Groucho. With Grace Kahn at the piano, he launched into "Oh, How That Woman Could Cook," which Grace had cowritten with her late husband, Gus.

Although Groucho still had a song or two left in him for friends at home, this would be his final performance before the public.

TWENTY FIVE

The GrouchoPhile was published in early November. Although Groucho was pleased with how it turned out, there was no book-launching party this time around. Erin liked the book except for one minor detail. Toward the front was a reproduction of a piece of Groucho's stationery, and on it Groucho had written his "You Bet Your Life" catchphrase, "Tell 'em Groucho sent you." On the flip side there was another copy of Groucho's stationery on which he had written: "This book is dedicated to my secretary. To Erin Fleming from Groucho." (I wasn't insulted, incidentally, that Groucho continued to refer to Erin as his secretary. He never stopped introducing her as such, despite my official status as the occupant of that esteemed position.)

Erin was upset about the inclusion of the second inscription. Bobbs-Merrill, the same company that had published the *Beds* reissue earlier in the year, published *The GrouchoPhile.* While the former was a cheap paperback edition, the latter was a large, expensive coffee-table book. There would be no recalling the entire first printing this time. Instead, as a compromise, Bobbs-Merrill agreed to delete the Erin Fleming dedication page in subsequent editions.

One might have assumed that Erin, who had hitched her wagon to Groucho's star in 1971, would feel supremely triumphant that he had dedicated a pictorial history of his entire life to her. Once again, however, there is danger in second-guessing the whys and wherefores of Erin's actions and reactions. For some reason that I'm sure made perfect sense to her, Erin objected to having Groucho dedicate the book to her.

I thought *The GrouchoPhile* had turned out nicely and was happy to see that a photo of Groucho and me on Bruin Walk was given its own page and a nice lengthy caption about the *Animal Crackers* campaign and my subsequent employment. Granted, Hector had a lot to do with the selection of photos and the content of the captions, but I was flattered nonetheless, especially since I'd missed out on getting my picture into the *Beds* reissue.

Despite Groucho's gradually weakening condition, he had agreed to appear at a fund-raiser for Ralph Nader's consumer-advocate organization in Washington, D.C. I had strong reservations about Groucho taking such a long trip, especially in the chilly month of November. Nevertheless, Groucho was very much looking forward to going. On the strength of his official OK, Groucho's name became the centerpiece of the publicity campaign surrounding the event, which would also include Chevy Chase, George Fenneman, Valerie Perrine and the popular husband-and-wife mime team of Shields and Yarnell, who had recently been signed as Rogers and Cowan clients and were being handled by Tom Wilhite.

In addition to the fund-raiser, Groucho was set to attend a special display of some of his letters at the Library of Congress and to donate the first portion of his memorabilia to the Smithsonian Institution. I felt uneasy about the latter, since it served to reinforce Groucho's mortality.

Several days before the event Erin started having doubts about the trip. Although pulling out at such a late date would certainly be considered poor form, I was encouraged that Erin might actually be starting to come to grips with Groucho's increasingly fragile condition. Then, during a lunch at Groucho's, Erin explained the reason for her hesitation: "I just can't get up and perform in front of people anymore."

She can't get up and perform in front of people anymore?

Erin called Lauren Bacall, who happened to mention that she felt the event should be held at the prestigious Kennedy Center rather than the smaller, historic theater that had been selected as the location. As it turned out, the Nader people had tried for the Kennedy Center but it had already been booked. Erin didn't care. If it wasn't going to be held at the Kennedy Center, it was going to have to proceed without Groucho Marx and Erin Fleming, and that's all there was to it.

So the day before they were scheduled to leave for Washington, Erin canceled, citing Groucho's intermittent bladder trouble as the reason for the last-minute cancellation. (Maybe if she hadn't been *yelling* at him so much his bladder might have been in better shape.) Fifteen thousand dollars of this nonprofit organization's money had already been spent publicizing the fact that Groucho Marx would be making a rare personal appearance. The Nader people had to scramble to rework the show without Groucho, whose already shaky reputation suffered as a result.

Not surprisingly, Erin's suffered even more.

Toward the end of November, Hector went to New York to begin researching Groucho's roots in preparation for the projected biography. Shortly after his arrival, Erin also went to Manhattan. During dinner with Hector one night Erin suddenly announced that she wasn't returning to California until Groucho had made up with his children.

I suppose it was typical of Erin's contradictory personality: She spends four years slowly and methodically turning Groucho against his children, then suddenly declares that he must make peace with each and every one of them or he'd never see her again.

This would have been a particularly sadistic form of emotional blackmail except that Groucho never learned of Erin's ultimatum. Erin called Henry Golas and told him to tell Groucho about her decision, but instead of telling Groucho he *had* to do it or Erin wouldn't return, Henry simply asked Groucho if he'd like to see Arthur and Lois. As if this were nothing out of the ordinary, Groucho said, "Certainly."

Henry sent a telegram to Arthur which said, "PLEASE CALL ME. WANT TO SEE YOU. LOVE, FATHER." When Henry told Erin about the telegram she said, "You should've signed it 'Padre,'" since that had been Arthur and Miriam's nickname for Groucho. Indeed, when Arthur received the telegram he knew it must have been ghostwritten, because it hadn't been signed "Padre." Ironically, Henry had written down the wording of the telegram *exactly* as Groucho had dictated it, "FATHER" and all.

Henry arranged for Arthur and Lois to come to dinner the following night, and it was arguably just as awkward as when Arthur had come to lunch that day in 1974 and left in such a hurry. Arthur didn't seem like such a bad fellow after all, but I took an immediate dislike to Lois, who struck me as something of a domineering shrew who wielded considerable power and influence over her comparatively passive husband. It occurred to me that they were sort of a scaled-down version of Erin and Groucho, although I have no reason to believe that Arthur was being abused by Lois, verbally or otherwise.

The awkwardness was exacerbated by the sense that Henry and

I were being viewed as part of the enemy camp. It's true that Erin had hired us and, indeed, had orchestrated the rapprochement. But I certainly didn't feel much of an allegiance to her by the end of 1976. Just the same, between the things I'd heard about Arthur, the palpable tension in the room and my negative reaction to Lois, I could hardly be said to have had an *affinity* for the two of them.

Henry and I tried to impress upon them that regardless of who had hired us, our primary loyalty was to Groucho and no one else. Nevertheless, Arthur still felt that his every movement was being monitored by either Henry or me. Admittedly, since we'd been made to feel suspicious of Arthur's motives and knowing that Erin would want to know how everything had gone, we probably were watching over things.

The color of truth is gray.

Erin had told Henry to inform Arthur that he was welcome to examine Groucho's financial records, just to prove that nothing untoward had been going on. Lois commented, "Now that she's taken everything, she wants to drop them on us!" But Arthur had a gentler reaction and declined Henry's offer to check the books. After dinner I brought out a fresh copy of *The GrouchoPhile,* which Groucho laboriously inscribed to his only son. Henry told Arthur that he could always call the house if he had any questions or if he wanted to talk to Groucho.

The air could hardly be said to have been cleared of ill feeling, but at least some sort of rudimentary civility had been established. Obviously, had Erin been there it would've been exponentially more difficult to accomplish even *that* much.

Arthur saw Groucho a few more times before the end of the year. Since he didn't feel comfortable sitting at the table with Erin, Henry or me, Arthur would occasionally take Groucho out to lunch. I felt badly that he didn't feel "safe" with me around, because I *wouldn't* have run to Erin and told her what had been said if I felt it wasn't any of her business. Of course, what went on between father and son wasn't any of *my* business, either, and I was happy to see the lines of communication reopening between Groucho and Arthur. Somehow, it felt right.

Bringing Groucho and Miriam together was more of a challenge. My conversations with Miriam had consisted almost entirely of answering Groucho's phone, hearing a boozy voice ask, "Is my father there? This is his daughter, Miriam," and then either putting Groucho on the phone or, if he wasn't home, taking the message that she'd called.

It was the opinion of several of Groucho's friends that of the three children, Miriam had been the brightest and the most promising. Unfortunately she also appears to have suffered the most, battling alcohol, pills, mental institutions, a broken marriage and unhealthy relationships throughout most of her life.

Miriam accepted two invitations to visit Groucho during the month of December, then didn't show up for either of them. Consequently, after Erin had returned from New York, she drove Groucho and Henry to visit Miriam at a house in Culver City where she was living with another couple. Once again, the atmosphere was awkward, but at least some sort of effort was being made.

Groucho and Miriam stayed in sporadic touch over the next few weeks and then we received a call from Cedars-Sinai Hospital, informing us that Miriam had been admitted as a patient. She had been savagely beaten by the couple who had been "taking care" of her, although, in the classic tradition of the perennially battered, she claimed that she'd simply fallen. Eventually Miriam admitted that the couple had locked her in her room for several days with only a bedpan at her side.

Once Miriam had recovered from her beating she was transferred to St. John's Hospital in Santa Monica to begin an alcohol rehab program. Consequently, Groucho's contact with her was once again reduced to intermittent phone calls, but there seemed to be a glimmer of hope that Miriam was going to be in a better place, physically and emotionally.

As 1976 drew to a close, Groucho, at Erin's prodding, had reestablished contact with two out of three of his children. This left only Melinda. Since she had been the apple of his eye for so many years, this might have seemed the easiest gap to bridge. But despite the happy atmosphere of her visit a year earlier, Erin had resumed her task of chipping away at Groucho's feelings. He had recently cut off Melinda's allowance, reluctantly agreeing that she'd been a neglectful daughter. Erin said that all Melinda had to do to get her allowance back was to pay a little more attention to Groucho.

That *sounded* simple enough, but what resulted was anything but simple.

Twenty Six

On January 16, 1977, Groucho was inducted into the Motion Picture Hall of Fame. Despite its impressive sound, it was essentially a gimmick concocted by a promoter to drum up business for a movie memorabilia convention that was being held at the Wilshire Hyatt House in Hollywood. One dealer, who had brought along a large poster from *Horse Feathers* in the off chance that Groucho might stop by, was delighted when he saw Groucho actually drifting toward his table. He eagerly thrust a felt-tip pen into Groucho's hand and peeled away a portion of the plastic wrap that had been protecting the poster.

The dealer had told me he had no intention of keeping the poster; he only wanted Groucho's autograph on it to so that he could jack up the price. I was grimly amused when Groucho inadvertently signed the first three letters of his name on the poster and the last three on the plastic wrap, rendering the signature worthless and actually marring the visual impact of the poster.

The induction ceremony started off with George Jessel reciting his perennial ode to Old Glory. Then George Fenneman introduced Groucho by saying that a recent poll taken at a New York university revealed that the three men admired most by incoming freshmen were Jesus Christ, Albert Schweitzer and Groucho Marx.

Groucho shuffled up to the microphone, apologized for Jesus' not being able to make it and then thanked the Hall of Fame "for this award—shabby as it is." The packed banquet room ate it up. Groucho was still his irreverent self, more or less, though the toll that time was taking seemed to be accelerating.

After the ceremony I spoke with Victor Heerman, a tiny, dapper old man who had directed *Animal Crackers,* of all things. He said he was glad that my efforts had helped trigger its rerelease, but that he would have liked to have attended the repremiere in 1974. I didn't have the heart to tell him that the reason he hadn't been invited was that everyone assumed he was dead. He was quite alive, however, and had had a lengthy, interesting career, starting out as an editor of Mack Sennett two-reel comedies in the twenties before moving on to directing.

Also in attendance were George Seaton, who had cowritten *A Day at the Races*; Fritz Feld, who had appeared in *At the Circus*; Virginia O'Brien, who had performed a song in *The Big Store*; and Dan Seymour, who had the distinction of having appeared in both *Casablanca* and *A Night in Casablanca*. They would never see their former colleague again, as this would prove to be the last time Groucho would make a public appearance of any kind.

Before leaving the hotel I spent a little time with Morrie Ryskind, whom I discovered on the sidewalk trying, without success, to summon a cab. Since this wasn't New York, I suggested he ask the doorman to phone for one. As we watched cab after cab pass by, I said, "Maybe if they knew you were a Pulitzer Prize-winning playwright they might be more inclined to stop." He smiled and said, "I don't think it'd make much of a difference to them. It's a little like the fellow who won the Heisman Trophy in 1926: What have you done *lately*?" Eventually one of the cabs stopped. I helped him in, he waved, and off he went.

Shortly after the convention, Hector returned from his research-gathering trip to New York. When he asked Groucho how discreetly he would prefer some of the more sensitive aspects of his personal life be treated in his official biography, Groucho, perhaps sensing that the end wasn't far off, simply said, "Tell it all." Little did either of them realize how *much* there'd be to tell by the time Hector had finished his manuscript.

Melinda came to visit Groucho toward the end of January, but not because of Erin's request that she pay more attention to her father. She came because she'd begun hearing stories that Groucho was being mistreated by Erin Fleming. And she came with a lawyer. Rather than denying the allegations, Henry confirmed that Erin could, indeed, behave in an abusive manner toward Groucho. Then Melinda told Henry that she never received any money from Groucho, despite the fact that Henry had seen canceled checks proving otherwise.

Realizing that he was stuck in the midst of a vicious game of "Who Do You Trust?" Henry decided the best thing to do would be to tell Erin that Melinda was beginning to question how Groucho was being treated. This was a little like trying to clear the air by lighting a stick of dynamite and tossing it into the room. Erin came storming into Groucho's house screaming about how Melinda was accusing her of *abusing* him, of all the ridiculous things. Then Groucho blew up, exclaiming, "That little bitch! She'll never set foot in this house again!" A few minutes later he began to shake and cry. It looked as though the iron door had been closed on Melinda for good. If this was Erin's idea of bringing everybody together, she had an interesting concept of family unity.

People have asked me if Erin was "on drugs." It was common knowledge among the household staff that Erin smoked pot, popped Valium, Elavil and Quaaludes and indulged in cocaine. Although I saw her taking pills with some regularity, I never saw her doing coke. Many's the time, however, that I would see her go into her office with a few friends or business associates, close the door and a few minutes later come out cackling maniacally in a mood that was 180 degrees removed from the one she was in when she'd entered the room.

Technically speaking, I couldn't *prove* they were doing coke, but I had little doubt that that's what was going on. It reminded me of when I was reading through Groucho's deposition from 1969, when Eden had divorced him. He had been talking about how her drinking had increased over the years. Eden's lawyer asked him how he knew she'd been drinking. Groucho said he'd go into her bathroom and there would be seven or eight empty champagne glasses on the counter. The lawyer said, "If they were empty, how can you be certain they had, at one time, contained liquor?" Groucho answered, "Well, I know they didn't contain *Jell-O!*"

Likewise, I don't believe Erin and her friends were going behind closed doors and eating Jell-O. But writing off Erin's schizophrenic behavior as a side effect of drugs would be grossly unfair—to the pharmaceutical companies. I suspect the pills and powders, at best (or worst), merely inflamed her existing psychological problems.

A few days after the blowup over Melinda, Groucho and Erin attended George Burns' eighty-first birthday party. Things did not go smoothly. First off, Groucho became annoyed when he discovered he wasn't going to be asked to entertain, and he ended up snapping at Milton Berle, "I don't think you're funny." Berle countered with, "Everything I know, I stole from you," to which Groucho responded, "Then you weren't listening."

Then Erin encountered some of Groucho's former attorneys who had recently resigned, and she decided the best thing to do would be to scream at them in front of all the partygoers. As a result, Erin and Groucho were asked to leave. Once again, as with the ill-fated Ralph Nader affair, their participation in a public event had turned into an embarrassment.

It should have been obvious to anyone with eyes and ears that Groucho was spiraling steadily downward. He was walking more slowly, he was more disoriented and his sense of time was becoming more and more distorted. It *was* obvious—to everyone but Erin Fleming, who decided in January that Groucho was going to star in his own television special. It would be taped right in Groucho's living room and would feature the biggest names in show business entertaining, and being entertained by, Groucho Marx. And it was going to be carried by one of the major networks in prime time. That's the way Erin envisioned it: sort of like his eighty-fifth birthday party, only with commercials.

After Groucho's shaky appearances on the Bob Hope special and "Donny and Marie," I thought she was crazy to even *think* of letting him make another television appearance, much less be the star of the show. But as she so often did, Erin surprised me. She actually managed to convince a production company to back the show. Of course, her list of the "biggest names in show business" dwindled to Bud Cort and Sally Kellerman, and the "major network" turned out to be Channel 13, the lowest-rent local station on Los Angeles television. But the fact remains that she swung the deal.

The taping was set for March 5. Most of the creative decisions would be handled by Erin and a director she had lined up named Stanley Dorffman. All Groucho had to worry about was rehearsing. So that's just what he did—he worried about rehearsing.

The nurses started reporting that Groucho was spending his nights twisting and turning fitfully, then getting up every morning at 5:00 A.M., insisting, "I've got to rehearse! I'm doing a show!" He'd shuffle into the living room, sit down at the piano and begin plunking out tunes and mumbling lyrics. It was obviously stressful for Groucho to know that he was expected to be the centerpiece of a television special that was only a few short weeks away.

To make the show more distinctive, Erin hired a young composer to write a theme song. It was her idea that if the taping went smoothly it might become a series, or at least a series of specials, and her career as a television producer would be off and running. The composer came up with a rock-oriented melody and Groucho-oriented lyrics:

Who is the man with the cigar in his hand,
And the walk that's the talk of the town?
It's Groucho! It's Groucho!
Now tell me, what's the secret word?
It's Groucho! It's Groucho!

I hated it. It makes Barney the dinosaur's "I Love You, You Love Me" song sound sophisticated by comparison. What was worse, when the composer would come over to rehearse and play his theme song, Erin would goad Groucho into getting up and dancing to it. Since he was in such creaky shape, all he could manage to do was rock back and forth and move his arms up and down stiffly, like the Frankenstein monster when he was listening to the blind violinist. In an effort to make Groucho look good, Erin would join him in dance, mirroring his awkward, robotic movements.

It was a grotesque tableau.

All throughout this rehearsal period I worried that Groucho was being pushed to a point beyond his endurance, that he and the show were skating on the thinnest of ice. Erin could only see that a marvelously entertaining television special was in the works, and she was sure it would be a big hit.

Groucho continued to sleep poorly and get up at five each morning, pleading with the nurses that he *had* to rehearse or Erin would be upset with him. Toward the end of February, Hector told me that Groucho seemed more out of it and more easily fatigued than ever. He would excuse himself to go to the bathroom and then wander into the kitchen or the hallway by mistake, having forgotten his original destination.

On the Saturday following Hector's bleak report, I showed up for work and found Groucho to be in a total daze. I'd witnessed a wide spectrum of mental states in recent months, everything from bright and alert to groggy and hazy. But I had never seen him so completely zonked out, like a zombie, bumping into walls, staring blankly at nothing in particular, and only partially responding to our voices. And he seemed to have lost part of his peripheral vision, focusing only on what was directly in front of him.

One of the nurses told Erin that Groucho had had another stroke. Did Erin call for an ambulance? Or call Groucho's longtime internist, Dr. Kert? Or even give Groucho a cursory once-over? No. Instead, in her infinite medical wisdom, Erin *denied* that Groucho had had a stroke and admonished the nurse not to make such ridiculous, alarmist statements again. As if that weren't enough, Erin insisted that the show must go on. I'd always admired that show-biz adage—up until that Saturday afternoon.

Shortly thereafter an incident occurred that I found extremely suspicious. Groucho was helped into Erin's office, where she placed some legal documents in front of him and, without telling him what they were, showed him where to sign. After Groucho scrawled his name at the bottom of each page, the nurse helped him back into his bedroom.

It reminded me of the time a couple of years earlier when *I* had been called into Erin's office to sign a document I'd never seen before. It had to do with the creation of Groucho Marx Productions, of which Erin and Groucho were equal partners. The company was being formed to develop and oversee various film and television productions as well as the licensing of Groucho merchandise. I was instructed, by Erin and by Groucho's business manager, Bill Owen, to sign as "secretary" of the company. I asked what exactly this position entailed. They laughed at my query and told me, "Just keep doing what you're doing and you'll be a millionaire by the time you're thirty!"

I'm still waiting.

Erin had enormous drive, but there was only so much she could accomplish through sheer force of will. As we were about to discover, nature had other plans. Since Groucho's overall condition had been improving somewhat, Hector thought that Groucho might enjoy a visit from Olivia de Havilland, who was in town to attend the AFI salute to Bette Davis. During World War II Groucho had been romantically interested in de Havilland, but as Groucho had explained it, "She was stuck on John Huston." Nevertheless, they had seen each other socially from time to time over the years.

Hector called her up at the Beverly Hills Hotel and explained the situation. Miss de Havilland agreed to come and have afternoon tea with Groucho on March 3. That morning Groucho fell, and since this resulted in his having difficulty walking, he was put to bed. He insisted that he would be able to get up when Olivia arrived, but when he tried to put weight on his leg, he crumpled. So it was decided that he would receive her in his bedroom.

Olivia de Havilland was warm and gracious while Groucho looked her over and said, "You're not getting any younger." Rather than taking offense, she laughed heartily at Groucho's assessment. During her visit Groucho inscribed a copy of *The GrouchoPhile* for her. After she left, Erin assured Hector that a doctor would be called at once to check Groucho out.

Later, when Hector couldn't get hold of either Groucho or Erin to find out what the situation was, he called me up and we went over to the house. By this point I had my own key to the door that three years earlier had seemed so imposing.

We walked in and found the house completely deserted and Groucho's bed neatly made. Puzzled by this discovery, Hector called Erin's legal secretary, Dena Brown, to ask what was going on. Dena told him that Erin had taken Groucho to visit Zeppo and Gummo in Palm Springs. We barely had time to digest this outrageously suspicious piece of news when Dena called back and said, "I forgot to tell you. Erin said the house should be shut up for the weekend and that Steve shouldn't work." I looked in my office and found it stacked with cartons bursting with what looked like legal papers.

Things were getting curiouser and curiouser.

Completely at a loss to explain any of what we'd seen or heard that day, we followed Erin's instructions and left the house. As I closed the door, I remember thinking, *Well, here it is. I lasted a lot longer than I thought I would. It's been a helluva ride.* What I didn't know was, what the hell was going *on?!*

The next day answers started to trickle in. Erin called Hector and said, "Do you know where we are?" Obviously not. It turned out they were not in Palm Springs, as had been claimed. They were at Cedars-Sinai Hospital. When Groucho had fallen, he'd fractured the top of his femur where it sockets into the hipbone. He'd managed to get through his afternoon tea with Olivia de Havilland with a broken hip. The ball at the top of the hip was immediately replaced with an artificial one.

Hector felt that Arthur should be told about Groucho's accident and hospitalization. Erin said, "You know how Groucho feels about Arthur. He doesn't want him around." But the surgeon and the hospital's public relations man agreed with Hector that Arthur needed to be informed of his father's condition. Erin acquiesced, saying that Groucho's lawyer, Martin Gang, would call the three children and let them know what was going on.

The next day Hector talked to Arthur, who claimed he knew *nothing* about any of this and was understandably angry that he appeared to be the last to know. Eventually word leaked out to the press that Groucho was in the hospital. As usual, the news reports said that Groucho was alert and wisecracking. As usual, the reports of his alertness were greatly exaggerated.

The doctors also confirmed that Groucho had, despite Erin's emphatic denial, recently suffered a mild stroke. That diagnosis, coupled with his recent hip surgery, caused them to doubt that Groucho would ever walk again. His progress was extremely erratic. One day he'd be responsive and actually make an effort to take a few steps with someone supporting him on either side; the next day he'd be completely incapacitated. At one point his heartbeat became irregular, causing all of us to expect the worst.

As it turned out, my job hadn't ended after all. Erin had wanted the house closed up that weekend just until things settled down. I visited Groucho the Saturday after he'd been admitted to the hospital. He recognized me and didn't seem to be in much pain. His major complaint was that they didn't give him much of a chance to sleep—the old wake-you-up-to-give-you-a-sleeping-pill dilemma. But that's what he said he wanted most: sleep.

By mid-March, Groucho began to show signs of improvement. His vital signs had stabilized and his hip was coming along nicely. Then, just as I was allowing myself to get a little optimistic, Groucho developed pneumonia. It seemed so unfair that all these maladies were being visited upon him, one on top of the other.

As a result of the stroke he was often more disoriented than he'd been before. At one point, he didn't even recognize Erin. *That* was a first. It was only a temporary lapse in recognition, but it began to give me a strange sense of hope that if she were somehow to be removed from the picture, he might not be as lost without her as he would have been before his mental condition had taken such a drastic dip. It was a strange "upside" to a very grave situation, but an upside nonetheless.

Groucho's surgeon said, "He may be eighty-six, but he has the arteries of a man of a hundred and five." Given his bleak condition, I held out little hope that he would pull through. Even if he did, I was certain his ability to create even the weakest of wisecracks was gone for good. Nothing about Groucho's situation looked promising.

Incredibly, Erin *still* hadn't canceled the TV show; she'd only postponed it.

Hector divided his time between visiting Groucho in the hospital and continuing to work on the biography. At one point, he needed to look through some papers at Groucho's house. When Erin heard that Hector had been there, she told him that he couldn't go into the house anymore because their insurance covered only the household staff.

En route to the hospital to visit Groucho, Henry Golas confided to Hector, "Erin said to get you out of the house, but that I can go back as soon as I get rid of you. She said you don't understand about her and Groucho. She thought you did, but now she feels she was mistaken." It looked as though Hector was about to join the ranks of the pipsqueaks and impostors, or worse. Hector said that Erin had been getting increasingly more erratic and suspicious, not only of him but of everyone she dealt with on a regular basis.

Hector had dinner with writer Norman Krasna, one of Groucho's oldest friends. Krasna had moved to Switzerland many years earlier and was in town only for a brief visit. Hector told Krasna about Erin's increasingly paranoid behavior, and Krasna told him that the two of them were expected at Arthur and Lois's house after dinner. *This* was a surprise, at least to Hector. If he was feeling uncomfortable before, his discomfort was about to increase tenfold.

Once at Arthur's, Hector was informed that a string of former employees—mostly nurses—had come to Arthur complaining about Erin's mistreatment of Groucho. As a result, Arthur said, action was going to be taken. Hector didn't ask what this consisted of, but he assumed it was some sort of plan to have Erin removed. As a result of his visit to Arthur's, Hector felt more in the middle of things than ever before. First Erin felt that he could no longer be counted on as an ally (something he never claimed to be), and then he was viewed by Arthur and Lois as a dubious visitor from Erin's camp. Curiously, Erin never asked Hector about his visit with Arthur. Maybe she didn't want to know.

On the morning of March 22, Groucho left the hospital and returned home. Although this sounds encouraging, he hadn't been officially discharged. Erin and a physical therapist had in essence kidnapped him and taken him home. The doctor was upset that Erin had "stolen" Groucho before he was due to be released, but the feeling was, now that he's home you might as well let him stay, rather than putting him through the hassle of being driven back to the hospital.

As a result of this final outrage on Erin's part, Arthur went to his lawyer, J. Brin Schulman, and then, on Schulman's advice, to Santa Monica Superior Court. There, as Groucho's son, Arthur had himself officially declared Groucho's conservator along with the Bank of America, which would oversee money matters. It was a surprisingly simple move.

Deceptively so.

The following day Erin urgently summoned Hector to the house. Naturally, he assumed that Groucho had died. When he showed up, however, he found Groucho resting comfortably in his bedroom. At the front end of the house, things were markedly more tempestuous.

Arthur, Lois, Schulman and some representatives from the Bank of America had shown up ready to take command. As a result, Erin had summoned *her* lawyers, and the two factions had set up camp in two rooms—Arthur's in the den and Erin's in the living room. Arthur delivered an ultimatum to Hector: He would cooperate on the biography only if Hector would testify on Arthur's behalf as to Erin's abusive behavior.

This was considerably more than Hector had bargained for when he'd agreed to write the book. Additionally, as in my case, while he certainly had a lot of complaints about Erin's behavior, Hector didn't feel any particular warmth toward Arthur and Lois and had many reservations about the deleterious effect removing Erin might have on Groucho.

Now both factions thought of Hector as a traitor because he

refused to declare his allegiance to either side. Hector strongly considered throwing in the towel on the whole biography business, but Norman Krasna convinced him to stick with it since he had such a unique perch.

Groucho had signed a paper in 1974 appointing Erin as his conservator should the need ever arise, so the judge agreed to postpone his decision to appoint Arthur until he'd had a chance to look over the document and give the situation some thought.

The next day Erin told Hector that the judge had decided that the 1974 document was binding, and that as a compromise she would be made Groucho's conservator while Arthur's bank controlled the financial end. A final decree would be made in court on April 15.

It was expected to be a routine proceeding.

This *appeared* to be a solution of Solomonic wisdom: Erin could stay by Groucho's side but his children would also be welcome, and the Bank of America would watch over the money end of things. It looked good on paper. In practice it proved to be something else entirely.

Although Groucho had improved somewhat during his two and a half weeks in the hospital, he was still in an extremely fragile state and for the first time in his life was confined to a wheelchair when he wasn't in bed. Erin told everyone that he was making terrific progress at home, but her idea of "Groucho walking" was a nurse and a physical therapist carrying Groucho up and down the hallway while his feet barely touched the floor, like a marionette. While Erin thought that Groucho was coming along just fine, I feared that the slightest setback, physical or emotional, could prove fatal.

Two days after the big showdown in Groucho's house, Nunnally Johnson died.

It was just the sort of traumatic event we'd prayed wouldn't crop up during Groucho's precarious convalescence. My mind immediately flashed on a letter I'd found that Groucho had written to Nunnally in October of 1961 shortly after Chico had died. In it Groucho had said, "If you, Thurber, Ruby, Sheekman and a few others knock it off, I'll be about ready to say the hell with everything."

James Thurber had died the month after Groucho had written the letter, Harry Ruby had died in 1974, Arthur Sheekman was mentally and physically incapacitated and now emphysema had finally overtaken Nunnally Johnson. In a strange twist of fate, after a lifetime of devouring the morning paper Groucho had ceased keeping up with the news on a regular basis after the last stroke and the broken hip. Consequently, although it was emotionally and logistically difficult, we managed to keep Nunnally's death from him. Groucho never knew he'd lost his old friend.

Erin felt that the proper thing to do in light of Groucho's absence was to pay her respects to the Johnson family, so she showed up at the memorial service wearing an extremely low-cut blouse. When Hector questioned her choice of wardrobe she laughed and said, "Oh, Nunnally would've *loved* it!" Well, Nunnally might have loved it, but his family was less than enthused by her taste in funereal attire. Never one to pass up the chance to make a scene, she also managed to get into a shouting match with Norman Krasna over the conservatorship battle. I suppose she figured Nunnally would have loved *that,* too.

After the funeral, Hector took Erin back to Groucho's house. One of the nurses wheeled Groucho into Erin's office, at which point, without warning, he suddenly told Erin to "get out." Startled by Groucho's sharp directive, Erin said, "Who's going to take care of you?" Ignoring her question, Groucho simply repeated, "Just get out."

As it turned out, this did not represent a permanent shift in his attitude. Not long after he'd ordered her out of his house, Erin was back in Groucho's good graces. Nevertheless, it was an extraordinary thing for Groucho to have said to her, and it reinforced my hypothesis that Erin's removal might not prove quite as traumatic as I'd once feared.

Groucho's mental state during this period continued to be up one day, down the next. We could never be sure how sharp or how foggy he'd be, or what he would remember from the previous day's events. His banishing of Erin, followed by the almost immediate reversal of that decision, was indicative of the erratic nature of Groucho's psychological makeup.

Likewise Erin and her paranoia, now that things were really starting to heat up. On Easter Sunday, convinced that Arthur had somehow managed to install listening devices in the house so that he could spy on her, Erin hired two private eyes to methodically check out the house and its environs in search of sophisticated surveillance equipment. The two detectives, Norman Perle and Fred Wolfson, failed to find any bugging devices.

But they did find a plastic grocery bag containing a medicine bottle, three yellow pills and twenty-nine syringes in the storm drain in front of the house. Perle showed them to Erin, who said they must've been planted there by Arthur's sinister forces in order to frame her. When Wolfson asked Erin what she wanted to do with the suspicious-looking pharmaceutical supplies, she told him to bury them in the yard.

Instead the two detectives took the drug paraphernalia straight to the Beverly Hills police. Toxicological tests were performed on the syringes. The results showed residual traces of Nembutal, a short-acting barbiturate. A criminal investigation was soon under way.

It was at this point that all hell broke loose.

TWENTY SEVEN

"Threat to Groucho Marx's Life Claimed"
"Possibility of Plot to Kill Groucho Marx Probed"
"Saw Manager Give Marx Tranquilizer, Nurse Says"
"Marx's Manager Threatened to Kill 2, Court Told"

The lurid headlines came fast and furiously. I couldn't believe what I was reading in the *L.A. Times* over my morning bowl of Grape Nuts almost on a daily basis. Something that had seemed like such a private, personal part of my experience was now being bandied about in the newspapers and on the evening news. It was as if everyone had suddenly learned of a deep, dark secret that I'd been carrying around with me for years. Understandably, everybody I'd ever met was calling me up asking me what the hell was going on at Groucho's house.

Before the shit had hit the fan, I'd been trying to be as discreet as possible, giving a fairly vague account of what things were like at 1083 Hillcrest—especially to my coworkers in the Universal steno pool. I felt protective of Groucho in his weakened condition, and out of a combination of fear and vestigial loyalty I tended to downplay Erin's volatile personality. My close friends knew what was happening.

I also wrote to Dick Cavett about what had really been going on. Since he had told me that I "could speak freely" and since he had a genuine affection and concern for Groucho's welfare, I clued him in as to what was happening in regard to Groucho's condition and Erin's behavior. He wrote back saying, "None of the Fleming news surprises me, although it *is* shocking."

That pretty much sums up how I felt at the time. Did I really think Erin had been trying to kill Groucho? No. And yet, given her mercurial personality and unpredictability, nothing I heard about her would really have *surprised* me. She seemed capable of almost anything, given the right set of circumstances. When someone sprints up and down the behavioral spectrum as madly as Erin had, there's no such thing as doing something out of character.

For the record, everything had come unglued on Friday, April 15, 1977, during what was supposed to have been a routine court proceeding. On the strength of that 1974 document naming Erin as Groucho's personal choice for conservator, Arthur had withdrawn his petition. But in light of recent events, J. Brin Schulman had asked the judge to reconsider his decision to allow Erin to become Groucho's conservator. Schulman maintained that Erin presented "a clear and present danger" to Groucho.

She may have been present, but she was rarely clear.

As evidence Schulman put detective Perle on the stand. Perle gave testimony for two hours, informing the court of the discovery of the syringes and Erin's directive that they be buried in Groucho's yard. Then Wolfson took the stand and described how Erin had tried to get Groucho to sign a check for $650 to cover the private detectives' fee. According to Wolfson, she had propped him up in bed, stuck a pen in his hand, and when he had trouble writing, screamed, "Sign the fucking check! What's the matter with you? Can't you write your own name?"

Since the judge hadn't anticipated needing a lengthy period of time in which to consider the petition, he had to move on to other cases, so they adjourned until the following Monday.

As with Nunnally's death, we kept Groucho in the dark as best we could about the bitterness of the legal battle between Erin and Arthur. One night, however, he was in the mood to watch the news. Ironically, he managed to catch the first brief story about the conservatorship struggle and the ugly allegations about Erin's behavior. Groucho was angered by the report, but his anger didn't stick. By the next day he'd forgotten all about it. I suppose that on occasion, advancing senility can be something of a blessing.

The conservatorship mess even made it onto "Saturday Night Live." Jane Curtin was giving her "Weekend Update" news report, and in discussing Erin's petition she said, "In addition to asking the court to appoint her conservator of the ailing Marx, she has also requested that her name be legally changed to Flemmo."

When court reconvened on Monday, there began a slow parade of former employees who either had been fired by Erin or had quit on their own. After the two detectives had finished telling their syringe story, Groucho's former cook, Martha Brooks, was put on the stand. She recounted what life had been like with Erin and Groucho: how Erin had pushed Groucho to perform when he wasn't up to it, how Erin would drum into Groucho that his children didn't care about him and would put him in a home, and how Erin had talked Groucho into tearing up photos of Melinda and her children because, according to Erin, Melinda didn't love him anymore. It was heartrending testimony.

The following day, some of Groucho's former nurses gave extremely damaging testimony about how Erin had treated Groucho. But the first person to speak on Tuesday was the man who had been Groucho's internist and heart doctor for the previous twenty years, Dr. Morley Kert. He testified that Erin could "stimulate and cajole" Groucho to respond in ways neither he nor the nurses could ever do. He also testified that he never prescribed barbiturates or tranquilizers for Groucho because they might affect his balance and slow down his mental processes.

But nurse Linda Ponce, who had worked at Groucho's until August of 1976 (and who used to dance the Hustle with John Ballow in Groucho's kitchen), testified that she occasionally gave tranquilizers to Groucho and then listed the dosage in the nurse's log, which was kept in Groucho's bedroom at all times.

Another nurse, Jean Funari, whom I had always found to be competent and compassionate, testified that she saw Erin give Groucho a tranquilizer to make him sleep so that she could go out on a date without having to worry about him. According to Jean, Erin had threatened Groucho that she would "slap him all the way to Pittsburgh" if he didn't take a nap, and she ended up giving him a tranquilizer. This had taken place in Las Vegas, a considerable distance from Pittsburgh.

Jean characterized Erin's behavior as "abusive treatment of a little old man," saying that Erin often screamed at Groucho using filthy language, and that on one occasion she had seen Erin push Groucho back down into a chair when he'd started to get up from the dining-room table. She also said that once, when Groucho had been particularly difficult to handle, Erin had told her, "I wish he'd die."

Maybe *A Stranger in the Mirror* was more on the mark than I'd initially thought.

As if all that weren't enough, on Wednesday detectives Perle and Wolfson were put back on the stand because, according to them, they had run into Erin the night before and she had threatened them. The confrontation had occurred at the condominium of Carolyn Benoit, the nurse who had accompanied the detectives when they had found the syringes. Apparently fearing that Benoit would also testify against her, Erin had gone to the condo to talk to the nurse and had encountered the two detectives there. According to their testimony, Erin had said, "I'm going to kill you!"

Also testifying on Wednesday was Terrie McCord, the nurse who had asked Groucho to write me that little note a year earlier. She told the court that she had seen Erin give Groucho the prescription tranquilizer Meprobamate "on many occasions," in direct contradiction of Dr. Kert's testimony. Terrie also stated that she saw Erin push, shake and slap Groucho, and that after Erin's tirades Groucho would often be left trembling, and sometimes in tears. Once she saw Erin angrily hurl a book across the room, which hit Groucho in the chest.

Terrie also described the incident that had resulted in her quitting the year before. Terrie had complained to Erin that one of the nurses had been smoking marijuana while on duty. Instead of getting mad at the other nurse, Erin had started shouting obscenities at Terrie, accusing her of trying to run things. As if that weren't bizarre enough, Erin then unzipped her jumpsuit, stripped down to her panties and started playing with her pubic hair. Taunting Terrie, Erin had said, "Why don't you fuck me? Come on! You want to wear the pants around here? You think you're a man? Fuck me!" It was at that point that Terrie had walked out.

According to Terrie, John Ballow also witnessed the above incident and had quit shortly thereafter.

On the strength of all this damaging testimony, Judge Edward Rafeedie was prepared to award Arthur temporary conservatorship of his father, but Erin's attorney, Stanley Gold, managed to convince the judge to hold off until Groucho himself had been heard from. Rafeedie and the principal parties came by Groucho's house that night. The lawyers and the judge spent about an hour talking with him.

Rafeedie wasn't convinced that Groucho was in any condition to make important decisions about his life, although he did ask Groucho if he wanted Arthur to take care of him. "No," was Groucho's tearful reply. Obviously all of this was quite stressful for Groucho.

The following day, Thursday, April 21, Gummo died of a heart attack in Palm Springs. It's safe to assume that he and Zeppo had been following the progress of the court proceedings rather closely. Gummo was the brother to whom Groucho had felt closest, and we worked hard to keep his death from Groucho. We prayed he wouldn't ask for a newspaper or click on the news again. Thankfully, he didn't. Groucho would never learn of Gummo's death.

On the day Gummo died, Zeppo wasn't in Palm Springs by his brother's side. He'd come to Santa Monica Superior Court to say a few words on Erin's behalf. Zeppo had nothing but glowing things to say about Erin and her relationship with his surviving brother. Zeppo contended that if Erin were to be taken away from Groucho, "It would kill him." He also declared that Erin was "the finest woman in the world."

Well, they always *said* that Zeppo was the funniest one off-screen.

I wasn't surprised by the flattering things Zeppo had to say about Erin. For one, he was an older man with an eye for younger women and he probably thought Groucho was one lucky bastard to get such a relatively young chick to look after him. For another, Erin had persuaded Groucho to give Zeppo a thousand dollars a month, since he had no real income and tended to be a heavy gambler. If the status quo were to be upset, there's no telling what effect it might have on that particular arrangement. A lot of people heard Zeppo's remarks and concluded, "Well, he should know. He's Groucho's brother."

But frankly, Zeppo simply wasn't around often enough to get any kind of accurate picture of Erin's personality or her ongoing relationship with Groucho. There was no shortage of celebrities Erin could have called upon to try and bolster her contention that she had a salutary effect on Groucho, because at first glance they appeared to be made for each other. That had been my conclusion when I'd seen them together on Bruin Walk. It was only after I'd spent a considerable amount of time at Groucho's house on a daily basis that my opinion began to shift.

Whether or not removing Erin would constitute a threat to Groucho's health was another matter. Someone might be addicted to a dangerous drug, but there's no use taking them off it if the withdrawal is going to kill them. So it was with Groucho. Although I'd been encouraged by his not recognizing Erin that day in the hospital and tossing her out of his house a few weeks earlier, I still wasn't convinced that removing her wouldn't have a deleterious effect on Groucho.

But I almost felt that it was worth a try.

Since Judge Rafeedie felt that Groucho's health was of immediate concern, he decided to appoint a neutral, temporary conservator until a final decision could be made. This seemed like a wise solution. He asked that both sides put forth names for consideration.

Almost immediately, Erin's side nominated—big surprise—Zeppo Marx. Arthur initially wanted Bert Granet, one of Groucho's oldest friends and a former television producer, but Granet declined when he learned that the job might last longer than a few weeks. Arthur's second choice was Nat Perrin, who accepted only on the condition that it wouldn't last much more than a few weeks.

Rafeedie dismissed Zeppo, who lived so far away and who thought Erin was a wonderful person. That left only Nat for serious consideration. Consequently, on Friday, April 22, Nat Perrin was made temporary conservator of his onetime employer, Groucho Marx. A date of May 13 was set for the formal hearing, at which time the judge would decide whether Erin or Arthur would be Groucho's permanent conservator.

The judge told Nat, "Be fiercely independent. You're under no obligation to anybody in this case. You may change the locks at the house and determine who has the keys. You have the power to dismiss any employee, although you should maintain the status quo in respect to those who are performing satisfactorily."

On the strength of that directive, I was certain I was about to be let go. It wasn't so much that I hadn't been performing satisfactorily; it was a combination of factors: Nat Perrin didn't really know me very well, I'd been hired by Erin the Terrible, and how much need was there, at this late date, for someone to handle the fan mail of a dying man and keep his archives organized? No. This was it. I was sure of it.

So when Nat called me up a few days after he'd been appointed Groucho's conservator, I was fully prepared to be let down gently. It had been an amazing three years, but the best of times were clear-

clearly behind me and, truth be told, this might be a convenient place to hop off the trolley.

But Nat had another reason for calling. As a result, I would end up performing one final service for Groucho. It was probably the most important thing I would ever do for him. More important than getting *Animal Crackers* off the shelf. More important than handling his fan mail. More important than helping Hector on those books.

The irony was, Groucho would remain completely unaware that I was doing it.

Twenty Eight

Henry Golas was going to be staying at Groucho's house during the week to look after things, and Nat wanted to know if I would be willing to stay there on weekends to give Henry a couple of days off. Between my devotion to Groucho, my friendship with Henry and a guaranteed thirty-five dollars a day, how could I refuse? From that point on, however, my paychecks would no longer be signed by Groucho. Instead, a Mr. Strickland from the Bank of America would be signing them.

What an extraordinary responsibility, and how flattered I was by the obvious faith that Nat placed in me. Since he wasn't going to be staying at the house, I would essentially be Nat's proxy. I was to make sure the nurses came and went according to their prescribed shifts. I was to regulate and assign times to Groucho's friends who wanted to visit him. And I was to referee the visits of Erin and Arthur, since neither of them had any authority over the household or, more important, over Groucho. In a sense I was responsible for Groucho's life, such as it was, each and every weekend.

To keep things from getting confrontational, we arranged it so that Arthur and Lois would visit in the morning, Groucho's friends would visit in the afternoon and Erin would come by at night for dinner and beyond. The average visiting time for friends was about twenty or thirty minutes, but things were kept fairly flexible if the visit was perceived to be having a beneficial effect on Groucho. If I felt that someone was overstaying his or her welcome or was upsetting Groucho, I was to ask them to leave.

That included Erin Fleming.

As you can imagine, Erin *loathed* everything about this arrangement. Stripped of all authority, she was at the mercy of Henry's or my discretion regarding her visitation rights. I "overheard" her screaming to a friend over the phone, "Fucking *servants* are running this place! They're treating me like a cockroach!"

What a remarkable turning of the tables.

I loved it.

Despite the fact that Groucho was down the hall, slowly fading away, a certain calm accompanied Nat's appointment. He hadn't wanted his position to last much more than three weeks; it ended up lasting three months. The Nat Perrin Regime, as I dubbed it, was bookended on one side by the vicious, tabloidy court battle and on the other by Nat's stepping aside and Groucho's death shortly thereafter. But in between was a pocket of relative tranquility, like when the Five Good Emperors ruled Rome in between the madmen.

One of Nat's first official acts was footing the bill for airplane tickets for Melinda and her kids to come down from Mendocino and visit Groucho. All of the bitterness, accusations and Erin-generated venom melted away the minute Melinda walked into Groucho's bedroom and clasped his outstretched hand. Although he was frustrated by his own physical deterioration, Groucho enjoyed grabbing hold of someone's hand tightly and impressing her or him with how much strength he still had left. It was almost as if he were saying, "I may be in lousy shape, but don't count me out just yet."

The visit of Melinda, Miles and Jade was enormously beneficial to Groucho. And to Melinda. Their love for each other was obvious to anyone who watched them together, and he never seemed to tire of kissing her. They could finally feel free to spend time with each other without fear of Erin suddenly bursting through the door and throwing a fit. Groucho couldn't get enough of Melinda, and she ended up staying for several days, boosting his spirits markedly.

Miriam was still in the process of recovering from her chronic alcoholism, but all reports were pointing in an encouraging direction. Although she wasn't quite up to visiting Groucho, she would soon be sober on a permanent basis—tonic enough for her father, who had seen her through so many dramatic ups and downs over the years.

And when Arthur would visit, I saw none of the bitterness and awkwardness that had marked earlier get-togethers. His concern for Groucho was genuine, and in time Arthur and I got to be on fairly friendly terms, though I don't think he could ever fully shake the feeling that I was one of Erin's minions. For my part, I never quite warmed up to Lois. Can't win 'em all.

One day I brought along a copy of Arthur's book, *Son of Groucho.* As I handed it to him to sign, he said, "Was that you honking at me on your way over here?" I assured him it wasn't. So he took my book and wrote, "To Steve, the one who didn't honk, and a nice guy."

And I'd always thought that Groucho, Chico and Zeppo were the ones who didn't honk.

By this time I was officially pulling for Arthur to win conservatorship, although I never verbalized it. My main hang-up with his appointment had been my fear that Erin's removal might, as Zeppo had feared, kill Groucho. But I began to notice that Erin wasn't really on Groucho's mind when she wasn't around. During his first couple of weeks out of the hospital he would say, "Where's Erin?" or "I wish Erin were here." But after a while he didn't seem to notice her absence. On one occasion, he couldn't even remember her name. And we felt that his needs were being met by Nat, the nurses, the family and friends who stopped by, Henry and me.

Even Nat admitted to me that he was getting mixed signals from Groucho with regard to Erin. Sometimes Groucho would say, "I love her," while other times he'd tell Nat, "That woman is stealing all my money."

When Erin was there, Groucho was certainly affectionate toward her, like old times, and he would perk up considerably. But things weren't so bad for him when she wasn't around, and I began to really enjoy the feeling of operating in an Erin-free atmosphere. On the one hand I was hoping that Arthur would get the appointment, and on the other hand I was praying that I wouldn't be swept out along with anyone else who had had anything to do with the Erin Fleming administration.

Incredibly, as far gone as Groucho was by this point, I was still witnessing vestiges of his old wit. Blackie the cat had run away some months earlier, and Groucho had a new cat, Suki, who walked into the bedroom one day, startling the nurse.

Nurse: "How long have you had cats?"

Groucho: "I've always had cats. And before that I had measles."

The nurse's car had recently been in for repairs. For an incapacitated man, Groucho was in a gallant mood.

Groucho: "Tell me where you live and I'll take you home."

Nurse: "But my car has already been fixed."

Groucho: "Well, then, you can take *me* home! You know, you're cute, but it's too late."

Nurse: "Too late for what?"

Groucho: "Too late for you."

Also around this time, the famous Richard Nixon/David Frost

interviews aired, marking the first time the former president had appeared on television since his resignation three years earlier. Groucho managed to catch some of the interviews. His pronouncement on Nixon's rationalization of the Watergate affair? "A lot of horseshit!" Apparently he still retained something of his keen political awareness.

One of the more bittersweet aspects of looking after the place during this period was meeting more people from Groucho's circle, although the circumstances were certainly more somber than they'd been before. In late April Norman Panama, who had cowritten *Road to Utopia*, *Monsieur Beaucaire* and *Mr. Blandings Builds His Dream House*, came by to visit Groucho along with Julius J. Epstein, who was best known for having cowritten *Casablanca.* At one point, Panama made a playful reference to their wives.

Panama: "You can have your pick of either of them."

Groucho: "Why? They *both* love me."

Panama: "Everybody loves you, Groucho."

Groucho: "Everybody except *me.*"

During their visit, the nurse was watching *Casino Royale* on Groucho's TV. Julius Epstein looked up at the screen and said, "Oh, there's Woody Allen!" Misunderstanding Epstein's reference, Groucho began looking around the room saying, "Woody? Where? Where's Woody?" He thought Mr. Allen had arrived in person, and he was understandably disappointed to learn that Epstein had only been referring to the television set.

As Panama and Epstein prepared to leave, Epstein said,"We've got to go. We're going to be playing poker later this evening."

Groucho: "I don't play cards."

Epstein: "I remember years ago you used to play for very small stakes."

Groucho: "And french-fried potatoes."

I was pleasantly startled to hear Groucho resurrecting one of Chico's lines from, of all things, *Animal Crackers,* and Panama and Epstein obviously felt good for having been able to elicit this humorous response from their ailing friend.

George Burns stopped by one day. He never made any reference to Groucho's depleted condition in front of Groucho. It was as if nothing were out of the ordinary as he filled Groucho in on what was happening in show business and then reminisced a bit about the old days. Seemingly forgotten was the embarrassing scene at Burns' birthday party a few months earlier.

Another George—Fenneman—came by to pay his respects as well. It was nice to see him again. During his visit, the nurse asked if someone would help lift Groucho from the wheelchair to the bed. I had been assisting in that department, but Fenneman wanted to help out so he grabbed hold of Groucho's upper body while Groucho put his arms around Fenneman's neck. As they were making their way to the bed Groucho said, "Fenneman, you always were a lousy dancer."

In late May, Steve Allen came by. Groucho was wheeled into the living room, where Allen sat at the piano. Because the most recent stroke had affected his peripheral vision, Groucho had a little trouble focusing on Allen and comprehending who he was. It was an awkward start to what turned out to be a wonderful afternoon. Allen started to play a variety of Tin Pan Alley standards, most of them at my request, and Groucho began to perk up, actually singing along to a few of them. While he played, Allen talked about a variety of show business–related experiences. He mentioned a program he'd seen recently.

Allen: "It was one of those shows where the emcee got some guy out of the audience. Groucho, did you ever get people out of the audience?"

Groucho: "Yes. We got them out and *kept* them out!"

A little later, talk turned to unusual acts.

Allen: "This fellow would be shot out of a cannon. Groucho, were you ever shot out of a cannon?"

Groucho: "No, but I was shot *into* one once."

Allen: "Well, this guy had a novel approach."

Groucho: "Yeah, he didn't use a cannon."

It felt more like old times than it had in a long while, as I watched Groucho sitting in his wheelchair, tossing off a bit of his patented absurdity. During each song Groucho would turn to the nurse and me and say, "He's great! Isn't he great?" After one number, the nurse said to Groucho, "So you like Steve Allen's piano playing?" Groucho replied, "No, he's lousy," then asked him to keep playing.

Although Allen had only intended to stay for a half hour or so, it was obvious that Groucho was having a good time so he ended up spending a couple of hours there. Before he left, I thanked him for having done such a thorough job of lifting Groucho's spirits, and I asked him to sign a copy of *The Funny Men*, a book he'd written about popular comedians in 1956. Allen took a pen and wrote, "To Steve, from a great piano player, despite what Groucho says!"

Several years later, Allen wrote a follow-up to *The Funny Men*, entitled *Funny People*. In his chapter on Groucho he recounted the above incident, but for some reason he kept referring to me as "Steve Sharian." I wrote to him asking why he had decided to change my last name, and he wrote back apologizing for his lack of accuracy and closing with, "I hope this sets the record straight, which is more than my Pioneer turntable can do."

It was a bittersweet experience, orchestrating the slow procession of friends who were coming by to say hello or, depending on your point of view, goodbye. Many of them hadn't seen Groucho in a long time because they hadn't wanted to risk running into "her." With Erin's visits now restricted to the evening, they could come by without fear of disruption. It's too bad Connie August hadn't lasted long enough to see this come to pass.

There was an almost unspoken feeling that Erin's hangers-on weren't quite as welcome as Groucho's longtime friends. In addition to not wanting to run into Erin, some of Groucho's older friends didn't want to run into anyone associated with her. So, when Bud Cort showed up unannounced at the door one day accompanied by director Colin Higgins and a few other people I'd never seen before, he was in for a surprise. Bud smiled and said, "Hey, Steve! We just dropped by to say hi to Grouch!"

I told Bud that he couldn't just "drop by." All guests had to be cleared with Nat ahead of time and a specific visiting time arranged. I suppose I *could* have let them in, had I wanted to. But the truth was, I didn't want to. Bud couldn't believe I was pulling this on him. He kept saying, "Oh come on, Steve, it's *me! Bud!*"

Precisely.

Later that evening, when Erin came by, she told me in no uncertain terms that I'd made "a *big* mistake" with regard to my future in this town. I'm still waiting for the fallout from not having let Bud Cort and Colin Higgins in to say hi to "Grouch" while he was lying on his deathbed.

I got to know Nat Perrin a lot better during this period of relative calm, and the more time we spent together, the higher my already high opinion of him became. In addition to stories and anecdotes about working with Groucho in the thirties and forties, Nat had another experience for which I envied him to no end.

When he was a teenager, he had sneaked into Aeolian Hall in New York City one night in 1924 when George Gershwin was going to debut a new piece he'd written just for the occasion. Nat said it was stiflingly hot inside the music hall and a lot of people had left long before Gershwin had gotten around to playing, but he was such a big Gershwin fan that he simply had to stick around and hear his latest composition. It was a little something called "Rhapsody in Blue."

Years later, Nat attended a party at Groucho's house and was startled to discover Gershwin at the piano. Nat's nervousness at encountering his idol was compounded exponentially by Groucho announcing, "George, I'd like you to meet Nat Perrin! He's the only person I know who can whistle the entire 'Rhapsody in Blue!'" Luckily for Nat, he wasn't called upon to back up Groucho's claim.

Bit by bit, Nat let down his wall of neutrality around me. One afternoon he sighed, turned to me and said, "Let's face it, Steve. Erin's a little whacko." I said, "Let's face it, Nat, Erin's a *lot* whacko, and I sometimes wonder if it isn't *she* who needs the conservator." I had a paperback copy of a book that contained the scripts to *Monkey Business* and *Duck Soup*, both of which Nat had worked on. I asked him to sign it, and he wrote, "For Steve, who is authorized to make any script changes he deems necessary."

Frankly, I'd always been happy with how both scripts had turned out. It was the last act of Groucho's life that could've used a good rewrite.

I don't know that Nat fully realized the extent of the burden he had taken on. Although he only came by the house once a day, preferring to keep in touch with us by phone, everybody dumped on poor Nat whenever there was even a hint of a problem: Arthur, Erin, the nurses, Henry, me. It was like the babysitter calling up the parents while they were out and complaining all the time, except it wasn't the baby who was the problem. Nat tried to be diplomatic and take everything in stride, but it was clear he was getting stressed out.

Much of this was either generated by or concerned Erin

Fleming. Although she was on good behavior at the beginning of Nat's "reign," she hated the fact that she had restricted access to Groucho, and she was slowly trying to turn Nat against Arthur in the hope that he'd just throw in the towel and recommend Erin as Groucho's conservator. I don't think she ever understood that Nat hadn't *sought* that position at all and that he was actually looking forward to handing over all the responsibilities, either to her or to Arthur, when the time came.

Erin's wild accusations continued, although mercifully, they were less frequent. One evening both she and Groucho got upset stomachs after eating something that Jules Plourde had prepared. Rather than assuming that some of the food had somehow gone bad, Erin immediately leapt to the conclusion that Arthur was trying to poison them. As a compromise, Nat said that nobody but Jules could touch the food and only the nurses would be allowed to feed Groucho.

Then there was the time that Erin was running a slight fever and was told she needed a doctor's permission before she could see Groucho. Instead, she blew off the doctor and insisted on coming over to see Groucho despite the clear and present danger of exposing him to her cold. Arthur was understandably upset and told Nat that he shouldn't have allowed that to happen.

Deluged by the constant stream of complaints from both sides, Nat petitioned the court to be relieved of the responsibility of being temporary conservator. He told the press, "I get calls all the time from the house—when I'm home, when I'm out to dinner and when I'm at parties. It's a continuous job and I can't even get out of town. It has become quite a responsibility."

The judge's final decision was supposed to have been made on May 13, but Erin's lawyers petitioned for an extension in order to give them time to prepare witnesses and arguments favorable to Miss Fleming. As a result, Judge Rafeedie agreed to postpone his decision until July 18. To his credit—and to my eternal gratitude—the much-beleaguered Nat agreed to stay on as temporary conservator until that time.

Staying at the house was a strange blend of sadness and fun. At night after Erin and Jules had left, it was just a sleeping Groucho, his longtime evening nurse, Happy Cooper, and me. By Nat's decree, I had the run of the house. I could get a late-night snack, browse through some of the many wonderful books or, more likely, watch a new and wondrous gizmo called cable TV.

Groucho was the first person I knew to have it installed. There were brown plastic boxes connected by long, skinny wires to each of his TVs, containing a couple dozen channel buttons. While pushing most of them simply gave me menus of what was on the other stations, he did have Z Channel, a now-defunct station that showed commercial-free movies: recent releases, classics, art films and old shorts.

After a numbing week of typing "Kojak" scripts at Universal, going home to my crumbling North Hollywood apartment and acting as traffic cop to the various warring factions at Groucho's house, it felt sinfully luxurious to be able to spread out on the king-sized guest bed, turn on the set, kick back with a Coke and watch an uncut movie. I could almost forget that Groucho Marx was in the next room, dying.

Almost.

One night there was a strange occurrence—strange even by the standards I'd come to expect in that house. It was rather late; past midnight or so. Groucho was sleeping soundly, Happy Cooper reading quietly beside his bed. I was, as usual, stretched out in the guest room enjoying a movie on Z Channel. Suddenly and without warning, the house was plunged into total darkness. Since we were perched high atop the appropriately named Hillcrest Road, away from the city, everything was pitch black. It was one of those deep, all-consuming darknesses where you can't tell if your eyes are open or closed. Just to complete the picture, the phones had gone dead as well.

Here I was, defender of the castle, and I had no idea what was going on. I was scared shitless.

My heart pounded as I felt my way out of the bedroom and into the hallway, where I was startled to run into Happy, who was also trying to feel her way along the wall. Since no flashlights were at hand, our goal was to locate some candles, which we guessed were somewhere in the dining room. The dining room was, of course, clear at the other end of this dark, sprawling house.

Being plunged into total darkness is unsettling under any circumstances, but recent events had caused my mind to inflate this occurrence beyond all reason. First, Erin had accused Arthur of installing surveillance equipment. Then, sinister drug-tinged syringes had been discovered in the storm drain, causing questions to arise as to Erin's methods and motives. This was followed by Erin's threatening to kill the two detectives who had refused to bury the syringes. And last but certainly not least, Erin had recently accused Arthur of trying to have her poisoned.

Given Erin's volatile temperament and her resentment that fucking servants were running the place, I couldn't be certain what had happened or, more to the point, what was about to happen. It was like when they found those syringes. I didn't *really* think she was trying to do him in, but I couldn't be *sure.* I tried to prepare myself for the unexpected: A burglar? Erin and some accomplices coming in to kidnap Groucho? Hit men? I really didn't know what to expect, only that I couldn't rule anything out at that point.

Happy and I managed to find the candles and some matches, so we seated ourselves in the dining room, lit the candles and waited for *something* to happen. Although the candles enabled us to see our surroundings more clearly, their glow also served to create an even eerier mood. After a while, Happy took one of the candlesticks and wandered off to look in on Groucho, who was sleeping soundly through the entire crisis. As she drifted down the hall, the glow of the candle's flame illuminated the framed pictures on the walls, enhancing the gothic atmosphere of the place. All that was lacking were thunder and lightning.

As it turned out, we weren't experiencing anything more sinister than a temporary power outage. After a couple of hours (at least it *seemed* like a couple of hours), the lights came back on, Happy returned to her reading and I went to bed, although sleep was a little harder to come by than usual that night.

When I say that Groucho would never be aware of what I was doing for him, this is not to imply that he wasn't aware I was *there.* But I'm sure he just figured I was doing whatever I'd been doing for the previous three years, nothing out of the ordinary. What he would never know was that I was spending the night there, looking out for him and helping to ensure that his final days were as comfortable and stress-free as I could manage in terms of friends, family and the rest of the household.

I had been telling people that it looked as though Groucho was on his last leg for years, but it was becoming increasingly apparent that this was to be his final battle. Despite Erin's contention that he was making great progress, Groucho wasn't responding to the physical therapy and he was starting to develop respiratory problems resulting from having been so continuously bedridden. From any angle, things were looking bleak.

Goddard Lieberson, Groucho's longtime friend and the head of CBS records, had been named executor of Groucho's will some years earlier should the sad occasion arise. Unfortunately, as May turned to June it was looking more and more as though that sad occasion was imminent.

And then, on May 29, Goddard Lieberson died.

As with Nunnally and Gummo, Groucho was never informed that he'd lost yet another close friend. It seemed as though the news of any one of their deaths would have been enough to finish Groucho off, and so it was all the more ironic that he was "tuning out" just as these grim returns were coming in.

After having convinced Hector not to abandon his work on Groucho's biography, Norman Krasna had returned to his home in Switzerland. There he found an inscribed copy of *The GrouchoPhile* awaiting him, which Groucho had asked me to send off several months earlier, before his hospitalization and rapid decline.

Krasna carefully looked through the book, which covered Groucho's entire life from early childhood through old age in vivid photographs. Then he wrote a warm, sentimental letter about how much Groucho had meant to him over the many years they'd known each other. It closed with, "You have been one of the great influences in my life and I love you very much." Krasna had sent the letter to Arthur to make sure Groucho got it, since no one could be certain who would be in charge of the house by the time it arrived in early June.

Arthur brought along the letter on his next visit and read it to Groucho, who wept openly. Groucho kept the letter near him for days, asking the nurses to read and reread it to him often. He cried each time it was read, as though he'd never heard the words before. Finally, I was called into Groucho's bedroom. He wanted to dictate an answer to his old friend.

Despite the fact that Groucho was still capable of engaging in sporadic repartee with his nurses, I was skeptical that he would be able to formulate a legitimate letter. Nevertheless, as I'd been accustomed to doing for three years, I took pen in hand and awaited his dictation. Slowly and deliberately, Groucho spoke: "Dear Norman, I miss not seeing you. We had a lot of great times together, until you moved to Switzerland. Come back. We need you. Love, Groucho."

At first I wasn't sure I had heard him correctly, but then I figured Groucho must've meant that since he hadn't taken enough advantage of seeing Krasna when he was living in the States, he missed "not seeing" him now that he lived in Switzerland. I took the piece of paper into my office, zipped a sheet of Groucho stationery into the Smith-Corona, and typed up what would turn out to be the final Groucho letter.

After checking it over to make sure I hadn't mistyped anything, I brought it in to Groucho and handed him a pen. Between the "Love" and the "Groucho," I'd left ample room for him to sign his name, which had by this point become a particularly challenging task. Groucho looked it over, muttered "Good," took the pen and proceeded to make two vertical lines instead of a *G*. I thought, "Oh no. He's really blowing it this time. I can change a Y into a G, but there's no way I'm going to be able to turn whatever he's trying to do into *Groucho*."

While I was wondering how I was ever going to fix it, Groucho made a horizontal mark between the two vertical lines, like a goal post, creating a capital *H*. This was followed ever so slowly by *a-c-k-e-n-b-u-s-h*. Hackenbush. It was the name of Groucho's character in *A Day at the Races*, and it had been Krasna's nickname for him over the previous forty years. I felt a lump in my throat as I realized that Groucho hadn't misspelled his name at all; he'd simply been continuing a long tradition with an old friend.

About this time, testimony resumed in the Erin/Arthur conservatorship battle in the form of depositions. Former cook John Ballow spoke for the equivalent of 368 pages in his characteristically melodramatic style. He told how Erin had bullied Groucho and how she "had enough drugs of her own in her purse to kill a bear! I used to say, 'Where do you get all these drugs?' and she'd say, 'I have ways.'" His testimony certainly didn't do anything to disprove the harsh things the nurses had said in April. Everyone had been waiting to hear from Erin herself, but her deposition kept getting postponed, usually for "medical" reasons. Her lawyers blamed one delay on colitis, which is frequently caused or at least aggravated by extreme stress.

As excerpts of each person's testimony hit the papers, I was glad I hadn't been asked to testify. The two sides seemed to be interested only in hearing from *former* employees. I figured Erin's lawyers weren't in any hurry to subpoena me because I'd probably have some unflattering things to say about her. And I figured Arthur's lawyers weren't going to subpoena me because they still saw me as someone from Erin's camp and I'd never given them much of a reason to think of me as an ally. Those reasons, coupled with the fact that neither Hector nor Henry had been subpoenaed, led me to feel fairly safe that I'd be spared the undoubtedly uncomfortable experience of being hauled into some lawyer's office and made to answer questions.

As early June arrived, I was anticipating the arrival of Diane Szasz. She had decided to move out to L.A. from Ohio and seek her fortune, possibly as a computer programmer. The plan was for her to stay with me in my tiny apartment just until she could find her own place. Our long-distance relationship was finally going to have a fighting chance to develop.

Meanwhile I was still typing scripts in the Universal steno pool. Although the job could certainly get tedious, there were certain perks. Universal was in the midst of filming a television remake of *It's a Wonderful Life*, entitled *It Happened One Christmas* and starring Marlo Thomas. This otherwise blasphemous venture had one saving grace: The villain, Old Man Potter, was going to be played by Orson Welles. I dug up an original photo from *Citizen Kane* and kept it in my drawer at the office in anticipation of the day when Welles would be on the lot: June 14. If I could arrange entry to the soundstage, I was determined to ask him to sign my picture.

I was having lunch at Groucho's the following Saturday with Arthur and Lois. We were finally getting along a little better than we had at the onset of all the craziness. Suddenly there came a knock at the door. Jules answered it and discovered a man with an envelope in his hand.

It was a subpoena for me to appear before attorneys from both sides, in J. Brin Schulman's office. In addition to summoning me, it said, "STEVE STOLIAR has in his possession or under his control the exact matters or things designated below: The originals and all copies of all documents, records, books, and other writings, as defined in California Evidence Code S. 250, and other things relating to or concerning JULIUS H. MARX/GROUCHO MARX and/or ERIN FLEMING and/or GROUCHO MARX PRODUCTIONS, INC., or to any of the personal, business, or financial affairs of said persons and/or said corporation."

A wave of nausea swept over me, as though the D.A. finally had everything he needed to put me away for good—except I hadn't done anything. I toyed with the idea of pretending I'd never gotten the notice. Lois quickly chimed in with, "No! You can't do that! You *have* to go!" Thanks gobs, Lois.

The date on which I was ordered to spill everything I knew was June 14.

So much for asking Orson Welles to sign my picture.

Twenty Nine

I had never given a deposition before and I was scared to death of the very idea. I was hoping that maybe Muriel Gregory wouldn't grant me permission to miss work in the steno pool. No dice. If I failed to show, I would be held in contempt of court.

It was my understanding that despite the intimidating, official-sounding language of the subpoena, they were only going to ask me some questions about my work at the house and whatever I knew about the personal and business relationship between Erin and Groucho. In all likelihood it would last until sometime that afternoon. That didn't sound too bad.

I spoke for three days.

At Schulman's office, high atop a Century City office building, I was led into a posh, oak-paneled conference room where I was introduced to Schulman and Joe Donahue, who was one of Erin's attorneys. Correction: One of Erin's *new* attorneys. She changed law firms almost as often as she changed her mind. The only other person present was Noeleta Lacy, the court reporter.

Schulman asked me if I'd ever been deposed before. I told him in a nervous voice that I'd never even been *elected.* Then he attempted to put me at ease, saying that it really wasn't a complicated process; it was just a matter of answering the questions to the best of my recollection. If I didn't remember something, it was OK to admit to that. Simple enough.

Then I was sworn in, with Ms. Lacy busily typing up everything I was saying on her stenotype machine. I was so rattled by the whole setup that I temporarily forgot my phone number. After all, since I lived alone and had only just moved into the apartment six months earlier, I'd never had occasion to *call* it. It wasn't any big deal, but my hesitation in answering only served to make me more nervous. I started imagining the two lawyers thinking, *What is this? The guy says he can't remember his own phone number? What's he trying to* pull *here anyway?*

Once we got under way, the going was a little smoother, but I never got over my worry and discomfort. I felt that if I were to say something that put Erin in too flattering a light Schulman would pounce on me, and if I said something damaging about her Donahue would let me have it with both barrels.

As it turned out, Schulman had little reason to worry. Merely by my telling the truth to the best of my recollection, things didn't look too good for Erin. This was not lost on Mr. Donahue, who quickly realized that he must fall back on the two classic forms of discrediting a witness in order to cast doubt upon the value of the testimony: Attacking my memory and attacking my character.

Lucky me.

With regard to the former, my memory was fairly reliable. But after I discussed how Erin had berated Groucho and how she would have frequent screaming fits, Donahue bristled at the fact that I was unable to give him the dates these incidents had occurred. He wanted to know how it was that I could quote lines from a forty-year-old Marx Brothers movie yet couldn't pinpoint the specifics of events that had taken place at Groucho's house during the previous three years.

My reply: "Because I've seen that same movie over and over again, reinforcing the same lines, but each of the three years I've been working at Groucho's has been made up of 365 separate days, which start to slur together after a while." I thought that was a fairly good answer given the fact that I was trying not to piss myself.

Many years later, as I sat glued to my television set watching the O.J. Simpson trial, I felt a certain kinship with the many reluctant witnesses who were mercilessly torn to shreds by both sides. True, the eyes of the world weren't exactly trained on J. Brin Schulman's conference room while I was giving my deposition, but given how nervous I was to begin with I doubt it would have made much of a difference to me at the time.

I didn't go out of my way to praise Arthur, but frankly, there really wasn't much to say about him that was of a negative nature: I was aware of a chronic estrangement between him and Groucho, I'd heard unflattering things about him from Erin, there was that awkward lunch in 1974 when he'd suddenly left Groucho sitting alone at the lunch table, and that was pretty much it.

Neither did I begrudge the positive things about Erin, such as hiring me and selling me her Pinto at a discount. Donahue asked if

I didn't credit Erin with helping to make Groucho into a living legend. "Yes," I said, "but what price glory?" I also spoke of how I'd initially been concerned that taking Erin away might hurt Groucho since he'd been so dependent on her for so long, but that I no longer felt that way because he didn't seem to miss her when she wasn't right in front of him. Not surprisingly, Donahue didn't like that at all.

I began to think of Schulman as something of a friendly face, if only by default. And I suppose Schulman was thinking along the lines of the old Arab adage: The enemy of my enemy is my friend. Whenever Donahue would really start to lay into me, Schulman would interrupt with something like, "Counselor, Mr. Stoliar is not on trial here. His deposition is simply a part of the discovery process. I believe he is answering your questions to the best of his ability."

Yeah, what *he* said.

With regard to attacking my character, when I started talking about how Groucho's signature had deteriorated over the previous year or so, Donahue objected on the grounds that I wasn't a professional graphologist and was in no position to intelligently discuss such matters. While we were still on the subject of Groucho's signature, Donahue asked if I'd ever signed Groucho's name to any checks, letters or legal documents. Since Groucho almost always signed the "Groucho's," I quickly answered, "No." Then I suddenly remembered something and said, "Well, there *was* this one time..." Donahue leaned forward, expecting to get a confession out of me proving that I'd been an accomplice in some nefarious scheme.

I told them about the day Groucho had received a letter from a distraught woman who said that her son had dropped out of junior high school because he wanted to be a comedian like his idol, Groucho Marx, and since Groucho hadn't gone past grammar school, neither would he. She pleaded with Groucho to write to her son and urge him to return to school.

I knew that if I showed the letter to Groucho, he would at best have instructed me to send the kid a picture. So instead I decided to do something I never did. I zipped a piece of Groucho's stationery into the typewriter and proceeded to fake a letter from Groucho. I wrote, "When I was your age, things were different. My brothers and I had to go into vaudeville in order to make a living. But I've been trying to compensate for not having had an education ever since. These days, I always try and read the latest best-sellers. Back then, I was *living* in the best cellars." And on it went, telling the kid he could always go into show business, but urging him to go back to school for the time being.

Although Groucho hadn't written it, nothing I said was inaccurate, technically speaking. I forged Groucho's name, sent it off and told no one what I'd done.

Several weeks later the kid's mother wrote back to Groucho, thanking him for having turned her son's life around. He was back in school doing wonderfully, and she owed it all to Groucho Marx.

After this heartrending tale of redeemed youth, how could Donahue attack me for having forged Groucho's name? He didn't. He wisely chose to go on to something else entirely.

At one point, on the third day of my grilling, Donahue asked me if I thought that Groucho loved Erin. I started to make a delineation between loving and being in love. I felt that Groucho had been superficially infatuated with Erin, which was more along the lines of being in love, whereas I saw loving as a deeper, more durable feeling that built over a longer period of time.

Donahue said he didn't understand the difference, and proceeded to set up a hypothetical situation wherein he and I would go out for beers and begin discussing women and dating and love. After he'd spent a couple of minutes setting the scene, I said, "This could never happen." Puzzled, he said, "Why not?" I answered, "Because I really don't like beer."

Donahue blew his top, admonishing me, "Mr. Stoliar, if you would refrain from *ad-libbing,* we might actually be able to *finish* this deposition!" I calmly replied, "Mr. Donahue, are you implying that I should prepare my answers *ahead* of time?"

It was a minor victory but a victory nonetheless. The rest of the time, I was just trying to make sense and not embarrass myself in front of these high-priced, high-powered attorneys. As I recall, I succeeded on both counts.

After three days of watching me being slowly roasted over hot coals, the court reporter, Noeleta Lacy—who had remained mostly silent throughout my testimony—told me that she enjoyed taking my deposition more than any of the other witnesses because my loyalty and affection for Groucho had come through so clearly. It was a little out of character for her to tell me that, but I was glad she did.

Since I'd been talking at length about how difficult Erin could be and how harshly she had treated Groucho over the years, it would be safe to assume that I wasn't looking forward to crossing paths with her at Groucho's house. I was sure Joe Donahue had filled her in on my traitorous testimony, so I girded myself for an onslaught of verbal abuse when next we saw each other.

As it turned out I didn't see her that weekend, but my relief was tempered with sadness. Groucho had taken a turn for the worse and had been rushed to Cedars-Sinai. I was still expected to stay at the house in order to keep an eye on things and to field phone calls from friends, family, the press and so on. Since Groucho wasn't at the house, Erin saw no reason to stop by. This, of course, was fine with me.

Groucho had managed to dislocate the new hip joint, so another operation was required. Additionally, Groucho's lucidity had been steadily declining over the few weeks preceding his return to the hospital. The nurses would help him to get dressed and then he would immediately insist that he needed to get dressed. Likewise, he would eat a hearty lunch, then after he was wheeled back to his room insist that he had to have lunch. Happy Cooper also said that Groucho was starting to hallucinate, seeing wild animals at night, which was something he'd never done before.

After spending a week in Cedars-Sinai recuperating from the second hip operation, Groucho was released. His return home was short-lived, however. The following day, June 23, he was rushed back to Cedars-Sinai because he was having difficulty breathing. Once in the hospital, he contracted pneumonitis, a form of pneumonia. I'd gradually begun to accept the idea that Groucho would be better off quietly slipping away rather than trying to bounce back from so much adversity. It was a hard thing to admit to myself.

Since I was working until eight at Universal during the week and watching over Groucho's house on weekends, I had no opportunity to stop at Cedars. Truthfully, I don't know what it would've accomplished, given Groucho's tendency to drift in and out. Instead I relied on Hector's reports. He said that Groucho still liked to impress visitors with his strong grip and that he still enjoyed kissing women: the nurses, Erin, even Lois Marx, whom he would continue to kiss until she'd eventually get tired of bending over the bed. It was as though, with the end nearing, all former bitterness toward others had quietly vanished.

But Groucho was hardly incoherent. Unfortunately. During one visit he looked up at Hector and muttered, "This is no way to live." It saddened me all the more to hear that Groucho was sometimes painfully aware of his increasing deterioration. Why couldn't the bliss of ignorance be more consistent, dammit?

Toward the end of June, Diane arrived. Since we got along so well it was difficult to leave her alone in the apartment to go house-sit at Groucho's, particularly during those early weeks. After a while, Diane would come up for dinner on Saturday, watch a movie with me on Z Channel and then drive back into the Valley.

In early July, Erin finally gave her deposition. It was 912 pages long, and in it she declared her love for Groucho and categorically denied any hint of having abused him.

What a surprise.

One night, after enjoying *One Flew over the Cuckoo's Nest* on Z Channel, Diane left Groucho's at two in the morning and started back to the apartment. In the middle of serpentine Laurel Canyon her car broke down, frightening her considerably. By this point Nat Perrin was about to abdicate the throne and it was obvious from the avalanche of negative testimony that Erin was never going to be awarded custody of Groucho. Assuming that Arthur was on the verge of being put in charge of things (and after having consistently defamed his adversary during three days of testimony), I asked him if it would be all right if Diane drove up with me and stayed over until Sunday. Arthur had no problem with that.

For a few brief weeks, Diane and I were able to enjoy a strange sort of weekend getaway in Groucho Marx's home. We had the house and pool to ourselves and a gourmet chef preparing our meals. But even though Groucho wasn't there, a thick black cloud hung over the place. While we were playing house and enjoying Jules' incomparable omelettes, somewhere in the back of my mind I was anticipating "the call." I thought how strange it was that this new life with Diane was beginning just as my days with Groucho were drawing to a close. And I was saddened that she and I would never be able to thank him for having brought us together, however indirectly.

With the July 18 deadline for appointing a permanent conservator fast approaching, Joe Donahue asked for a postponement so more testimony could be gathered favoring Erin. Judge Rafeedie acceded to Donahue's request, circling August 31 on the court calendar. But Nat Perrin had taken just about all he could take. He'd initially agreed to play traffic cop until mid-May, then he'd promised to try and hang in there until mid-July, but nobody had said anything about the end of August.

Consequently a compromise was reached. After considerable haggling behind closed doors, both sides agreed to a new conservator on July 15. Like Nat, he was someone without apparent bias, who could be counted on to be as fair as possible given the difficult circumstances. He was someone who had worked around Erin for years with minimal friction, yet had always gotten along well with Arthur Marx. Who was this mystery man? None other than Arthur's son, twenty-seven-year-old Andy Marx.

Initially Erin only agreed to make Andy a temporary conservator, giving him a few weeks in which to prove himself. But after a brief meeting in Groucho's hospital room on July 27, Andy was made Groucho's conservator on a permanent basis. Now Nat Perrin could go home and get some well-deserved rest.

Andy's appointment was altogether fitting and proper, from my viewpoint. I'd met him at Groucho's on my first day of work, and now he was going to be there on my last. I was glad that I'd always remained on friendly terms with him and that he understood that my allegiance—like his—was to neither party, but to Groucho himself. It seemed unlikely that Andy would feel compelled to get rid of me on the grounds that I was somehow in cahoots with one side or the other.

Groucho continued his downward spiral. By now, most of his conversation, if he said anything, was restricted to "Yes" and "No." The rest of the time he drifted in and out of lucidity. In mid-August, however, when a nurse wanted to see if he had a fever, she approached his bedside with a thermometer. According to Andy, Groucho opened his eyes and said, "What do you want?" The nurse smiled and said, "We have to see if you have a temperature." In a voice barely above a whisper, Groucho muttered, "Don't be silly. *Everybody* has a temperature." Then he drifted off to sleep again.

While his other senses may have been failing rapidly, his sense of humor was remarkably tenacious. As with all the other Grouchoisms he'd uttered during my tenure, this one had been worded just as the younger Groucho would've worded it, only more slowly and softly. It would turn out to be his last reported witticism.

I sensed the end approaching and I had accepted the inevitable. After all, it was Groucho himself who had said, "This is no way to live." I began to envision the lengthy tributes in the newspapers and magazines and on television that were certain to follow his death. He'd attained the status of living legend toward the end of his life, and now he was about to become immortal. I hoped the journalists would get the names and dates right as they prepared their big stories on "The Death of Groucho Marx." I wondered if any regular programming would be preempted in order to do full justice to the passing of a giant who had conquered the worlds of vaudeville, Broadway, Hollywood, radio and television.

Then, on August 16, at 3:30 in the afternoon, death came to Elvis Presley.

The shocking news that at the tender age of forty-two, Elvis had suddenly "left the building" caused such a massive, nonstop media frenzy that people hardly seemed to take notice when, three days later, Groucho Marx died of natural causes at the age of eighty-six.

I heard about Groucho's death on the car radio while I was driving home from Universal in my Pinto—the "crummy old car" he'd originally bought for Erin. I didn't feel like crying. There was actually some vague sense of relief that the long hard struggle was finally over. I had talked to Andy that afternoon and he'd said that the doctors were amazed that Groucho was still hanging on.

He had reconciled with Arthur and Melinda, and although Miriam didn't get to the hospital in time to say goodbye to her father, she had made her peace with him and was on the road to a healthier life than she'd ever known.

Erin had been at Groucho's bedside until Arthur and Lois had shown up, at which point she glared at them and then went out into the hospital corridor. Arthur, Lois and Andy watched over Groucho until he slowly slipped away at 7:25 P.M. According to Arthur, it was a peaceful exit.

Shortly before Groucho died, Andy had been besieged at the hospital by phone calls from reporters. He refused to talk to them, so Erin decided to give them a statement: "Groucho's just having a nice little dream now. He's just going to have a nap and rest his eyes for the next several centuries. But he's never going to die. He told me."

For all I knew, she still hadn't canceled the television show.

I assumed that my job had ended along with Groucho's life, but when I asked Andy if I should bother going to Groucho's house the next day, he surprised me by saying that I might as well spend the weekend there as I'd been doing for the previous several months. Although I was certain this would be my last weekend, the house still needed looking after, and Andy said it would be helpful if I could handle all the phone calls that were sure to come in. For my final weekend there, I felt it was proper to go it alone, without Diane.

It was a strange feeling to be in the house knowing—with certainty, this time—that the owner was never going to walk through the front door again. As expected, the phone never stopped ringing the entire weekend. Most of the callers were reporters trying to get the lowdown on whether Erin was watching over Groucho's body and what sort of funeral arrangements had been made. I had no idea, and I told them so. Nobody believed me; they thought I was just being evasive.

One of the callers was Groucho's longtime friend Betty Comden, who with her partner Adolph Green had written the scripts to *Singin' in the Rain*, *On the Town* and *The Band Wagon*.

Comden: "Is Erin there?"

Me: "No."

Comden: "Is Arthur there?"

Me: "No."

Comden: "I don't know who to console."

Me: "I guess we should console ourselves."

I felt badly for her. Betty Comden had been close friends with Groucho for decades and she deserved a more personal response than I could give her. But what I'd said reflected exactly how I felt: There was no longer any sense of allegiance to Erin Fleming, and I'd spent a lot more time with Groucho than Arthur had during the previous three years. So I believed it was up to each of us to deal with our thoughts, feelings and memories about Groucho and his passing in our own way.

I coped with his death by talking over the recent chain of events with Henry and Hector. We Three Musketeers, perhaps more than anyone, understood the dynamics of what had been going on and how raggedly it had ended. And there was that strange sense of relief, now that the battle—Groucho's battle, anyway—was over.

On Saturday afternoon I received a call from Mr. Strickland at the Bank of America—the fellow who had been signing my checks—who informed me that my services would no longer be required after that weekend. It was a perfunctory ending to what had been an astonishing three-year run.

Before leaving on Sunday, I took one last stroll through the house: Groucho's bedroom, the bookcases jammed with all those wonderful books; Melinda's old room, which had been my home away from home every weekend for the past several months; the hallways filled with photographs spanning eight decades; the trophy table with all the awards; Erin's office, where I'd met Andy on my first day; my office, where I'd worked for three years trying to make the other fans happy; the living room, where all those parties had taken place; the dining room, scene of countless delicious meals and ugly scenes; the den, where I'd watched all those episodes of "Best of Groucho"; and the kitchen, where I'd had that tuna-fish sandwich with Martha Brooks about a thousand years ago.

I was briefly tempted to take a few things with me—the inscribed Benchleys, the Thurber drawings, the wire-rim glasses—but I knew that if I did, I would forever feel like a vulture who had picked over Groucho's bones. So I left everything just as I'd found it.

I took one last look down the hallway, then pulled the door closed behind me, got into my car and headed back toward the Valley.

THIRTY

Although Groucho's struggle had ended, the bitterness between Arthur and Erin extended far beyond his death. On Sunday afternoon, while I was packing up my things in preparation for my final departure, Arthur held a brief memorial service at his house, along with thirty or so friends who had never felt comfortable when Erin had been around, including his sister, Miriam, and Harpo's widow, Susan.

Other friends, such as Georges Jessel and Burns, expressed surprise and disappointment that they hadn't been invited to Arthur's house. Zeppo, the sole surviving Marx Brother, was also left off the invite list, the result of his unbridled endorsement of Erin Fleming during the conservatorship fight. He had to learn of his brother's death on the evening news. Angered by the snub, Zeppo gathered the press together and reiterated his belief that Erin had extended Groucho's life beyond measure. He also decried the tackiness with which the news of Groucho's death and subsequent memorial service had been handled.

Zeppo chose to decry this tackiness from the showroom of a local car dealership where he had recently purchased an automobile.

The following morning Groucho's body was cremated, per his wishes, while Arthur and Andy said prayers at Temple Beth El in Hollywood. That night Erin held her own memorial service at her house on Vista Grande, which was attended by thirty or so of *her* friends. There were no reports that Jessel or Burns had any complaints about missing out on that one.

Needless to say, I hadn't been asked to either gathering, since I'd managed to fall neatly in between the two opposing factions during the course of the previous several months. As far as each side was concerned, I was simply obsolete.

Several days later, Groucho's ashes were taken to Eden Memorial Park in Granada Hills and placed in the cemetery's columbarium. The bronze plaque that marks Groucho's niche says simply: "GROUCHO MARX 1890–1977." The columbarium is located just on the other side of the wall where my mother was interred in 1969 and where my father joined her in 1992.

Although the coverage of Presley's death greatly eclipsed Groucho's, there were tributes in print and on television. The predictable clips were shown: the mirror scene from *Duck Soup*, the stateroom scene from *A Night at the Opera*, Groucho toying with guests on "You Bet Your Life." And there were also, unavoidably, references to the recent unsavory battle between Erin and Arthur. But generally speaking the press did a reasonably adequate job of allowing Groucho to take his rightful place alongside the other comedy greats: Laurel and Hardy, Charlie Chaplin, Buster Keaton and W.C. Fields.

Surprisingly, *Time* magazine, whose cover Groucho had graced twice in his lifetime, provided extensive coverage of Presley's death yet devoted only a small amount of space to Groucho. As a result, angry letters from Woody Allen and Dick Cavett complaining about this sorry imbalance were printed in a subsequent issue.

One tribute that *wasn't* lacking was a half-hour retrospective ABC ran in prime time, composed of clips from the various Dick Cavett shows on which Groucho had been a guest over the years. Cavett and Harry Reasoner were on hand to introduce the different segments. Although I would have liked it to have gone on for hours, it did serve as a reminder of how nimble-witted Groucho had once been—not so many years earlier—and it helped chase away a few of those lingering images I had of a Groucho Marx who had become completely helpless.

I assumed that with the end of my days at Groucho's certain other things would come to an end as well, such as my correspondence with Cavett. I figured that the main reason he'd been answering my letters was because I'd been a pipeline into Groucho's house and I could fill him in on all the lurid goings-on. Now that that was over, why would he bother staying in touch?

A week after Groucho died, the phone rang in the steno pool at Universal: "Stoliar? Cavett. Listen, I hope we're not gonna lose touch just because Groucho's gone. By the way, I hope you don't mind, but I've shown some of your letters to Woody and he says they're very well written."

We've been good friends ever since.

Hector Arce continued to work on the Groucho biography. If nothing else, at least he now had an ending. I was called upon to conduct a few of the interviews for the book, including one with Nunnally Johnson's gracious widow, Dorris, and another with Dick Cavett. It was interesting to be able to talk to them after the fact, so to speak, when they felt freer to express their opinions than they might have had Groucho still been around to hear them.

The book, simply titled *Groucho*, was published in early 1979. Lyn "Charlotte Chandler" Erhard had beaten Hector to the punch by having her Groucho biography come out the year before, but although her book contained many positive elements, Hector's was the better chronicle of Groucho's life. I'm only sorry more people didn't hold off on *Hello, I Must Be Going* until they'd had a chance to browse through *Groucho*.

The story of the *Animal Crackers* campaign and my subsequent employment was described in both books, but since Lyn had left toward the end of 1975, Hector's was the only one to discuss my involvement in the events surrounding Groucho's final months. My dad was mighty proud of the fact that there were two lines of entries in the index under "Stoliar, Steve."

A few months after Groucho died I was approached by a writer named Jeanie Kasindorf, who was doing an article on Groucho's last years for *New West* magazine. After having lunch with Ms. Kasindorf and telling her something of my experiences at Groucho's, I received a call at Universal from Dena Brown, Erin's legal secretary, wanting to know if I'd spoken to anyone who happened to be doing an article on Groucho. I saw no point in denying it, so I told her that I had spoken with Kasindorf. Dena wanted to know what I'd said. I replied, "I told her the truth about what things were like at Groucho's house." Dena thanked me and hung up.

A short time later, I received another call. It was Erin. I hadn't spoken with her since before I'd given my three-day deposition in June. It was creepy hearing that voice again, and naturally I knew why she was calling.

Without knowing anything about the content of my conversation with Kasindorf, Erin had a message for me. It was the sort of thing you usually hear in bad movies, when someone is being threatened but the bad guy doesn't want to be caught saying anything that could specifically be construed as a threat. Erin said something along the lines of, "I think what you need to do is call this Jeanie Kasindorf person back and tell her that you might've been mistaken about a few things. You have your whole life ahead of you, Steve. It would be a shame to ruin it over something like this."

At that point I was starting to feel pretty shaky. Even over the phone, she had the ability to reach out and make me feel extremely uncomfortable. I almost considered rethinking what I'd told Jeanie when Erin added, "I want you to do this—and I know Groucho would want you to."

That was the clincher. How *dare* she drag Groucho's ashes out of their urn? I decided then and there to stick by what I'd told Kasindorf, regardless of the consequences.

That was the last time I had any contact with Erin Fleming.

Despite the fact that Andy's appointment—and more to the point, Groucho's death—had put an end to the struggle over Groucho's conservatorship, the war between Erin and Arthur pressed onward. In late October of 1977 Erin was sued by the Bank of America, with the full support of Groucho's children, for having fraudulently taken $400,000 out of the estate. The suit asked for punitive damages as the result of Erin's having used undue influence in order to receive gifts and money from Groucho, including the Mercedes 450 SEL and half of the two thousand shares of Groucho Marx Productions.

In February of 1978 Erin countered with a claim that *she* was owed money for, among other things, royalties for having been Groucho's personal manager during numerous book and record deals. In May of that year, the Bank of America responded with a request that the court prevent Erin from receiving those monies. From their point of view, Erin had wheedled, extorted, inveigled and otherwise manipulated Groucho into being foolishly and extravagantly generous to her, and they felt she was entitled to nothing.

The case wasn't heard for another five years. Then, in early February of 1983, I was startled to turn on the news and see none other than Erin Fleming pointing an accusatory finger at J. Brin Schulman and in a booming voice, declaring, "Mr. Brin Schulman is an assassin and he *murdered* Groucho Marx!" Judge Jacqueline Weiss gaveled Erin into silence and instructed her to curtail her outbursts.

There was no such thing as Court TV in 1983, but the trial of Erin Fleming received a great deal of attention from

"Entertainment Tonight" as well as many of the network news shows. Although it never reached Simpsonian proportions in terms of gavel-to-gavel coverage or media frenzy, the celebrity angle of the trial made it one that many people followed as closely as possible.

Later in the week, Erin caused another in a series of stirs by refusing to allow the bailiff to look through her purse as she entered the courtroom. Staring daggers at the bailiff, she demanded, "Give...me...my...*pocketbook!*" in the very same tone of voice the Wicked Witch of the West had used when she'd demanded that Dorothy give her back "those slippers." Concerned about Erin's ability to control herself, Judge Weiss asked Erin if she felt she could continue to testify. Erin responded by announcing rather defiantly, "There's nothing wrong with *me! You* may have a few problems!"

Erin's lawyer, David Sabih, then pleaded with the judge to excuse Erin from further testimony since it was obvious she was distraught. The judge acquiesced, and as a result a court-appointed psychiatrist examined Erin and found her to be "severely mentally ill, psychotic and paranoid." What a strange irony, given the fact that eight years earlier it had been Groucho whom a court-appointed psychiatrist had found to be of unsound mind during the ill-fated "adoption" of Erin Fleming.

With great fanfare, Sabih announced that a parade of big-name celebrities including Barbra Streisand, Woody Allen, Jack Lemmon, Walter Matthau, Jane Fonda and Sammy Davis Jr. would testify that Erin had been the best thing that had ever happened to Groucho. But when the time came, none of the aforementioned luminaries came to her defense. Instead the jury and the spectators heard from Bud Cort, Sally Kellerman and George Fenneman, who all gave their opinion that Erin Fleming had been extremely beneficial to Groucho Marx in his declining years.

The only really big names who spoke on Erin's behalf were Carroll O'Connor, who said that Erin had kept Groucho alive, and George Burns—although Burns' testimony could hardly be said to have been a wholehearted endorsement. When Sabih asked Burns if he'd seen the obvious love between Groucho and Erin at the parties he'd attended, Burns responded, "How could I see anything? There were a hundred and fifty people there!" When J. Brin Schulman got up to ask Burns a few questions, he said, "I've never cross-examined God before, so I'm going to do it carefully." Burns replied, "I'm only God when they pay me."

If you're wondering why Zeppo didn't come up from Palm Springs to testify on Erin's behalf as he had during the conservatorship battle, there's an excellent, albeit unfortunate, reason: Zeppo had died of lung cancer in 1979. Given his youthful appearance and zest for living, I'd figured Zeppo would be around for many years after Groucho's death. I'd figured wrong. By the end of the seventies, all the Marx Brothers were gone.

Zeppo, by the way, had his own brush with infamy shortly before his death. In 1978 a former girlfriend, Jean Bodul, alleged that Zeppo had beaten her up in his car some years earlier. Zeppo's explanation was that it was "just a little pushing and shoving" after she'd tried to drive away with his keys and credit cards. Although Bodul had asked for $350,000, in deciding against Zeppo the jury awarded her only a little over $20,000. After breaking off her apparently unhealthy relationship with Zeppo, Bodul sought refuge in the loving arms of noted Mafia crime boss Jimmy "The Weasel" Fratianno, whom she later married.

Talk about your frying pan and your fire.

Witnesses for the prosecution against Erin included former cooks Martha Brooks and John Ballow, who testified that Erin had threatened Groucho's life; Miriam Marx, who testified that Erin had been verbally abusive to her father; and Lois Marx, who proudly recounted the story of dumping water on Erin's head at Matteo's restaurant some years earlier.

The jury also heard from Groucho's ex-wife (and Melinda's mother), Kay, with whom he'd maintained a cordial relationship for many years after their divorce in 1950. He had even continued giving her money regularly, long after he was legally obligated to do so. Kay fought back tears as she told about a phone call she'd made to Groucho wherein she'd heard Erin in the background saying, "Tell her you don't want to see her and you don't want to talk to her anymore," after which Groucho had weakly repeated, "I don't want to see you and I don't want to talk to you anymore."

After two and a half months of testimony, the jury finally began their deliberations. During that time, Erin gave her opinion as to what was really at the heart of the Bank of America's legal action against her: "There's something about this that really stinks, and it has to do, I believe, with the fact that I'm a woman." As bizarre a statement as this is, there's probably some truth to it: It's unlikely any man would've had nearly as much success taking advantage of Groucho Marx as Erin Fleming had.

Initially the jury deadlocked on whether Erin had actually cheated Groucho, but they eventually reached a verdict that Erin had used undue influence over him. She was ordered to pay back more than $400,000, which it is doubtful she still had.

Indeed, Sabih declared that Erin was "totally penniless." He also insisted that the verdict had been racially motivated because there were four blacks on the jury and someone had been spreading vicious rumors that Erin hated black people. But when reporters asked the jury foreman—who was white—about the basis for the verdict, he explained that it was Erin's own testimony that had hurt her case the most. "We felt she was evading the truth and had things to hide," he revealed.

After the decision came down, a glassy-eyed, perpetually grinning Erin Fleming appeared on "Nightline" and gave Ted Koppel a real run for his money in terms of weird answers and awkward silences. When asked about the allegation that she had taken advantage of Groucho, Erin declared somewhat cryptically, "It's an impossibility to defraud Groucho Marx! It's like saying that Groucho Marx was crazy when that was his trademark!" When Koppel asked her how she intended to come up with more than $400,000 to pay back into Groucho's estate, she said she was going to put it on her MasterCard. Koppel was speechless. One has to assume she was joking. Then again...

A short time later, Judge Weiss reduced the amount of the damages by $200,000. Nevertheless Erin elected to file an appeal, which didn't reach court until 1986. In February of the following year, the Court of Appeals upheld the original verdict against Erin. Consequently Erin's attorney, Melvin Belli, petitioned for the verdict to be overturned by the California Supreme Court. In July of 1987, they refused to hear the case.

In short: She lost.

Finally, in 1988, what was left of Groucho's estate was divided among Arthur, Miriam and Melinda. Unfortunately, the years of expensive legal battles had eaten up much of what had been estimated at just under $2 million in cash, property and various holdings at the time of Groucho's death.

In the course of assessing the value of Groucho's estate after he had died, professional appraisers had gone through the house and made a tally of his personal memorabilia. They had concluded that its total worth was $53,000—a small fraction of its actual collectible value, even by 1977 standards. Among the items listed were a pair of "white metal spectacles without lenses," which they estimated at $100, and Groucho's prized medal from the French government, which they deemed to be worth a dollar.

In addition, Groucho's holdings included stock in AT&T, General Motors and Texaco, worth hundreds of thousands of dollars. He also owned a thousand shares of something called Groucho Marx Productions. Estimated value: One dollar.

Erin, you may recall, owned the other thousand shares. Maybe she could sell them off and use that big dollar to begin paying back the hundreds of thousands the court had decided she owed the estate.

That's assuming she could unload those shares.

Epilogue

Arthur Marx is now older than Groucho was when "You Bet Your Life" went off the air. I ran into him on the Universal lot in 1981. In between writing a number of celebrity biographies, he had come in to pitch story ideas to Bill Dial, an underappreciated writer-producer for whom I was working as a production secretary. It was nice to see Arthur again after so much time had passed. We chatted a bit and I asked him how Miriam was doing.

"Miriam's fine now. She stopped drinking around the time my father died. I guess she didn't have a reason to drink anymore."

Miriam, incidentally, has been sober now for more than fifteen years. She put together a wonderful and revealing book of letters that Groucho had written to her over the years, entitled *Love, Groucho*. When it was published in 1992, she inscribed my copy, "To Steve—Thank you for being there for my father, when I obviously wasn't able to be."

You're welcome, Mir.

Melinda Marx is still up in northern California, far away from Hollywood and everything it represents.

Andy Marx has written computer-themed articles for a number of publications including *Variety*, the show-business newspaper Groucho had so enjoyed reading each day.

After *Groucho* was published, Hector Arce proceeded to write two more Hollywood biographies, one on Tyrone Power and the other on Gary Cooper. He'd wanted to call the Power biography *Ty*, but the publisher vetoed that idea in favor of *The Secret Life of Tyrone Power: The Drama of a Bisexual in the Spotlight*. As a result Hector was mistakenly vilified by the press and the public for having chosen such a cheap, exploitative title for his book.

We remained good friends following Groucho's death, and we often got together for lunch to reminisce and to fill each other in on what was happening in our lives. Hector took a sort of big-brotherly interest in me and had high hopes for my eventual escape from the Universal steno pool. I assumed we'd be friends for many years. Then, in April of 1980, Henry Golas called to tell me that Hector had gone into a North Hollywood hospital for a simple hernia operation and had died of a heart attack during surgery. Since Henry and I both have rather black senses of humor, I assumed he was kidding. He wasn't, and I lost a real friend in Hector.

Henry has gone on to become an associate producer in motion pictures. He recently moved to Santa Barbara with his wife and young son, and although we haven't seen much of each other in recent years, we remain friends and make a point of keeping in touch.

Ours is an extremely exclusive club.

Daryl Busby is now an award-winning television writer, working both as a freelancer and a staff writer. Although we're not as close as we once were, we do keep tabs on each other.

John Ballow operates a florist shop in Palm Springs.

And what became of Erin Fleming after the trial? That's one of the questions I am most frequently asked. To a large degree, the answer is shrouded in mystery. For years I received sporadic bulletins. One had Erin shopping in a boutique, asking Groucho's ghost for advice as to which dress looked better on her.

Another concerned a different boutique. Writer Larry Gelbart's wife, Pat, had been purchasing a dress when Erin had walked in, greeted her and then proceeded to take a swatch of blue cloth out of her purse.

Erin: "Pat, what do you think of this shade of blue?"

Pat: "It's…nice."

Erin: "It's *exactly* the shade of blue they should've made the Pacific Design Center! It was designed by my father, you know."

Pat: "Oh?"

Erin: "Yes. I told him he should've made it this shade of blue, but he wouldn't listen to me! You do know who my father is, don't you?"

Pat: "No."

Erin: "Why, Laurence Olivier, of course!"

And with that, Erin did an about-face and walked out, leaving a speechless Pat Gelbart behind. For the record, Erin's father was not Laurence Olivier.

Dick Cavett told me that he had received a Christmas card from Erin in the mid-eighties after not having had any contact with her since before Groucho's death. Inside was a photo of her and Groucho. She had signed the card, "Erin Fleming Guccione."

Neither of us was aware of Erin's having married the noted publisher of *Penthouse* magazine or any of his relatives. Years later, she would explain—using her characteristically bizarre logic—that she had added the "Guccione" to her last name in order to frighten off all of the people who were out to get her. Whether she was assuming any Italian surname would conjure up underworld images, or that Bob Guccione himself had a tough-guy reputation, the answer is known only to her.

Another report had Erin moving back to her native Canada, while still another had her living in the same house on Vista Grande, although how she could get by financially after years of ruinous legal battles is something of a mystery in itself. I drove by the house recently and found two brand-new, expensive cars parked in the driveway—a further indication that it was unlikely that she still lived at that address.

Yet another explanation of Erin's whereabouts came to light by way of Nat Perrin. In 1982, I had run into Nat at a screening of *The Marx Brothers in a Nutshell*, a uniformly excellent and thoroughly enjoyable documentary put together by Bob Weide and Joe Adamson. When he spotted me, Nat had remarked, "Steve, you look a lot *calmer* than the last time I saw you!" I'm sure he was right.

In May of 1995 I again spoke with Nat, who had recently celebrated his ninetieth birthday. After complimenting me on having been "a very stabilizing influence on a very crazy household," Nat added rather matter-of-factly, "By the way, Erin's a bag lady on Santa Monica Boulevard now. A celebrity bag lady, I guess you could say." Stunned, I asked if he was kidding, and he said, "No. I'm serious. She's had a lot of problems over the years. My wife gave her money once and some of the restaurants give her food from time to time."

Could this be true? Could the same woman who had been wearing a full-length white fox coat when I'd met her and who had ruled Groucho's house with an iron fist now be reduced to poverty and homelessness? What a curious irony that the woman whom many had said bore a slight resemblance to Vivien Leigh should now, like Blanche DuBois, be dependent on the kindness of strangers.

When I told Daryl about my conversation with Nat, he said that he had seen Erin walking along Santa Monica Boulevard only a week earlier in the vicinity of a drug-and-alcohol rehab center. Hardly conclusive, but possibly significant (and certainly coincidental).

I became determined to try and unearth whatever information I could about Erin's post-trial activities and current whereabouts—if only to confirm or disprove Nat's sad account of her fate. Since there was no "Erin Fleming" listed in the phone book, I called the Screen Actors Guild to see if she still had an agent. There was no agent, but there was a phone number. With a certain degree of apprehension, I dialed it.

A recorded voice informed me that the number was no longer in service and there was no new number.

Next I contacted all of the Marx enthusiasts with whom I was still in even sporadic touch and asked them what they knew about Erin's recent activities. I was surprised and disappointed to discover that nobody had a single shaft of light to shed on the subject. Apart from accounts of the trial and its aftermath, they hadn't seen a thing about her in newspapers or magazines in years.

Frustrated, I called up the *Los Angeles Times* and asked them to run a computer search for any articles on Erin Fleming during the last ten years. A couple of days later, I received a copy of an article dated June 13, 1990, which carried the headline: "Erin Fleming Arrested with Gun." It went on to say that Erin had walked into the West Hollywood sheriff's station at 11:00 at night and had promptly been arrested for carrying a concealed—and loaded—.357 Magnum revolver, which had been protruding from her purse. She had been released on her promise to appear in Beverly Hills Municipal Court the following month. No reason was given for her having gone into the sheriff's station in the first place, much less why she was carrying a concealed weapon in her handbag.

No wonder she didn't want that bailiff going through her purse.

It wasn't much of a report and it still didn't answer any questions about her current condition, but at least I had a morsel or two of reasonably recent information on Erin for the epilogue of this book, since the deadline was fast approaching for me to turn in my finished manuscript.

Then, in a series of events that would be considered too contrived if I'd put them into a script, some extraordinary data came to my attention.

In late August, Dick Cavett called to tell me that he had just received what he characterized as "a four- or five-page demented letter from Erin Fleming." This was the first time he had heard from her since the "Erin Fleming Guccione" Christmas card almost ten years earlier. Knowing of my search for recent information on her for the conclusion of this book, he sent me a copy.

Although technically speaking the letter had been *sent* to Cavett, it hadn't been *written* to him. The letter, dated August 13, 1995, had actually been written to an attorney in Los Angeles, but accompanying it was an eclectic list of eleven others to whom she was sending copies, including Cavett, publicist Warren Cowan, attorney Melvin Belli—and Bob Guccione.

The letter is a long, rambling, angry tirade against this lawyer who, according to Erin, had been a fellow patient in the locked psychiatric ward of the County-USC Medical Center in 1992. According to her narrative, during their incarceration another patient—a black woman—had grabbed Erin's glasses and smashed them in order to get even for Rodney King (!). Erin is now furious with this attorney for not having gotten her an eight-dollar pair of eyeglasses from Thrifty Drugstore so that she could see. Erin claims to have been rendered blind by the loss of her glasses, although the four-page letter is written in the same neat handwriting she'd used twenty years earlier.

She goes on to state, "I thought I could save my sanity in a madhouse if I could see to read," then says she has lost her mind because this man never got her those glasses.

Erin continues to rail against this lawyer, accusing him of "not playing with a full deck" and urging him to commit harikiri (which Cavett felt compelled to change to the correct "hara-kiri" on my copy). Before closing, she states that "all of Canada would like to lynch you," cautions him to "beware the Ides of August" and ends by intoning, "God may forgive you, I never will."

As if having this astonishing document drop into my lap at the eleventh hour weren't enough, one of my Marx-enthusiast acquaintances ended up having a two-hour phone conversation with Erin—after not having spoken with her in many years—in which she reiterated many of the points she'd made in the letter, adding that she's been in and out of mental hospitals ("snake pits of human misery," as she referred to them) over the previous ten years, had only been released from County-USC in April of 1995 and has declared bankruptcy at least twice since 1986.

According to Erin, her initial commitment to a mental hospital was all a misunderstanding stemming from the fact that when Groucho had died she had told reporters, "He's never going to die." What she'd meant was, "He'll go on living through his films," but "they" had taken her literally and therefore had her put away. (Why none of the various doctors and hospital staff who have treated her over the years have been skilled enough to correctly diagnose this "misunderstanding" is a mystery.)

My acquaintance said Erin was rambling and delusional throughout the entire conversation, making sense one minute, then being totally paranoid and unrealistic the next. And she's convinced that there are a great many people who are out to get her.

In still another in a series of ironies, Erin had herself been in the care of a court-appointed conservator at one point, but she was planning to sue this conservator for having sold off her furniture while she was in the hospital.

I couldn't resist asking if my name had come up in the course of their two-hour chat. It had. Once. Apparently, in the midst of an antilawyer tirade, she'd suddenly blurted out, "Steve Stoliar killed Groucho, because he dropped Groucho and broke his hip. If Stoliar hadn't dropped him, Groucho would never have had to go into the hospital and he wouldn't have died. Look at George Burns!"

How strange to learn that after nearly twenty years, the only time she'd mentioned my name was to accuse me of having precipitated the death of Groucho Marx. Although it is probably unnecessary for me to state this, not only did I not drop Groucho, I wasn't even in the house when he fell, so Erin's accusation isn't even an embellishment of the truth; it's complete delusion.

Whether or not she is literally homeless, it's clear that Erin, now past sixty, has fallen upon the toughest of times mentally, emotionally and financially. There are those who would say there is poetic justice in Erin's sorry state. And there are probably some of Groucho's old friends and family members who would have no second thoughts about tossing her severe pronouncement of "God may forgive you, I never will" right back at her for her harsh treatment of an old man in his declining years.

There's certainly a case to be made for it.

I alternate between feeling very sorry for her and feeling very bitter about how she treated Groucho during my years there. A short time after Groucho died, Erin had called up producer Jerry Davis and said, "So, do you know any other rich old men in need of companionship?"

It wasn't the most sentimental remark she could have made to the man who had introduced her to Groucho way back when.

J. Brin Schulman—that other "assassin" of Groucho Marx—tried to get in touch with me in early 1983 regarding the possibility of my testifying against Erin in the civil trial, but I was in the process of moving to New York, so he missed me. Just as well. Since Groucho had been gone for almost six years, I had absolutely no desire to be drawn into all that again.

Why was I moving to New York? Dick Cavett had hired me away from my secretarial duties in Bill Dial's office in September of 1982 to serve as the writer for a monthly series he was doing for HBO. Despite the fact that I was going to be earning half as much as I'd been earning as a secretary in order to move to a town that cost twice as much to live in, I made the quantum leap from secretary to writer. I tested the New York waters for a few months and then returned to L.A. in January of 1983 to pack up my things and move eastward.

After spending two and a half glorious years devouring Manhattan, I reluctantly moved back to Los Angeles in 1985 to take a lucrative writing job on a short-lived television series that was being produced by my old boss and friend, Bill Dial, at my old stomping grounds, Universal. Since then I've been dividing my time between freelance writing and cartoon voice-overs. Things seem to be working out, more or less, and the very fact that you're holding this book in your hands may indicate that S.J. Perelman didn't waste that inscription on me after all.

Diane Szasz and I lived together for a couple of years and eventually married, but not each other. We do remain on friendly terms, however. One of Groucho's few pieces of advice to me was not to get married until I was thirty. I held off until I was thirty-seven, just to be on the safe side. It turned out to be a smart move.

When I look back on my years with Groucho, I sometimes have difficulty believing that it all really happened. Despite the ugliness of some of it, my experience was still that literal dream-come-true, and I wouldn't have missed out on it for anything. If I'd felt like Dorothy opening the door into glorious Technicolor on my first day at Groucho's house, the Oz analogy holds true for the end as well. As Dorothy put it, "I remember that some of it wasn't very nice, but most of it was *beautiful*."

That's pretty much how I felt as I pulled the door closed on my last day there.

I still have the key.

AFTERWORD

Somehow, more than fifteen years have passed since the hardcover edition of *Raised Eyebrows* was published. During that decade and a half, a number of events have occurred involving the people and places you've just read about.

In terms of the book itself, the response from Marx Brothers fans and other readers has been very gratifying. Quite a few said they felt as though they were right beside me during those remarkable years inside Groucho's house—which was my intention. Some said they were reminded of having to care for or say goodbye to an elderly relative. Some felt I was too easy on Erin Fleming; others felt I was too rough. I recalled 'em as I saw 'em.

I also heard from some of the people discussed in the book and the consensus seemed to be that I had an astonishing memory for details and was uncannily accurate—except for whatever I had said about *them!*

For starters, Bud Cort threatened to sue me.

Shortly after the book hit stores, I received a phone call from Bud. It was the first time I'd spoken with him in twenty years. He said I had remarkable recall of those long-ago events, but he was *very* hurt and upset that I'd said he was more Erin Fleming's friend than Groucho's and that he had taken advantage of Groucho's hospitality during the time he stayed at the house. He insisted he had gotten Erin's explicit permission to have that Christmas party and also said that he was already a good friend of Groucho's before he'd met Erin.

Since he brought up the name, I asked him if he was still in touch with Erin. He said, "Actually, I have a restraining order against her, but that's neither here nor there." (I thought it was at least "there," but that's neither here nor there.) I explained to Bud that even Hector Arce's contemporaneous Groucho biography had discussed the Christmas-party incident. He told me it was "lazy writing" on my part to rehash what Hector had said in his book.

Bud wanted my book recalled and reprinted without my comments about him. I told him that was impractical, but I did say that if the book ever went into a second printing or paperback edition, I would add that his recollections and mine differed. That seemed to extinguish the fire.

A week later, I received a very stern letter from Bud's attorney saying that my book had contained "numerous false statements" that were defamatory and had "already caused him damage," and that I had falsely cloaked my assertions with "a sheen of truth." The letter went on to say that, against the attorney's advice, Bud would not file a lawsuit—provided I lived up to the "agreement" I'd made with him over the phone, i.e., that if there were subsequent printings of the book, I'd give Bud the right to pre-approve—or reject—any statements made about him. I was to sign the agreement letter and mail it back within ten days. If not, they would proceed with the lawsuit against me, as well as against General Publishing Group.

I had never agreed to give Bud editorial control over subsequent printings, but I had also never been threatened with a lawsuit and I was concerned—especially with that ten-day deadline looming. I called the president of General Publishing Group, Quay Hays, and read him the letter. Instead of sharing my concern and offering the services of the company's legal representatives, Quay *laughed!* It seems the attorney who had written the letter worked at the same law firm as Quay's attorney—actually, worked *under* Quay's attorney—the same attorney who had personally vetted my manuscript before it had been published and had not found one potentially damaging statement.

Besides, Quay explained, Bud would have to prove in a court of law that *Raised Eyebrows* had "prevented him from earning a living." As Quay had predicted, nothing came of the lawsuit. But at least you now know that Bud's version of events differs from mine.

I also heard from Groucho's older daughter, Miriam, via letter rather than telephone. She said *Raised Eyebrows* was "a wonderful book," but she took issue with my having said that her caretakers had physically abused her. She admitted that "they were terrible people who were psychologically abusive" and they did lock her in her room, causing her to jump out the window and break her arm. But even though she was usually black and blue when Henry Golas had seen her, Miriam insisted she—and not the caretakers—had been responsible for the injuries: "That's what practicing alcoholics do. They fall around and bang themselves up, and most of the time they don't even remember how they did it." She thanked me again for being there for Groucho when she couldn't and added, "You obviously loved my father very much, as did I, and your book shows it."

Miriam also said I should "ignore Bud Cort" because it was a "known fact" that he was "one of Erin's buddies." She also advised me to watch my back with respect to Erin Fleming "because the woman is obviously insane."

I took both suggestions under advisement.

I sent Henry Golas an advance copy of *Raised Eyebrows.* He said, "It was like walking back in the door of 1083 Hillcrest Road and finding nothing changed or out of place. I am proud to be one of the group who locked protective hands around Groucho." Since Henry had been there for so much of what transpired, his review held a special significance.

In the course of promoting my book, I appeared on a television talk show on the East Coast, where I received an unexpected call—live and on the air—from Terrie McCord, the nurse whom Erin had confronted in her unzipped jumpsuit. Terrie had nothing but positive things to say, and it was great to hear her voice after so many years.

In May of 2009, I got a Facebook message from someone named Frederick Cooper. The name didn't ring a bell, but his *mother's* certainly did—Appline "Happy" Cooper—Groucho's wonderful evening nurse who had helped me through that frightening, Gothic-horror night when the power went out.

Frederick had thumbed through a copy of *Raised Eyebrows* some years earlier and had been pleasantly surprised at seeing his mother's name in the index, but he'd forgotten the title in the intervening years and so had been unable to show her the book. I was only too pleased to send Happy her own copy. Not long thereafter, she called me from her home in Florida and we had a warm and wonderful conversation about life inside 1083 Hillcrest.

Happy said whenever she would be at one of their lavish social gatherings and there was a celebrity she really wanted to meet, Groucho would introduce her by saying, "This is Happy, the woman I sleep with," rather than, "This is my night nurse." She chuckled at the memory of that.

I was surprised to learn that Happy had remained in touch with Erin for years after Groucho's death, helping her out with various hospitalizations and finding assisted-living facilities for her. Erin was fortunate to have had someone who cared enough to expend that kind of energy, especially since most of her other "friends" had long since abandoned her. My memory was accurate: Happy didn't have a bitter or vindictive bone in her body and truly lived up to her nickname.

In August of 2009, I received another long-distance phone call, this one from Northern California. It lasted an hour and a half.

The caller was the former Melinda Marx, by then a sixty-three-year-old *grand*mother. My longtime friend, filmmaker Bob Weide, had run into her recently, because Melinda's daughter, Jade, had a boyfriend who worked on the crew of *Curb Your Enthusiasm,* upon which Bob had toiled for years as an executive producer and director. It was strange to think of Jade having a boyfriend. After all, I had been one of the witnesses on the codicil to Groucho's will that added Jade as an heir when she was born, and my last image of her was as the innocent toddler who had accompanied Melinda when she'd visited Groucho shortly before his death. How could little Jade have a boyfriend?

Bob had asked Melinda if she'd read my book. She had not and, what's more, she was *very* reluctant to do so, because she hadn't liked any of the books that had discussed her father during the Erin years. Based on Bob's endorsement, however, Melinda told him she'd be willing to read *Raised Eyebrows.* I sent her a copy and awaited word. I hoped she'd like it, since the subject was so close to her heart and she'd been so disappointed before.

Melinda had just finished reading the book when she called me with her response: "You got it *all* right. You told the truth. Thank you so much for writing it. You have healed part of a hole in my heart and I only wish I'd read it years ago, so that the healing could've begun earlier."

It doesn't get much better than that. Actually, it doesn't get *any* better than that.

Melinda said she'd often contemplated writing about her life, but the Erin Fleming stuff would get her so upset and agitated, she would set aside the idea of writing and lose herself in playing the mandolin—her profession as well as her solace. She said, "You wrote the book that I don't have to write, because it's all in there. Justice has happened. The universe is a little more balanced." Melinda said other books had pulled their punches when discussing Erin, or even defended her treatment of Groucho, and she couldn't stand reading them. But Melinda felt she'd finally read a truthful account of those turbulent years.

Melinda told me the first thing she did was look up all the references to herself in the index and check them out, one at a time: "Yeah, he got that right...Yeah, he got *that* right, too..." Eventually she felt it was "safe" enough for her to read the rest of the book without fear of stepping on an emotional land mine.

Melinda represented a precinct I hadn't heard from, and not just in terms of the book. She hadn't participated in Hector's biography and was never willing to be interviewed for the various documentaries that had been produced since Groucho's death.

She explained that Groucho was really the only parent she'd ever had because his last wife, Eden, had seemed more like a high-priced call girl than a mother figure and Groucho didn't want her corrupting his youngest daughter, so he'd kept them apart intentionally.

According to Melinda, Eden drank a *quart* of vodka per day. The entire den bathroom used to be stacked, floor to ceiling, with *cases* of vodka. Melinda liked my reference to her father as a "Victorian" and believed that Groucho had a character flaw and an insecurity that resulted in his marrying young, uneducated women to whom he could play Pygmalion. Unfortunately, he would become angry with them for not knowing enough about various subjects and then they'd drink, which only made him angrier. This was very similar to Dorris Johnson's observations and assessment of Groucho as a husband, when I'd interviewed her for Hector's biography.

Melinda also talked about what it was like growing up with an alcoholic mother—Groucho's second wife, Kay. According to Melinda, Kay was already an alcoholic long before Groucho had married her in 1945. She and her first husband, *Dead End Kid* and *Bowery Boy* Leo Gorcey, would both get drunk and then get into some real knockdown, drag-out fights. Melinda vividly recalled Kay hurling empty liquor bottles at her when she was just a toddler. She confessed that it had actually been a *relief* when Kay was eventually placed in a sanitarium.

In later years, Kay had moved up to Mendocino to be closer to Melinda and her kids, but it was still very stressful because even though Kay had stopped drinking, Melinda said she was "still nuts and very manipulative," constantly pitting one family member against another.

Melinda didn't have many happy memories of 1083 Hillcrest, where she'd spent her teenage years, but she had a great fondness for 806 North Foothill. She'd gone back to her childhood house a few years earlier to discover that the same family had lived there continuously since Groucho had sold it to them in 1956, and the old Marx family furniture was *still there*—the dining room table where she used to sit as a toddler, the pool table featured in the 1954 *Person to Person* with Edward R. Murrow, Groucho's electric inclinator (upgraded and faster), etc. She even found her tiny childhood handprints in cement in the backyard.

Martha Brooks, Groucho's longtime cook, had kept Melinda informed on the various goings-on at the Hillcrest house—at least until Erin fired her. Reportedly, Erin had something sexually scandalous on kindly Dr. Kert, which is why Martha thought he had testified on Erin's behalf in court. "I'm sure your *wife* wouldn't be too thrilled to hear about *that!*" Martha had relayed to Melinda, doing her best Erin imitation.

When Melinda had testified at Erin's trial, she couldn't help but cry, the circumstances being so upsetting and overwhelming. As she was leaving the courtroom in tears, Erin's attorney, David Sabih, grabbed her arm and said—loudly enough for most to hear—"You are really a *great* actress, Melinda! I'm sure you will be *very* successful!" That mean-spirited comment only made her all the more upset.

Melinda told me that Erin used to phone her frequently, threatening to *kill* her and her two young children. She had even *kicked* Melinda when she was eight months pregnant with Jade!

When Melinda received the sad news that her father had died, Melinda had gone off by herself into the woods near her home and cried. She said she didn't feel at all like traveling down to L.A. and dealing with "the factions."

A few weeks later, she was strolling pensively through a friend's sprawling backyard field, thinking about Groucho's passing, and she suddenly detected the unmistakable aroma of cigar smoke! There was no apparent source: no one in the house was a smoker, there was no fire in the fireplace, no neighbors nearby, no trucks anywhere in the vicinity with drivers blowing smoke out their windows. Even though Melinda said she doesn't put much stock in supernatural "signs" such as those, she really did feel that it was Groucho's perfect way of saying goodbye to her.

It was an extraordinary conversation that covered many topics. Most significant for me, personally, was Melinda's belated blessing on my book and how it had touched her so deeply. That was enormously gratifying and I was very grateful that she'd taken the time to share her thoughts, experiences and memories with me.

In January of 2010, I flew up to San Francisco to visit with my family and to attend an 80th anniversary screening of *Animal Crackers*—the film that had brought Groucho and me together in 1974. Dick Cavett and Bill Marx were scheduled to speak at the screening and I thought it would be nice to see both of them again. I also hoped the trip might be therapeutic: My darling wife, Angelique (*nee* Linda) had died suddenly in August of 2008 after twenty years of togetherness, and my family had been trying—and failing—to lure me up there for a restorative visit ever since.

It was *wonderful* to hang out with my family and Messrs. Cavett and Marx. Dick had lost his own wife, Carrie Nye, in 2006 and had been particularly helpful with firsthand advice on dealing with spousal grief, but I hadn't seen him in person in several years. I hadn't seen Bill Marx since running into him at that screening of *The Marx Brothers In A Nutshell* in 1982. Bill had just written a memoir of his father—and his own life—entitled, fittingly, *Son Of Harpo Speaks*.

Once I got back to L.A., Bill and I exchanged copies of our books. His makes for fascinating reading. I learned an enormous amount about Harpo the dad and the person, and even more about Bill himself. Bill said my book was "dazzling" and that he thoroughly enjoyed it from start to finish. It was great to be back in touch with him.

I hadn't seen or spoken with Andy Marx since the weekend after Groucho died. Through mutual friends on Facebook, we reconnected and, in March of 2011, got together for a wonderful lunch wherein we began to catch up on what had happened to us in the nearly thirty-five years since we'd last been in touch. He's a successful screenwriter now—and a keeper of the Groucho flame—with a lovely family. He told me that, unlike me, Arthur could never, under any circumstances, give Erin Fleming a shred of credit for having done anything remotely positive for Groucho. In a strange irony, Arthur's health quickly deteriorated and, very shortly after our lunch, Andy was appointed Arthur's conservator, just as he had been appointed Groucho's. Arthur died in April of 2011, just a few months shy of his ninetieth birthday.

Like Melinda, Andy had steered clear of Groucho books for the most part—especially after sampling some of John Ballow's "fanciful" version of events, which included Erin pulling a gun on him. This was news to Andy—and *he* would know. I gave him a copy of *Raised Eyebrows* and, after reading it, he said I did a nice job of capturing those difficult years, especially the "weirdness" of Erin's unpredictable mood swings and the challenge of dealing with Groucho's physical and emotional ups and downs during his final days.

Sadly, in the years since this book was first published, some of the people I've written about have died. They include Steve Allen, Milton Berle, Irving Brecher, Red Buttons, Buddy Collette, Betty Comden, Bob Dwan, George Fenneman, John Guedel, Bob Hope, Dorris Johnson, Hal Kanter, Jack Lemmon, Arthur Marx, Kay Marx, Maxine Marx, Susan Marx, Nat Perrin, Lynn Redgrave, J. Brin Schulman, Sidney Sheldon, Red Skelton, Bernie Smith and Gloria Stuart Sheekman. It's to be expected that a number of notables would have passed away since my years inside Groucho's house in the 1970s, but it's hard to believe we lost so many of the *dramatis personae* just since this *book* came out in 1996.

Predictably, one of the people I am most often asked about is Erin Fleming. Is she still a bag lady? Where is she? Has she read your book? Have you seen her? Have you heard from her? For years, I had no hard-and-fast answers. The last personal contact I'd had with her was in late 1977, when she'd called the Universal steno pool with her thinly veiled threat after my interview with Jeanie Kasindorf of *New West* magazine about Groucho's last days.

When I was in the midst of working on the book, I realized that, however balanced I tried to make it, Erin *still* wasn't going to come off well in the end, so I decided to change my home address to unlisted—but not my phone number. My reasoning was thus: I did not want that woman popping out of the shadows some night and thrusting a rusty potato-peeler into my ribcage—but I'd still be willing and curious enough to talk with her over the phone.

For years, I waited uncomfortably for someone to inform me that Erin Fleming had finally read my book, had a nuclear meltdown, and was out gunning for me. Finally, in 2002, I talked to Paul G. Wesolowski—the Marx maven who had remained in sporadic touch with Erin over the years.

Apparently, the assisted-living facility in which she resided had a small library and an arrangement with other, similar facilities to circulate and exchange books. She had learned of *Raised Eyebrows,* requested it, had finally read it, and Paul was going to tell me about her reaction.

I girded myself for the inevitable nuclear blast. After all, she had the capacity for becoming a force of nature over the slightest slight or perceived insult, and, despite the many positive things I had said about her in the book, there was no getting around the fact that I had also detailed her abusive behavior, her descent into madness and her falling on hard times. What was Erin's reaction? She'd told Paul, "There's a lie on every page. I didn't charge him $1500 for the Pinto. It was *$1200!*"

The nuclear bomb I'd been fearing turned out to be barely a burp. Incredulous—and maybe a little disappointed—I said, "What?!? That's like screening *Schindler's List* for a former concentration-camp commandant and having him say, 'It is a tissue of *lies!* For one thing, we wore our SS insignia on the *right* lapel, not the *left!*'"

That was what Erin Fleming took away from my detailed narrative of our three tumultuous years together? *The cost of the*

Pinto?!? My therapist later told me that this was a classic reaction for a schizophrenic—missing the big picture entirely and focusing instead on a seemingly insignificant detail.

(Maybe it *was* $1200...)

In the fall of 2003, I began to receive emails from Marx Brothers fans asking if Erin had died. Well, if she had, I hadn't heard a thing about it, from Paul Wesolowski or anyone else within the devoted and well-informed "Marx Brotherhood." Apparently, an internet search of vital records had turned up an "Erin Fleming" who had died in April of that year. Well, hers was a distinctive name, but hardly unique. Paul had gotten a Christmas card from Erin the previous December and said nothing had seemed out of the ordinary.

On October 11, 2003, I received an email from a Marx fan named Scott Wilson. He had done some online sleuthing and confirmed that it was, in fact, "the" Erin Fleming. She had died on April 15th by firing a revolver into the roof of her mouth. Erin had committed suicide in her second-floor apartment at the *Hollywood Royale*—an assisted-living facility on Franklin Avenue—directly down the hill from the legendary HOLLYWOOD sign.

I had such mixed feelings upon hearing that she was dead and the tragic circumstances of her death—not unlike how I felt when I'd learned she had become a bag lady. I certainly hadn't wished death upon her and—obviously—we could never meet or speak again. Not in this life, anyway. Erin hadn't left a note and nobody knew—or would ever know—what the last straw had been that had led Erin to end her chaotic and erratic life so violently on that particular April day.

I contacted Paul Wesolowski, who was stunned by the news. He called the *Hollywood Royale* and they confirmed that Erin had, in fact, shot herself. Her brother, Russell, had come down from Toronto, arranged for Erin's body to be cremated, and had taken her ashes with him back to Canada.

Despite her years as an actress onstage and on film, after all the time she'd spent by the side of the legendary Groucho Marx, after the scandalous headlines and much-publicized trial—covered by all the major networks at the time—there hadn't been one word about Erin's death in the papers, on television, or anywhere on the internet. Having spent years trying to enter—and remain in—the limelight, Erin Fleming had died in complete obscurity, almost literally in the shadow of the HOLLYWOOD sign.

On December 20th, 2009, I stepped through the front door of 1083 Hillcrest Road and what used to be Groucho's house. I don't mean that the house had once *belonged* to him; rather, it was where Groucho's house had once *stood.*

A writer-producer friend, Mike Rowe, had emailed me a few days earlier, asking if I wanted to go "back inside Groucho's house." Apparently, realtors were having trouble getting the $13.5 million asking price and had drastically slashed it to a mere $10 million (it eventually sold in May of 2010 for the low, low price of $8.8 million), and they were having an open house that Sunday afternoon for prospective buyers. I had mixed feelings about it, but was intrigued by the idea of returning to the house. And so Mike; another writer, Guy Nicolucci; their wives and I made the trek up long and winding Hillcrest Road.

I'd seen recent photos of the interior and exterior, which—sadly—showed that the place had been gutted from stem to stern and that there were *major* structural changes, which is why I say that it was much more than just "Groucho's old house owned by someone new." It was essentially an entirely new house with but faint echoes of the old homestead. If the realtors were trying to pass it off as an original Wallace Neff-designed house from the mid-'50s, then they were misrepresenting the structure in which I stood.

There were walls where there had once been rooms and rooms where there had once been walls. The kitchen was now a library, filled with random books. The screening room/den was now a state-of-the-art kitchen. The giant fireplace in the living room was—gone! The swimming pool had been reshaped and moved a few feet to the south, for reasons that escape me.

"My" office was now a much larger office with an adjacent bathroom that had never existed when I'd worked there. There was a bathroom in the same spot as the one I would use most often, but it had been completely rethought. For old times' sake (and perhaps to mark my territory), I put it to good use during my walk-thru.

Erin's office, which had initially been Eden's bedroom when the house was built in 1956, still had a slight curve to the windows as it had originally, but the bathroom, with its gigantic, luxurious, marble-lined, sunken tub, was gone and another bathroom built elsewhere, with ultra-modern fixtures.

Melinda's bedroom, where I'd slept in those final, tumultuous months, was now a wall. And the final irony: At the end of the long hallway that once led to Groucho's bedroom and office, I was confronted by the unsettling image of Elvis Presley pointing a large pistol directly at me. Fucking Elvis upstaging Groucho yet again. It was, in fact, the well-known Andy Warhol print of Presley—the man whose death three days earlier had robbed Groucho of his rightful place in the headlines—hanging on a wall that had not previously existed. Groucho's inner sanctum—his bedroom, office, and bathroom—were totally reconfigured and greatly expanded.

Oh—and the new garage—again, for reasons that escape me—was fully carpeted.

Ignoring the realtors and the handful of other looky-loos, I led my friends through the house as though I were some sort of forensic psychic tour guide, staring blankly ahead while gesturing to different areas with my hands and describing how the place had once been laid out: This used to be the screening room where Groucho and I would watch episodes of "You Bet Your Life;" that's where the kitchen window used to be where I'd wave at tourist vans, letting them think that I just *might* be Groucho; that's where the big dining-room table had sat, with a buzzer on the floor near Groucho's foot so he could summon the cook, etc.

I flashed on the scene near the beginning of *The Time Machine* where Rod Taylor explains how the small model of his time-travel device hasn't *really* disappeared—it still inhabits the same space, only in a different time. That was me: I was inhabiting the same *space* as I had 35 years earlier, but in a different time. (Maybe the Morlocks had dragged Groucho's old house across the lawn and into the Sphinx and ---)

Had it been *slightly* less revamped, rebuilt and reconfigured, it probably would've packed more of an emotional wallop. But since it was such a from-the-ground-up "renovation," I really did feel as though I were merely occupying the same space, in another time, instead of being "back" inside Groucho's house.

Maybe it's the difference between being a ghost and haunting the house you had once inhabited—and having the ghost of the house haunt *you.*

On the way back to our car, I turned back and took a final look at the strange-looking structure that now received all mail addressed to 1083 Hillcrest Road. Glancing down at the entrance to the driveway, I noticed that the cement curb still had the name of the original paving company and "1956" pressed into it, right next to the infamous storm drain where the sinister syringes had been recovered. Finally, *something* that hadn't been torn out and rebuilt.

The tall front door with the large brass knob had, of course, been replaced. It's extremely unlikely that the key I've kept with me all these years would fit the new lock.

Steve Stoliar
Studio City, California
November, 2011

About the Author

Steve Stoliar has been a professional writer for more than twenty-five years, providing material for Dick Cavett as well as penning episodes of such television series as *Murder, She Wrote, Simon & Simon, The New WKRP in Cincinnati* and *Sliders.* He has been a consultant on a number of books and documentaries about Groucho and his various siblings. He has also written and produced documentaries on such diverse personages as John Lennon, The Marx Brothers, Elvis Presley, Shemp Howard and Dr. Martin Luther King, Jr. Additionally, he has provided voices for various animated specials including *Frosty Returns, The Oz Kids* and *Snoopy's Reunion.* Born in St. Louis, he now makes his home in Studio City, California. Mr. Stoliar hopes to see *Raised Eyebrows* become a motion picture, major or otherwise.

Index